Modes of Spectating

Alison Oddey and Christine White

intellect Bristol, UK / Chicago, USA

First published in the UK in 2009 by
Intellect Books, The Mill, Parnall Road, Fishponds, Bristol, BS16 3JG, UK

First published in the USA in 2009 by
Intellect Books, The University of Chicago Press, 1427 E. 60th Street, Chicago,
IL 60637, USA

A catalogue record for this book is available from the British Library.

Cover designer: Holly Rose
Copy-editor: Rhys Williams
Typesetting: Mac Style, Beverley, E. Yorkshire

ISBN 978-1-84150-239-7

Printed and bound by Gutenberg Press, Malta.

302·23 ODD

Modes of Spectating

Acknowledgements

We would like to acknowledge the assistance we have received in compiling this book, and the intellectual generosity of all the contributors. We would like to thank all those who have financed or funded this research project, including The International Federation of Theatre Research, The Society for Theatre Research and The Arts and Humanities Research Council. We would like to thank all the photographers who have kindly supplied the images for this volume.

We would like to acknowledge the International Federation for Theatre Research's research group, 'Digital Technologies, Visualisation and New Media in Performance', whose scholarly debate testifies to this burgeoning area of study for both academics and practitioners.

Lastly, we gratefully acknowledge the advisory board of *Scenography International* for all their contributions and comments.

CONTENTS

INTRODUCTION

Alison Oddey and Christine White

Visions Now: Life is a Screen

The mode of spectating that is *historical*, that is the film reel of news, the sports highlights of the event, what was happening previously, has moved through the sound and narratives experience of the film to the instant replay, the immediate historicizing of the present moment. In the twenty-first century, we can take an historical event of the nineteenth century and re-market it as a children's animated series to bring both a knowledge and an awareness to a new generation of the London Brighton Veteran Car Run (LBVCR), which is more than an historical celebration, a publicised tourist attraction on the internet.

What is it that we want to spectate on the screen and is there still a need or desire to share, to communicate with others about what it is that we have seen, viewed or witnessed? Spectating enables us to journey in an experience, where we meet with the unexpected, chance upon and incur the improvisational, know and feel, and become acquainted with what is given. People spectate the LBVCR. It is free of charge, viewed from the roadside and the comfort of the experience is determined by each spectator, according to their own initiative of bringing a seat, drink or snack. The exhibition of cars displayed in the London streets requests that the spectator does more than simply view. They are asked to vote on their favourite vehicle from the display, which results in a free draw and a special prize.

Such is contemporary culture: the vote, the prize, the viewers' decision. Spectators are guided on the Internet by 'feature viewing points', which offer the spectator opportunities to eat, drink, go to the toilet, park their car and, sometimes, view the cars at close quarters. To become a 'spectator-performer-protagonist', as posited by Alison Oddey,[1] the roadside spectator can participate in the 'participant services' of an auction, a reception, a lunch, a cocktail party or a dinner and dance.[2]

What is radically different about how we spectate now?

In live spectatorship, the spectator's frame of spectating focuses on their own self in relationship to what they view. On the other hand, the spectator may be the anonymous individual, the nullified being, participating as one of many at an event. Are we leading towards a mode of spectatorship, where the 'liveness' is simply a mode of entering the live event; a means of display? The audience is watching the screens installed in the Regency Theatre, not the actors on stage; the large-scale plasma screens at the music concert, not the performers.

Is this the end of the 'live' event? Life captured on screen? The spectator's function has to change into a role which takes and actively engages them into the action. Is it technology, and the potential of computer-enhanced television, which will change our perspective of how and what we view with pleasure? The new mode of spectating is to focus only on what 'I' want to see; on my perception of the world as 'I' see it.

This mode of spectating is beyond simply watching. It is about substituting a sensory, kinetic and cinematographic experience, in which Mark Leyner argues, 'neural-input units will become as standard a feature of your entertainment console as the remote control.' A technology, which sends 'complex algorithmic signals into your major cortex and parietal lobe, enabling the spectator of the event to experience what it feels like inside the performer's body.' Leyner suggests that gerontological research and biotechnological innovations will profoundly affect how a spectator watches sports. He argues that, 'cloning capabilities, discoveries in the genetics of longevity and advances in cryonics will bring about an end to discussions about how competitors from past times might have fared together as scientists will be able to "revivify long-deceased athletes" or "extend the lives of current players.'[3]

In the sports analogy of spectatorship, Leyner proposes that wrestling, with 'its intricate and interfacing narratives, its music, pyrotechnic stagecraft and glorification of oratory is the *Gesamtkunstwerk* – the total artwork', of the worlds of sport and entertainment.[4] Mark Rosenthal, with reference to installation art, suggests the *Gesamtkunstwerk*, where, 'the artist has total command of a space and might use any artistic means, including architecture, music, dance and theatre, along with the visual arts, to create a synaesthetic environment, has become an everyday occurrence.'[5]

This notion of a total artwork recognizes a jigsaw of parts for the spectator to encounter and to gain delight at such detection. Is the 'tele-vising' of the live art event the future, where the spectator is drawn into the 'liveness' through their own engagement to the extent that they re-act, re-enact or act out the event within the space of their own viewing world? They are there – in real time – in the liveness of their own vision.

The perceptual experience of the spectator comes through the subjective capabilities of their own body and nervous system. This is within a recognized shift of spectatorship, which must now understand the conditions of cultural creation and reception in the twenty-first century. Therefore, artworks have re-directed themselves, reconfiguring in expanding borders, new areas of content, changing modes of cognition and experience. The interdisciplinary nature of installation artworks means that the spectator is no longer content simply to view the work. More is required. The spectator wants to engage in a more active way, to play a significant part or role in the reception of the work.

Jacques Lacan: 'I see myself seeing myself...I see outside, that perception is not in me...it is on the objects that it apprehends.' Can the spectator see without being aware of being seen? 'Installation challenges the aesthetics of frontality, that is, the paradigm of cinematic screen and monitor.'[6] When the spectator participates in the work, they become 'fused with it'. De Oliverira argues that the challenge to spectatorship is to focus on the 'viewer's frozen immobility' an endless mirroring, return of the gaze.[7] In Gilles Deleuze's opinion, cinema offers an opportunity to disrupt self-centred perception, by giving competing viewpoints.[8]

By contrast an installation 'may be defined as anything the artist wants to do when given a room in which to work...a spatial experience...the viewer is usually in an enclosed space, swept up in a work of art much larger in expanse than an individual object can normally create.'[9]

The notion of spectatorship has become of increasing interest as artists develop new works and manufacturers try to produce the means for viewing such works. The content producers are also challenged by concerns over spectatorship behaviour. The questions of absence and presence involved in spectating new forms of content, production, and performance, whether live or mediated, are beginning to vex society. Professor Susan Greenfield in the United Kingdom has challenged the government to support a research enquiry into the effect of some spectatorship mediums and their effect on the spectator, not only how we view but also what we view. This has an obvious bearing on what artists create. The pleasure of viewing and spectating is also pertinent to these aspects of spectatorship. In Bertolt Brecht's *A Short Organum for the Theatre* he raised concerns for the viewing public and these concerns developed into his production style with intended alienating effects to awaken the audience from an otherwise passive reception of the theatrical experience unfolding in front of them. Whilst such concerns were understandably provoked by the sleep walk into National Socialism in Germany, which resulted in a fundamentalist political period of genocide and intimidation, Brecht's recognition of the dangers of passive reception as a tool of indoctrination needs to be revisited within the now many spectated experiences, which can adapt and change an individual's world view. The ways in which media and media entertainments, in the form of gaming and the televisual, are used by young people, are most pertinent to our studies and again require a consideration of the pleasures of spectating, alongside the pleasures of participation. If, as Greenfield asserts, these modes of spectating change young people's ability to concentrate on longer-term traditional tasks, such as reading a book, what are the challenges of this assertion? This is, of course, only one strand of research, which is pertinent to *Modes of Spectating*. We have selected those which we feel form the most interesting and challenging relationships for spectatorship, presenting an interdisciplinary snap-shot.

The questions, which this collection presents, are:

- ■ What are spectators doing?
- ■ How do we understand the way spectating performance modes has changed?
- ■ What is the nature of spectating multi-media projects?

- ■ What is the choreography of the spectators as an artistic control?
- ■ What do spectators of live performance want?
- ■ What level of disturbance is necessary for entertainments in the twenty-first century?

Art reinforces stereotypes of behaviour and how we respond to our culture when we spectate it. The new mode of spectating is not the art but the event itself.

The notion of the active spectator and the passive spectator requires us to distinguish if passive viewing is negative. Is this a hangover from the politics of Goebbels and Brecht and the atrocities of the Second World War? If we assume that passive is watching and receiving wisdom, what is active about reading that is different from the activity of watching a film? The same translation and interpretation process occurs – a process of communication. It is natural. Have human beings become less observant?

This book attempts to disrupt what we think ideas of spectating are and to challenge the notion that spectatorship is either passive or active, and to examine what spectatorship can be. We need to recognize the value of observation as an activity, which is a construct, and as valuable when related to text and books alongside images as complex expressions and receptions of culture. The value judgement made in relation to a child reading a book and that made of that same child watching a film or playing a video game needs to be challenged as all these modes of spectatorship develop.

Is there any difference between reading and non-reading, as has recently been argued, so that there is value in being able to speak about a book even though it has not been read. Professor of French Literature, Pierre Bayard, ponders over the question of how we should talk about books we have not read.[10] His intention is not to create a crib sheet for non-readers but to enable readers to conquer their fear of culture that is contained within books and to use a non-linear approach to the culture of reading. 'We are taught only one way of reading,' he says. 'Students are told to read the book, then to fill out a form detailing everything they have read. It's a linear approach that serves to enshrine books. People now come up to me to describe the cultural wounds they suffered at school. "You have to read all of Proust." They were traumatized. They see culture as a huge wall, as a terrifying specter of "knowledge"', he went on. 'But we intellectuals, who are avid readers, know there are many ways of reading a book. You can skim it, you can start and not finish it, you can look at the index. You learn to live with a book.'[11] His driving concern was to provoke reading by explaining the possibilities for the individual to navigate their way through culture and to also bring back those outside the reading culture who are more pre-disposed to image. His concept for success being to disrupt the inherited reading practice of linearity underlines the changes in culture reception that are provoked by alternate forms of spectating.

The spectator mode in gaming is the ability to watch others playing. The spectator in gaming is also a participant, and active engagement is necessary. The spectator has only relatively recently been used as the term for performance and cultural events; it had only been used for sport and competitive events previously. So why have we begun to use spectatorship as a critical term for performance and entertainment environments? What does it offer us, and how has the spectator's relationship changed in terms of power activity, and the dynamics of the engagement with the artwork? How has the spectator become the protagonist, the performer, the writer, the reader and critic rolled into one? Do we need the liveness of the event anymore, and if so, for what purpose?

What is liveness offering us? Is it just a different form of engagement, and if so, does the youth of today want/believe/relate to this definition of engagement? Their engagement is with the screen, with the imaginary worlds of *World of WarCraft*, *Donkey Kong* or Second Life, and the real and play-acted world of Bebo, MySpace and YouTube. The player/spectator controls the character, avatar or presence of self, directing, taking a particular journey, deciding their fate and presenting themselves in the various virtual environments, imaginatively.

If we suggest that passivity has reached a point of no return, where all spectatorship is no longer passive, where memory and creativity are clinically linked, and where sensory pleasures of spectating are sought, we must recognize the progress of technologies and their interfaces as imaginative and playful devices for engagement.

Shigeru Miyamoto, noted as the world's most influential video game designer, was asked about the interface for spectators of the Nintendo Wii. 'I see the Miis as the most recent character creation from Nintendo,' Miyamoto said. 'What's interesting is that regardless of the user's age, if they're looking at a Mii, it's their Mii. Before, when you're playing as another character, it's more typical of more passive entertainment, and by creating a Mii you're becoming more a part of the entertainment experience.' WiiFit and WiiMusic are Nintendo's further forays into modes of engagement with WiiFit offering interactive yoga and WiiMusic enabling users to capture feelings of composition and improvisation.[12] These tools are progressing towards imaginative provocations, which support brain activity rather than diminish it leading toward a soporific reception state.

So are new modes of spectating enabling a greater understanding of the positive benefits of imagination and creativity? Investigations are under way looking at the relationship between brain activity and the onset of dementia in ageing, in particular the influence of creative activities.

Simon McBurney argues that technology is simply another tool for playing with imagination and being creative. For an older population the cultural engagement can be problematic, as neither have they learnt the nature of instantaneous interactivity nor do they have the arrogance of youth and the sense that private experiences are of interest to others. We see this again in the televisual broadcast world of *Big Brother* and 'fly on the wall' documentary, extremely interesting to a youth audience and progressively so for others, but also an intrusion and an impolite viewing of living but no less engaging. There is a politics of politeness within modes of spectating.

What is interesting is that notions of interactivity, disrupted narratives and engagements, which are the developed culture of games, have permeated the seams of other cultural practices of art, film, performance and theatre.

Who the audience is becomes relevant at this point in terms of the viewing frame set up to engage with the event, the spectator's auditory awareness and the balance of seeing the artwork, hearing and listening to its text, and the spectator's sensorial and critical faculty, in the immediate engagement with the work. When handed the Tate Modern leaflet for the Unilever series with both images and text about Doris Salcado's *Shibboleth*, the instant decision for the spectator is whether to glance, look or read. This is the potential introduction to the work, in tandem with making contact (or not) with what appears to be a crack in the concrete floor within the enormous space of the Turbine Hall. The spectator will have a choice to read the text or read the work; the spectator choice is for personal interpretation and discovery or discovery within the critic or presenter's context: a choice to go into an imaginary world, which is created from the concrete crack itself of what the crack means, personally, culturally and socially and the time you are willing to give to spectating in the context of what your purpose was in going to visit the artwork. Cultural shopping, and a fleeting look, may reduce one's understanding of cultural context and artistic value.

How do we unpack what spectating is and identify what the differences are now in the twenty-first century? They come from changes in technology for communication and entertainment. The phone to contact friends is replaced by MSN or Skype; gaming and the Internet replace the television as the latest form of entertainment and the entertainment of choice for the under 25s. The significance of artistic manifestations in art and culture in human existence has long been a source of puzzlement and fascination. Do we simply want to be entertained in order to provoke our imaginations? What is interesting is the time, energy and economy that is developed around and for the spectator in order to do this. For it is only by the desire of the spectator to imagine that spectating is a successful marriage of creator and spectator.

The individual finds their place for imaginative provocation to be involved with their imaginary world. More choice and accessibility has enabled people to choose their preferred form, for their imagination. Before television we may have read the same books more than once; to return to capturing what we liked, we may watch films again and again; the games we play again and again are what we need in order to capture our imaginations.

Out-takes take us deeper into the practices of the filmic, showing how the conceit is achieved, they remove the aesthetic in the same way that theatre at one point in the twentieth century determinedly removed the overtly theatrical; reminding the spectator that this is no longer about the imaginary world.

Definitions
Audience – is a group of people who have come to watch, but more importantly to hear in a space that equates to an auditorium. Hearing related not necessarily to seeing, as the Elizabethans described going to hear a play.

Spectator – is an onlooker, wholly related to viewing and observation.

However, the definitions of both these activities in the twenty-first century collide. They not only require listening, but both looking and observation, action and integration, and interactivity.

The new definition of spectatorship is interactivity. It is the combination of hearing and observation and it has fewer of the negative connotations of the late twentieth century ideas of passive viewing, which have led to an uninformed binary of passive and active, valuable and non-valid cultural activities. Listening has become part of spectating.

Inter – in the sense of between and among and belonging in common to, and these terms all relate to the spectating activities. It is a prefix to the senses, as is all twenty-first century spectatorship. The definitions of reading and writing also have new parameters given the Internet and texting, which involve the active participant spectator. The spectator in this context is seeing less and moving more quickly with what they see. For example, the use of text language, a communication which can be read and understood very quickly. We don't need all the detail of language and words, but a shorthand code for the reader 'cul8r'. Instant spectatorship comes from the speed of this culture, and society claims a speed of activity, which perhaps militates against the languished time spent listening to a play of an evening to the exclusion of all other activity.

Watching – is being on the alert and keeping in view. This is the action of watching. This is the passive audience, who are watching what goes on before them. This is very different from observation, a sense of observing a prescribed act and not taking notice, in the same way that you can hear something and not listen.

The modes of spectating addressed in this book:

- Headset
- Television
- Internet
- Film
- Games
- Exhibition
- Theatre
- Walks
- Mobile phone
- Computer

1st Screen – cinema, 2nd Screen – TV, 3rd Screen – computer, 4th Screen – mobile. The content for all is called one thing, usually related to old formats, for example, film, video, DVD and DVR but the receiver device for the spectator is different, and so is the location of the viewer, in that it could be an auditorium, a living room, an office or the street. What difference does the playback device make to content creation and reception? Does it matter where you view it? Movies, or moving images more correctly, define the creative practice, rather than the format for recording. Is the mode of spectating the screen, or is it the movie or moving image? Content becomes a screen creative practice. However, the size of screen, and where you view it, for example on the mobile, makes the viewing environment become the living environment and the landscape.

Spectating covers a whole range of observation activities. This book encourages you to reflect on the questions we have set out and engage with the modes of spectating under discussion. We have presented these in relationships that suggest their synergies: interactive media and youth culture; imaginative escape; identity and the self-conscious spectator and the site of spectating.

What is clear is the scope and dimension of definitions of meaning for the range of language used across interdisciplinary landscapes, for example, the use of 'interaction' in terms of the spectator's interactivity with the space or landscape, the artwork, the movie, the computer-based art, the screen, or the object in the virtual world of 'Second Life'. One author understands interaction as perception in virtual space; another celebrates the human-computer interaction of interactive art, whilst another posits active spectatorship as the participatory relationship of actor and masked spectator in the immersive, theatrical environment. Connections are made through and between the past theories and histories of Herbert Blau's *Audience* or Augusto Boal's 'SpectActor', via street theatre and the mobility of walking the city through interactive performances, public spaces and public art, leading to definitions of the 'spectator-protagonist-performer' or the 'masked spectator'.

It is of course your choice as reader to skim, dip, browse or read from cover to cover. Whichever approach you take, we hope this enables you to consider modes of spectating that are relevant to new cultural practices.

Notes

1. Oddey, A. (2007), *Re-Framing the Theatrical Interdisciplinary Landscapes for Performance*, Palgrave Macmillan, Basingstoke, Hampshire and New York.
2. www.lbvcr.com
3. www.time.com
4. ibid.
5. Rosenthal, M. (2003), *Understanding Installation Art*, Prestel, p. 25.
6. De Oliverira, N., Oxley, N., Petry, M. (2003), *Installation Art in the New Millennium*, Thames & Hudson, p. 167.
7. Ibid.
8. Deleuze, G. (1983), *Image Movement Cinema 1*, Minuit.
9. Rosenthal, M. (2003), *Understanding Installation Art*, Prestel, p. 26.
10. Bayard, P. (2007), *How to talk about books you haven't read*, Minuit.
11. Riding, A. (2007), 'A guide for those who don't read, but wish they did, *International Herald Tribune*, 28 February 2007.
12. Schiesel, S. (2008), 'For Father of Donkey Kong Fun is a Serious Business', *International Herald Tribune*, 25 May 2008.

PART ONE: INTERACTIVE MEDIA AND YOUTH CULTURE

1

ALTERED STATES

Christine White

A beautifully designed videogame invokes wonder as the fine arts do, only in a uniquely kinetic way. Because the videogame *must* move, it cannot offer the lapidary balance of composition that we value in painting; on the other hand, because it *can* move, it is a way to experience architecture, and more than that to create it, in a way which photographs or drawings can never compete. If architecture is frozen music, then a videogame is liquid architecture.[1]

Steve Poole with these words attempts to raise in the viewer/user's consciousness the prowess of the art forms that develop/create and enable the process of developing videogames. He invokes the sacred geometry that lies behind the presentation of the visual, as architectures of maths and music but it is commercial and global concerns that have given videogames prowess and their artistic merit is seldom celebrated. Success rated by popularity and usually accruing commercial value too, has often achieved little critical repute.

In *The Location of Culture* Homi K. Bhabha proposes that globalization must begin at home as this enables us to recognize the 'predatory effects of global governance';[2] he argues for the rights of cosmopolitanism to be recognized, rights of diversity and the richness of the history of human civilization. In all this, the individual's claim for identity is a difficult path between the global and local, where ancestry and travel have changed our experiences, heritage and parentage beyond that of any other generation. In the last two decades more people have lived between or across national borders than ever before with one estimation from UNESCO as high as 40 million migrant workers, 20 million refugees and 20–25 million people displaced due to famine and civil war. The borders of culture are breaking down, and much of this breakdown is being determined by technologies of communication, be they computer, via e-mail or VOIP technologies, design images, which are part of a global culture transmitted via cable, wireless, terrestrial or extra-terrestrial technologies; the Internet and the interactive, downloads, pod casts, webpages and blogs, which contemplate and document human action and interaction in a way that could not have been thought possible 50 years ago.

A democratization is occurring which by offering the ability to speak in a global context, makes it far harder for oppressive regimes to maintain control, when the population of a country can get a perspective of their local world from a global context, from news media and local webblog comment.

The communications of people to people across the world have enabled many changes from local cultures and economies to global cultures and economies and these cross-border forays of cultural practice have altered ways of reading and perceiving. Professor Sue Thomas worked on a project called 'Transliteracy – Reading in the Digital Age'. In 2005, she ran a conference looking at the use of the Internet and its possible causes for anxiety or opportunity. The research was particularly concerned with reading in the digital age. The claim and concern for scholars was that the web is primarily a textual medium, which, therefore, requires reading – often of more than two languages, one being predominately English. This emphasis on reading gives an enormous boost to text, however, it caused some concern and anxiety by the fluidity of reading possible on shifting platforms. The platforms could be blogs, e-mail, hypertext and mobile media. The concerns were that text was being superseded by image, audio or even ideogram as the communication language of choice, and of course, in the context of the conference's research, that would change the nature of literacy.

The development of the global technology of communication has enabled an anarchic liberalism, where the evolving knowledge presented is not academically peer-reviewed but, as in the case of Wikipedia, is globally viewed, reviewed, and multi-edited by collaborators who are collaborating in providing edited definitions of knowledge. However, Wikipedia when launched in 2001, was originally inspired by the door-to-door selling of encyclopedia in the 1970s and a wish to use the computer to liberalize knowledge. Initially, the inventor asked academics to write definitions for the online-free-content-encyclopedia, but he decided that the entries were too dry and dull and so he opened the editorial role to everyone. Wikipedia encourages not only debate but in recent years has also been open to abuse, particularly with regard to, the number of times the entry on George Bush has had to be re-written or cleaned up.

The ways of reading the web are predominately visual, and it is rare for a viewer to simply read the pages one after another in a linear fashion; what is more usual is to edit as part of reading. We read a part, line or paragraph, skip irrelevant content and move through the information to find what we want. Often this is navigation done through visual structures, and by and through a sense of associative ideas. If this is the case, are we losing narrative structure and are the readers enabled by this seeming lack of coherence? This lack of coherence may in fact be what is attractive. This random kind of thinking/viewing is a very liberal response to creativity without a defining knowledge of narrative coherence. What impact does this liberalism and use of associative connections have on the brain if it is now so prominent a style of communication? Is there a problem with the lack of coherence? In his famous book, *Homo Ludens: a study of play-element in culture*, Huizinga writes, 'any thinking person can see at a glance that play is a thing on its own'.[3] This suggests that although, as he details in his book, play can be found in all human activity it is also able to be a thing/experience in itself. A feature of the new tools of communication has been their immediate integration into activities which constitute play.

In the global transliteration of information and the dissemination of thought and image, we may be able to chart the activity of human history changed or potentially changed by an endless communication, but what happens in the local sense to our use and absorption of images and information? What happens in the most local point of consciousness to this information and how do we process our reactions and behaviours accordingly? In this global arena, what happens in the local, locality of the brain? This chapter looks at questions for the local brought about by the global digitalization and visualization communications systems, which we take for granted and do not analyze with regard to the effect on our brains and brain function.

The separation of distinct reactions to image technology and image product has brought about a significant response to such technologies. In the late twentieth century we have invariably argued about the dangers of too much television watching for children and generally there is a perceived wisdom in limiting the time with which children have contact with computers, also based on a similar presumption. This sense of what is good for children is contrary to what is endured by most adults in both work-place and home situations – namely to sit for long periods of time, often several hours, working at the computer work-station. This rather hypocritical interaction between machines and humans of differing ages and experiences further confounds our responses to how we 'should' be responding to time in the company of technologies.[4] For what exactly are we protecting children from whilst not protecting ourselves as adults? We might be concerned for our children, thinking that prolonged activity on the Internet might lead them to unsuitable chat rooms or pornography sites where they could be groomed by paedophiles. A need to protect from this threat is therefore rational, sensible and some would say imperative. However, our response to the televisual world is negotiated by ideas of too much exposure. Certainly in the 1980s some sociological studies were made into the reactions of societies in non-televisual contexts and how their society communicated in the now lost ways of pre-TV communities.[5] However, what was the danger here? Indoctrination? The diminished conversational skills of these populations? The lack of work achieved due to this new technological distraction? It was more to do with the potential soporific nature of this technology on human behaviour and a perceived problem of visual imagery taking over and taking precedence from a literary or verbal culture, a culture of great art in terms of literatures, of poetry and prose.

In the latter part of the first decade of the twenty-first century, with many countries of the world investing in design and design research, we can see that the visual culture, which surrounds us, in many mediums and technological forms, is affecting our reception of and responses to communication. In the adage that 'a picture tells a thousand words', we as a global culture can quickly respond to televisual reports and fast moving images, and are able to determine messages in complex forms from the array of sequenced images put to us. Contemporary insights about the interconnections between modern imaging systems and their historical and perceptual impact on our human imagination can be both surprising and unforeseen. However, it is harder to promote new technologies as 'new', as they are not developing a unique category of perception. However, what these imaging systems do is privilege the cybernetic richness and sensory density fusing patterns of information that are mediated by technologies.

In the last twenty years, scientists have begun to take the phenomenon of synaesthesia more seriously as neuroscience has developed as a field of medical practice. However, the testing for synaesthesia as a mechanism must be countered by the notion of differences and similarities of perception that have arisen in the arts.[6] The implication of synaesthesia for theories of consciousness for painting, literature, music and performing arts are legion. Scenography embodies the arts of music, design, sculpture, paint, light and dimensional design and as such the notion of perceptions of spaces and responses to such design spaces is always based on an understanding, perhaps non-scientific, of the potential synaesthetics of such performance spaces.[7]

Harrison and Baron-Cohen produced their book on synaesthesia because they felt there was enough scientific evidence to warrant the discussion of different modes of perception.[8] Their definition of synaesthesia is where one sensory modality automatically triggers a perceptual experience when no direct stimulation to this second modality has occurred. This definition would be a natural explanation of what might be occurring in digitalized visualizations. In fact, one might from this premise suggest that performance and scenography have purposely set out to develop an audience's ability to respond synaesthetically to what is presented. Whilst states of synaesthesia can be reproduced through hallucinogenic drugs, performers desire such altered states for their audiences, and many audiences indulge in spectating to lose themselves by the nature of skipping through associative states, whilst being provoked by sound, light and form in space. This might indeed be one explanation for the popularity of contemporary and modern dance, which offers abstractions and visual stimuli for the spectator to enjoy. These altered states demonstrate the skills of design, the development of associative thought and the nature of artistic perception, which becomes a part of a less conscious art. This associative process may be a productive way of interrogating the design process, but what of the visualizations and their resultant effect on the audience?

The context of performance now encompasses the media of TV, film, theatre, DVD, Internet, web-blogs and people of all ages are interested in and intrigued by the possibilities that fast moving images and communication can offer them in describing their lives and stories. The content of the media is vast. Add to these wide-ranging opportunities and ideas of displacement, which might occur in virtual worlds, projections onto 3D objects and the integration of the anomalies in live performance and such immersive experiences. The Internet enables our imaginations in a display environment. It is polylinear in construction and it holds the promise of fulfilling a desire that was only partially expressed in the idiom of cinema verité – to create a kind of motion picture that lets the world reveal itself and permits discovery on the part of viewers.

The multiplicity of visual culture, then, in all these forms and the possible harnessing of associative skills may have an effect on younger viewers/users, which we haven't yet quantified or, more directly, been aware of, except in the notional sense of restricting the engagement with a televisual world, as an inherently positive response to a degenerate medium. How do these images and their corresponding changes and associations affect the health of young people due to what is produced by this sensory richness in the brain? The question is, therefore, what effect do images and multimedia experiences in a number of performative contexts have on concentration?

Human nature and the nature of spectating are both inextricably linked but what is the future of spectating in the developing landscape of technological change? I want to explore concerns, which rely on the presumption of the non-ambiguous nature of text-based knowledge as the premise for all other forms of knowledge. The presumption of this assertion being correct is at once alarming and quite sad as it is dependant on viewing the world of visual technological developments as a negative. The dystopia, which Professor Susan Greenfield expresses as a problem for our multimedia world, does not take into account the positive nature of multimedia entertainments technology – most notably the sophistication of the spectating undertaken by young people.

Whether we believe that Greenfield's bold attempt to describe how twenty-first century technology is changing the way we think and feel is correct, is debateable. Our increasing ability to manipulate electronic media, robots, genes, reproductive biology and our minds is dramatically changing the way some of us live. Whilst we may see some technologies as producing an individuated life, where the technology makes us fearful and alienated, the contrary is the case for gaming. The gaming nature of spectatorship is inclusive and censoring children's activities related to gaming, play-stations and movies, might conversely be interrupting the further development of these environments, as enhanced unambiguous knowledge, rather than as a negative environment of associative hypertext, which Greenfield finds disturbing.

Whether we can equate the private ego with the development of IT particularly, also challenges the nature of the gadgetry and spectating possibilities that are available to us and for young people in general. Any negative impact on the human brain and central nervous system is unproven, as is the assertion that the essence of the individual is lost.

At home, the toddlers play with their smart toys that mirror their development, as each grapples with its environment. They can amuse themselves assembling a kind of sub-atomic nanotech Lego. Meanwhile, their flexi-operative parents and guardians will plug-in-and-play their serotonin depleted brains, episodically provoked to virtual desk rage, as performance statistics are relayed to the virtual boss somewhere on the other side of the world. The family will socialise remotely on some days, the teenagers are promiscuously lost in virtual sex role-play with a designed partner of their choice. All the while, the Hyperhouse, with its electronic spine and communications hub teems with smart appliances, activated by bodily sensors adjusting ambience and functionality accordingly.[9]

And what's so wrong with that! The relationship of technology to our lives has almost overwhelmed any debate and the sense of technologies as dangerous *per se* for their anti-human and post-human properties is an irrational response to what we do with the technologies and what they can do to or for us. In many senses the surreal and surrealism as a form, is a natural precursor to our fears of multimedia performance genres. Multimedia contains all the dangers of the imagination and *l'amour fou* – obsessional love, of games and interactivity, which André Breton identified as the seduction of the surreal.

The extension of the notion of a fashion dummy into a 3D environment is both compelling and surreal – it is not a statue and not a person but it adopts the human. This use of the projected live human creates the incongruous, and therefore, it is in itself surreal – the young accept it and transgress the departures and adventures from the real that it enables and creates. Are the dangers of this type of play in need of analysis from Freudian psychoanalysis or a Marxist critique of the capitalist and consumer culture which is being promoted – is this what happens to Lara Croft in the *Tomb Raider* series of games?

Lara Croft is surreal – and the *Tomb Raider* series is one of the few gaming environments that addresses a proto-feminist position, which is why I like it. However, this mannequin, this fashion dummy, is no dummy – she's intelligent and cunning, swift and thoughtful and she wins! In this moment the game is a noisy culture. A neo-surreal environment, a digi-surreal context of the hypertext and inter-textual environment, and the complexity of irony within this environment and game as event is extensive. This ironic positioning of the event viewed can use violence and opulence as a communicative medium.

Lara Croft is a character, a film, a game, a look and a style. It/She, the concept/package of entertainment, defies category. It is a sophisticated viewing/playing experience. In this we have combined the televisual with the cartoon, the technology of viewing space with the artistic and added irony and surreality, into creating an ever expanding unilateral environment created by the intersection of all electronically visual media and all its transmission modes; TV, dvd, Ps2/3, Xbox, Internet, mobile, and Wii.

Fig. 1: Lara Croft.

In the 1970s wrestling was on the television every Saturday afternoon. It contained usually what seemed like extensive damage to individuals thrown against the ring ropes and slammed onto the canvas floor, the referee's count being beaten by the hero of the ring. The challengers came into this sport/entertainment already cast as good or bad, evil or naïve – and the crowd got behind their choice. The appropriation of hero or villain engages the spectator beyond their world; it transcends their own space and time. They can roar and shout for their choice and against the referee, whilst always understanding both the theatricality of the experience and the irony of the play which is being created. How much better then to engage in the spectatorship from within the ring, with *SmackDown! vs Raw*?

Fig. 2: *SmackDown! vs Raw.*

The game has all the irony and theatricality of the 1970s and of the live human version but without the pain – except that the shouts of pain as you play are within the construct of the game – of winning or losing. No one dies, it is violent but within the context of moves – a whole stratagem of physical engagement. There are even exhibition matches where you, with your mannequin or fashion dummy, can compete against players around the world. The moves and attacks mimic the human world of these events – why censor these?

The game-play skill improves eye to hand coordination, it encourages numeracy, and in thinking terms it encourages logic and strategy. No it's not real, but then *Hansel and Gretel* isn't either, however, I would suggest that only the most intelligent analysis really translates that story into a lesson for children not to go with strangers. We can add that meaning, now within an adult constructed world, and as a justification for frightening 5 and 6 year olds. But then that was only a story told. It used mainly words. Though sometimes illustrated, it doesn't have the terror of the moving image. It is this within the televisual mode of spectating, which has become unknowable. The sheer scale and rhizomatic complexity, has effectively taken the televisual beyond the reach of human control. This complexity breaks down the popular claim of the visual to represent reality.[10]

We look at the world via the televisual rather than just seeing it as an object of viewing – while images seemingly bring the world close, it never gets nearer. The televisual image always maintains its untouchability, coolness and spatial abstraction. What becomes important is how one sees what one sees through the televisually, ontologically designed eye of the mind. Effectively the televisual destroys the last vestiges of the innocent eye, of making everything that is seen a consequence of its designing. Therefore, the televisual designing, in significant part, transforms both us and the globalizing culture and economy that de-futures our world and the worlds of others.

The televisual encourages dreams, dreams of fashion and consumption, it becomes the dreamer stranded between a culture, she the spectator is unable to enter or return. It breaks the illusion of truth – the ultimate claim of the representational photo-televisual form. The televisual increasingly refracts everything that appears in its frame as entertainment and horrific events can be portrayed via the visual tropes and presentational conventions of the entertainment industry competition. This critical drift leads to an increasing intolerance of the serious.

To confront the televisual's ability to de-future, enables our action. The complex social process of mediation is no different within the 2D screen world of mannequins and dummies than it is in the world of humans. The knowledge of when characters are dummies, mannequins or even computer-generated images is part of the new cultural knowledge base. Up until 1968 what was permissible to be read and be heard was reviewed and censored. The word could be so dangerous. The sophisticated spectator can distinguish real from fantastical, as the art critic can determine the surreal. We dispensed with censorship of the word but still feel edgy about the image. 'It's only violence', said the 11 year old, 'I know what that is'.

In reviewing *Polar Express* what is noted by the viewer is the skill of animation, motion capture and CGI (Computer Generated Image). This is the position of the informed viewer, appreciating the out-takes, director's cut and documentary of how the film was made – all a part of the DVD experience. Far from destroying the 'magic' it enhances the experience. It is completely educational. If we want children to be informed what better way? Or when we say the 'magic' is exposed, do we really mean the illusion of the con – that took us in for so many years, has now been revealed? It's like reading *Lady Chatterley's Lover* after it was banned, which when my father finally got hold of a copy, he said it was a total let down. Better to be wowed by the effects, then see how it was done; better to be engaged in the game as the character, but know what you are viewing in your mind; better to be young now and informed about the truth of illusion than conned all your life!

In 'The Social Brain of a Teenager', Sarah-Jayne Blakemore disentangles some of the presumptions about the critical periods of brain development.[11] Knowledge of the human brain has begun to be more clearly understood with the development of Magnetic Resonance Imaging (MRI) and it has provided evidence of ongoing cortical maturation through adulthood. What is interesting in the more recent studies is the way in which we can now determine social cognitive development.

'Theory of mind' or 'mentalizing' refers to inferences that we naturally make about other people's intentions, beliefs and desires, which we then use to predict their behaviour. The ability to attribute mental states develops over the first few years of life and culminates in the ability to make complex false belief tasks by age four or five.[12] Most of these studies have concentrated on early childhood, but the development of cognitive abilities has not been further studied beyond these years.

Modes of spectating become relevant in studies of the developing social brain as the environmental factors, and contributions of hormones, culture and social environment are recognized as influencing behaviours and perceptions. Perceptive-taking ability is a skill, which is crucial for successful social communication. This involves individuals imagining either how they would feel (first person) or how a protagonist (third person) would feel in various scenarios. This skill enables us to reason about others, to understand what another person thinks or feels or believes, and it is necessary to step into their mental shoes and take their perspective. Blakemore cites: 'Functional neuroimaging studies have revealed that medial prefrontal cortex, inferior parietal lobe and superior temporal sulcus are associated with making the distinction between third and first person'[13] The speed of this skill develops and increases with age, possibly due to mature neural circuitry supporting social cognition and greater social experience.

It seems that pre-MRI, however, the value of spectating situations and having the opportunity to consider first and third person relations to actions was embedded culturally in our developments of storytelling, playing out and performance activities. We might consider these cultural practices as tools for cognitive health. There is certainly no lack of market for these opportunities – in books, movies and interactive games, and perhaps more traditionally theatre, the mode of spectating is the same; simply imagining.

The struggle for western societies is in determining the safety of these opportunities for simulation. Some of the inherent fear perhaps relates to our religious morals and to the need for no demi-gods. Simulated experience is seen as a nullified experience and yet we use these methods for teaching, flight simulators and practice driving tests to learn about hazards on the road. Of course the divergence and dangers could be seen to be in the map of the real, as in simulations outlined above as opposed to the simulation of something that has never existed.[14] The danger of the fantastic and fantasy was felt in the development of fantasy literature, which took a more imaginative turn. From the era of the original, we have developed a set of simulations which involve the counterfeit, the produced, the copy through to the simulated, third order of simulacra whereby the copy has replaced the original. The cognition of first and third person has developed and become more sophisticated, but is it dangerous or simply part of the expansion of cognitive concepts that the human brain is capable of discerning? This becomes the mode of spectating.

Borges' concern in 'On Exactitude in Science' is re-lived within the filmic and games media.

> ...In that Empire, the Art of Cartography attained such Perfection that the map of a single Province occupied the entirety of a City, and the map of the Empire, the entirety of a Province. In time, those Unconscionable Maps no longer satisfied, and the Cartographers Guilds struck a Map of the Empire whose size was that of the Empire, and which coincided point for point with it. The following Generations, who were not so fond of the Study of Cartography as their Forebears had been, saw that that vast Map was Useless, and not without some Pitilessness was it, that they delivered it up to the Inclemencies of Sun and Winters. In the Deserts of the West, still today, there are Tattered Ruins of that Map, inhabited by Animals and Beggars; in all the Land there is no other Relic of the Disciplines of Geography.[15]

The map of life set out is at a ratio of 1:1 but unlike Borges' maps the representations are not useless because they are the same size as life itself, and are more useful. The art of the mode of spectating interactive and passive fictions is to be able to assimilate and explore the fictions of false reality, to understand the complex perceptual differences enabled by the forms of communication and media. In the United Kingdom the stress in the creative industries on technology as the innovation misses the fundamental point about all modes of spectating, that is, innovation in creativity is about human expressiveness.

The complex narratives of games and complex language and narrative of the gaming structure – with parallel narratives and points of interactivity make a complex pattern for the spectator to follow and engage in. They work on both ergodic and ludic theories, the former that requires the active and non-trivial work of the viewer/gamer/player to follow pathways or derive routes through the games; ludic in the sense of play, but this play is extranoematic requiring thought and processing outside of human thought, extra thoughts and ideas beyond the immediate stimulus.

Gaming is described as a lean forward media rather than a lean back media, such as tv, film and books. Digital games bring players into a productive relationship with text and they create the text on each engagement. There is debate in game theory as to what creates the organizing structure. Narratologists suggest it is narrative, and play theorists determine it is play theory, Ludology. Do we have conflicts between plot, characterization, closure as opposed to setting, formula for setting, and settings for action? Or, we might conclude that narrative is not essential to games. Games are present and in the now not the future. They depend on action and performance, the goal of the game and the spectator being an actor in the game.[16] This enables us to draw some distinctions between the narrative and interactive – interactive using the algorithm as the procedure for participation, requiring ergodic engagement not simply on a mental plane. Contrary to narratives, which are not necessary for games or simulations – instead these are representations. There are different modes of writing; 1) procedural authorship of rules that promote motion; and 2) aesthetic landscapes of discovery with consequence-based threads of emotion. The interactive is in conflict with narrative if the game is to 'include' the player. We should celebrate the kinetic aspects of popular culture of motion and emotion and we need to, therefore, understand the mechanics of emotion within popular entertainment. The need is for thoughtful criticism of this new art form, and of the emotional impacts and aesthetic statements for the promotion of thoughtful game content rather than the promotion of censorship. The ideal is an ethically informed public.

A technological development without impact on society is meaningless. In 'Informing Ourselves to Death' Neil Postman states: 'Printing fostered the modern idea of individuality but it destroyed the medieval sense of community and social integration. Printing created prose and made poetry an exotic and elitist form of expression.'[17]

Other positive remarks for interactive spectatorship include Thompson who states: 'Arguably, what most people are learning from first-person shooter games in particular is an inordinate respect for law enforcement agencies and some very conservative values, especially about people who commit crimes. As many critics of games would not see respect for authority as in itself a bad thing, the findings do little to endorse assumptions that gaming is associated with anti-social behaviour.'[18]

The online gaming and massive multiplayer online games (MMOGs) were predicted by Alvin Toffler in 1980, as a means to ending mass media and creating a de-massification of media and the rise of the 'pro-sumer', where users are creators and not just consumers of their own media.[19] Spectatorship, interactivity and authorship become extremely blurred in the fourth party developer game content environment, using open source models of software and programming.

Digital games are proving to be ever more social and less solitary and now players are equally likely to be female and in their late twenties.[20] The clans, guilds and social groups, which are part of some games and in-world structures, enable the forming of communities and whilst the ends of these often have tasks such as raids, battles, and quests they create a community and offer an experience of belonging – a feeling often commended in an audience for theatre. The activities are bonding, therefore, in the same way as sporting teams are created to compete, play and win. The technology offers experiences to the masses that have in the past been reserved for the few, such as travel to far off lands, explorations and expeditions, which were once the privilege of nineteenth century male gentry.[21]

So games involve paid and unpaid labour and the consumer becomes the last worker on the production line.[22] Making use of and also engaging these audiences will be a challenge to the gaming industry but all the entertainment conglomerates, who aren't keyed up to move from their linear production line profit structure to something akin to a gaming service and R&D creativity network, which has a democratic knowledge-share at its heart, will fail.

> You can't stop time – you can only simulate it, by stopping change. There is no solution to the lack of mercy toward the aged flushed out into the open by the Internet. The state of mind demanded by a world that quests after ever more rapid technical change is alien to anyone over forty. The best one can aim for is to be a case of arrested development and remain forever a child, fantasizing about clocks that tick for ten thousand years and gray goo that eats you in the night...a celebration only of the aspects of the childhood that has market value: the child's gift for coping with the havoc he wreaks, and the child's ability to walk away from aspects of self without feeling like an amputee.[23]

In order to judge the effect of games you need to be able to play them. The controversy of the classification over *Manhunt 2* highlights this issue. The judge who made the court ruling had not had experience of playing the game and understanding the concept whether termed narrative or interactive. A lack of knowledge about games and that specific works are operating on a different level, neglects a fundamental sense of other cultural arts – in the same way that certain horror fiction writing would not be recommended for the under tens. In this wider context we need to understand that games aren't just aimed at kids and there are very definitely modes of spectating.

Notes

1. Poole, S. (2000), *Trigger Happy: Video Games and the Entertainment Revolution*, Arcade Publishing, p. 226.
2. Bhaba, H.K. (1994), *The Location of Culture*, Routledge, p. xv.
3. Huizinga, J. (1938), *Homo Ludens: a study of play-element in culture*, Beacon Press, p. 3.

4. Byron Report 2008 – http://www.dfes.gov.uk/byronreview/

5. Contradictory reports and studies have been made over the last 50 years to determine the danger or damage of televisual experiences with no conclusion being reached. These range philosophically from Aristotle to Freud and sociologically and psychologically include arousal theory, social learning theory, disinhibition theory and aggression reduction theory. See also, Aronson, E. (1995), *The Social Animal*, New York, W.H. Freeman and Co., 7th Edition; Bandura, A. (1973), *Aggression: A social learning analysis*, Englewood Cliffs, NJ, Prentice-Hall; Berkowitz, L., 'Violence in the mass media', in Berkowitz, L. (1962), *Aggression: a social psychological analysis*, New York: McGraw-Hill, 1962, pp. 229–55.

6. Whilst medically synaesthesia refers to the involuntary confusion of the senses, for the arts synaesthesia expresses a multi-modal experience producing a sensory fusion pushing aside analytic explanations of art. See also Cytowic, R.E. (1993), *The Man who tasted shapes: a bizarre medical mystery offers revolutionary insights into reasoning, emotion and consciousness*, New York, Putnam.

7. Oddey, A., White, C.A. (2006), *The Potentials of Spaces*, Bristol: Intellect.

8. Baron-Cohen, S., Harrison, J.E. (1997), *Synaesthesia: classic and contemporary readings*, London, Blackwell.

9. White, C.A. (2007), *Transliteracy*, keynote address 'Transliteracy Conference for Prague Quadrennial and Scenography Internationa' l, July 2007.

10. Mass mediaras 1996, *R/U/A/TV? Heidegger and The Televisual Power* 1993

11. Blakemore, S.J. (2007), 'The Social Brain of a Teenager', *The Psychologist*, Vol. 20, no. 10, The British Psychologist Society, October 2007.

12. Barresi, J., Moore, C. (1996), 'Intentional relations and social understanding', *Behavioural and Brain Sciences*, 19, pp. 107–54. False belief tasks mean the ability to put yourself in someone else's position.

13. Blakemore, p. 601. The further studies are: Ruby P., Decety, J. (2004), 'How would you feel versus how do you think she would feel? A neuroimaging study of perspective-taking with social emotions', *Journal of Cognitive Neuroscience*, 16, pp. 988–99; (2001) 'Effect of subjective perspective taking during simulation of action: A PET investigation of agency', *Nature Neuroscience*, 4, pp. 546–50.

14. Baudrillard, J. (1996), *Simulcra and Simulation*, (trans.) Glaser, S., University of Michigan Press.

15. Suárez, Miranda (1658), 'Viajes de varones prudentes', Libro IV, Cap. XLV, Lérida, in Borges, J.L., 'On Exactitude in Science', p. 325 in *Collected Fictions*, (trans.), Hurley, H., Penguin Books.

16. Jesper, J. (2001), 'Games Telling Stories? A Brief Note on Games and Narratives', *International Journal of Computer Games Research*, vol. 1., no. 1, www.gamesstudies.org.

17. Postman, N. (2003), 'Informing ourselves to Death' in Ermann, D.E., Shauf, M.S., *Computers Ethics and Society*, 3rd edition, Oxford University Press, p. 102.

18. Thompson, C. (2002), 'Violence and the Political Life of Videogames', in King, L., (ed.), *Game On*, London: Laurence King Publishers, pp. 21–31.

19. Toffler, A. (1980), *The Third Wave*, New York: Bantam Books.

20. Economic Science Association 2004.

21. Cassell, J., Jenkins, H. (1998), 'Gendered Games' in *From Barbie to Mortal Kombat: Gender and Computer Games*, MIT Press.

22. Leadbetter, C. (1999), *Living on Thin Air: the new economy*, London: Penguin.

23. Lewis, M. (2002), *The Future Just Happened*, Hodder & Stoughton, p. 257.

2

A QUICK WALK THROUGH 'UNCANNY VALLEY'

Saint John Walker

An ex-animator's personal perspective on the development of animation in the digital domain, and how the tools generated by 3D technologists came from a particular mimetic ideology, that skewed its development. This chapter attempts to plot the emergence and migration of the 'Uncanny Valley' concept into common parlance; a term borrowed from robotics that found a home within the field of 3D animation. This is a consequence of a world-view that was present from the early digital animation tools, which heavily leaned towards mimicking the physical world rather than unleashing the artist's inner world.

It's been 21 years since I paid a friend 50 pounds to give me a day's tuition on his Amiga 500 computer. As an animator at the time, I was desperate to get an idea of this new technology's capabilities. The Amiga's 'Workbench' interface flummoxed me at first. On the screen an icon of a trashcan and a series of drawers with names like 'Utilities' or 'Workbench' gave me no clue as to how I could make stunningly creative work on this computer. There, for a brief moment, I understood I had entered an alien world. The interface had been designed by someone who belonged to a very different culture from me. This chapter represents a personal perspective on the development of animation in the digital domain. It looks at how a certain technology-primed cadre appropriated animation concepts, and led development along a certain path until it encountered and indeed resuscitated the concept of the 'Uncanny Valley'. Each medium's development is enslaved to its own history, but also the history of its antecedents. Even in the shiny world of seemingly unlimited pixels and bits, 2D digital animation still seems to be chained to the look of 'economy of line', that sprang from the economy of the production line; the need to produce twelve or 24 frames a second within a hand-drawn, yet industrial setting. Even though those days are gone, vector-based digital programs are still complicit in maintaining a flat unmodulated simplicity of style. Today, cartoons fly off the digital production-line with the same economical look as before, as a brief look at the Nicklodeon channel will confirm.

Whereas the development of the 2D digital animation concentrated on providing limited colour palettes and comfortable, craft-based flipbook metaphors within the graphic user interface, 3D digital animation developed within another industrial culture and sphere of influence. 3D animation was the fiefdom of the software technologists; the kind of people who understood CPUs and CLIs[1] but not sculpture or anatomy, never mind the pegbar, graticule and lightbox. From the start, the *cri de coeur* was 'it may not look like much now, but Moore's Law is on our side! We'll get there!'[2]

From very early on the promise of 3D Computer Generated Imagery (CGI) attracted a certain kind of optimist prepared to defer artistic gratification for the present, and just marvel at what could be achieved in terms of mips (millions of instructions per second – a measure of computer power). 3D CGI was a visual art without a fixed viewpoint, wherein the virtual artefact could be framed from any angle, modified, copied and reused elsewhere; offering easily changeable lighting and surfaces, where nothing was fixed until the final render. To many, the instruction code that described the image was more impressive than the image itself. The new 3D technologists didn't like to appropriate from traditional animation, nor from sculpture. What craft animators had called 'fairing' (a delightful term from sailing), the new 3D techies called 'acceleration' and 'de-acceleration' (more at home in the physics department); what animators called 'squash' and 'stretch' (summoning up fun and possibilities) became 'deformation' – a term that could be read to problematize departure from true scale.

Partly due to the early gravitation towards CADCAM (Computer Aided Design, Computer Aided Modelling) and its attendant mathematical simulation, the tools that 3D software programmers developed concentrated on mimicking the 'real world' rather than enabling an artist's inner world of imagination. It was all about manufacturing rather than creating. The functions of the virtual tools within 3D software were taken from the automotive and shipbuilding industries, and the nomenclature persists; hull, spline, loft, bevel, lathe. Bezier curves, the main means to design the characters in Pixar's flicks or Shrek the Umpteenth, emerged from the offices of Renault cars.[3] Mimesis was the trajectory along which 3D modelling and animation developed. From the start, the 3D software interface tended to stifle the artist, whilst at the same time sneakily appropriating the artist's nomenclature. Programs had names like Sculpt 3D and Imagine, but in reality Graphic User Interface (GUI) operations and menus led to thousands of Commodore Amiga home-computer kids trying DESPERATELY to build scenes that WEREN'T spaceships or cars, and usually failing[4]

From the early days of 3D software, the holy grail of photorealism was evident. The top selling Amiga 3D modelling program was even called Real 3D. You only had to look on the boxes that the software were shipped in, which were decorated with reflective chrome balls on tiled floors or glass objects. Well, at least that was what you 'thought' a real chrome ball on a tiled floor would look like. There was even lens flare in some pictures, for god's sake, to imply you were looking at a real object through a lens; a telling admission of 3D software's collective jealousy of the camera's seeming ability to capture 'the real'.

The inclusion of what became known as the 'Utah Teapot' model in major commercial 3D software in the 1980s and early 1990s, such as 3D Studio, AutoCAD and POVRay could be said to be symptomatic of both a bankruptcy of imagination and the mimetic urge. The Utah Teapot,[5] so called because of its inception at the University of Utah in 1975, was an early 3D reference model, a protean digital form that joined the pantheon of sphere, cube, cone, rod and torus as building blocks for the user in early software. Sure, it was a joke, but the inclusion of such a depressingly quotidian form belied the idea that your imagination could really be free to soar in this new medium. Here, one definitely gets the idea that the code that described the image was more impressive than the image itself. The 'Utah Teapot' computer graphics in-joke lives on; 'Utah Teapots' can be found in *Toy Story*, *Monsters Inc.*, and Disney's *Beauty and the Beast*, as well as in *The Simpsons*. Of course, 3D modelling wasn't the only art form pushed by technologists towards verisimilitude. That same holy grail had been approached with fervour in the field of robotics, too.

In 1978, the Japanese roboticist Masahiro Mori published an article in the Japanese magazine *Energy* entitled 'Bukimi No Tani', translated as 'The Uncanny Valley'. In it he made the

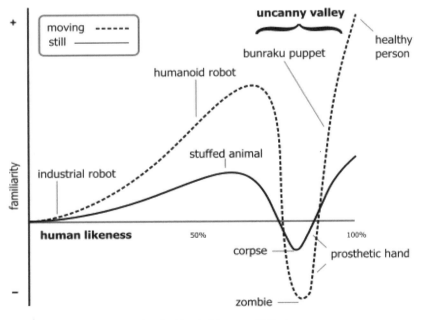

Fig. 3: Mori's 'Uncanny Valley'.

observation that the more humanlike his robots became, the more people were attracted to them, but only up to a point. If an android started to become too realistic and lifelike, suddenly people were repelled and felt a little disgusted. Mori called this emotional plunge the 'Uncanny Valley', referring to the dip in a diagram he plotted of anthropomorphic robots and our emotional reaction.[6]

As visual consumers of animation and games, we become engrossed with characters of all kinds, but if they approach photorealism we become hyper-critical. Our brains seemingly magnify the slightest imperfections. We note the soul-less eyes, the rigid lips. Our empathy with the character is curtailed, and in some cases we feel a form of revulsion. Oddly, we can empathize more with Woody and Buzz Lightyear in *Toy Story* than we can with their owner, Pete; we feel more empathy for characters in Pixar's *Cars* (who don't even have limbs) than, say, the perfectly proportioned Dr. Aki Ross, the main character in 2001's *Final Fantasy: The Spirits Within* – the first animated feature to seriously attempt photorealistic CGI humans.[7]

Now seen in some quarters as the hubristic consequence of the relentless scramble for the photorealist holy grail (the technologist's agenda) at the expense of story, empathy and emotion, *Final Fantasy*'s critical fate was ignominious. With losses of over $124 million at the box office, it effectively bankrupted its makers, Square Pictures. It was, however, an important point on the trajectory that had started with the first 3D polygon. With their special relationship with software and hardware manufacturers Alias Wavefront, (now assimilated into Autodesk, Inc) and rammed to the gunnels with Silicon Graphics Octane workstations and SGI Origin 200 servers, *Final Fantasy* was very much a product of 3D's dominant technology-first ideology. However, the public didn't seem to share the messianic fervour for synthespians and digital verisimilitude. Only Disney's *Treasure Planet* (2002) has lost more money as an animated film at the box office. It seems *Final Fantasy* had fallen into Mori's 'Uncanny Valley'.

Fig. 4: *Final Fantasy.*

Peter Plantec, author of *Virtual Humans*, likens the 'Uncanny Valley' to animation's own 'sound barrier' and states that, 'when a virtual human actor looks very, very real, you want to believe it is real, but a subconscious protective mechanism in your brain starts looking for flaws to prevent you from being fooled. The result is simultaneous belief and disbelief. Movies are all about suspension of disbelief and this kind of dissonance disturbs that process – ditto for games'.[8]

The concept of the 'Uncanny Valley' conveniently seemed to explain why all that motion capture, IK (Inverse Kinematics) and superb rendering technologies had failed to engage us. There was something a little 'icky' about the characters; a kind of cognitive dissonance. They looked mostly real, yet little imperfections disturbed the viewer.

In 2004 the 'Uncanny Valley' concept came to the fore again as a talking point in the CGI field during the box office 'battle royal' between two blockbuster CGI films, Pixar's *The Incredibles* and Warner Brothers' *The Polar Express*. The comparison between the emotional warmth we felt for Pixar's stylized plastic family and our uncomfortable feelings about the more accurate yet eerie characters in *The Polar Express*, which were described by many critics as being disturbing, was a subject for much critical debate, partly because their releases coincided.

The story of how 3D modelling and animation developed down a different path is interesting, and it should be noted that the 'Uncanny Valley' concept only really migrates across disciplines from late 1970s robotics into the late 1990s animation sphere thanks to the prevalence of 3D CGI generated human characters in games and films. 2D CGI had taken hold in the early 1990s and had not been linked to Mori's theory, because there was little or no need. It is very hard to find examples of 2D animation characters falling into the 'Uncanny Valley'. Of course, at the end of the day, both 2D and 3D animation techniques produce a flat image on our screens. So why do only 3D models appear in the 'Uncanny Valley', with the paradoxical point at which the simulation is so good, it's bad? My answer is that we are seeing the consequences of the different paths that 2D and 3D animation took into the digital arena, and how the development of 3D software and its interfaces continue to be all too readily wedded to the ideal of photoreal mimesis and its near attainability, rather than the expression of interior imaginative worlds. 3D advances such as ray tracing, caustics, sub-surface scattering and dynamics have now moved simulation and description to a new level. Autodesk, the company behind 3D software Maya and 3DS Max, have a section on their website called 'Is it fake or foto?' that challenges the viewer to decide which images are real, and which are 3D software originated, as if fooling the eye is a benchmark of success?[9]

It's instructive to compare two recent films: one using 3D technology, the other using 2D, and to note what kind of language is used by critics to describe them. Firstly, the aforementioned *Polar Express*. The characters move just like actors, thanks to the comprehensive use of motion capture techniques, applied to 3D models. They are almost convincing, but the critic Philip French notes, 'the human figures look like shop-window dummies brought to half-life as zombies'[10] and the BBC's Stella Papamichael states: 'Forget Christmas cheer – kids will run screaming from *The Polar Express* after seeing Tom Hanks looking like he's been killed, embalmed and resurrected by lightning' and talks of 'its dead-eyed cast'.[11]

We can contrast this with Bob Sabiston's heavily rotoscoped 2D animation process, seen in *Waking Life* (2001) or *A Scanner Darkly* (2006). Should this too not arouse unease? The characters move just like us, thanks to the comprehensive use of 2D rotoscope techniques. They are almost human. You could argue that their eyes are soul-less (an oft-repeated characteristic of the residents of 'Uncanny Valley'), yet when reviewers speak about the technique, it is words like beautiful and dream-like that get used. 'Director Richard Linklater, using the same dreamlike rotoscoping animation he showcased in *Waking Life*...It's never less than incredibly beautiful to watch', wrote Paul Arendt of the BBC.[12] The *Observer's* Philip French said: 'The actors retain their voices, but they're turned into cartoon figures clearly resembling themselves yet becoming somehow dreamlike and abstracted'.[13]

You can see 3D animation's plunge into the 'Uncanny Valley' as the result of the software/hardware peddlers and computer gurus who envisage the accurate cloning of our world, its occupants and its physics as the ultimate goal. In contrast, it was never part of the 2D animation culture to desire to replicate the real. However, nowhere is the Uncanny Valley more pronounced (and accepted) than in games, where the belief that immersion and superior game-play can be enhanced by simulating the real world as a touchstone to many. Clive Thompson, a digital media journalist and 'Uncanny Valley' commentator, seems to think so. He said:

> Unfortunately...gaming's Uncanny Valley could be here to stay, simply because players have become used to it. In the real world of plastic surgery, face-lifts used to look horrifically strange but now go unnoticed. Likewise, we've played with dead, fish-eyed characters for so long that they seem kinda normal. Creepiness, like beauty, is in the eye of the beholder...It's part of the malaise that currently affects game design, in which too many designers assume that crisper 3-D graphics will make a game better...game designers may never be able to capture that last one percent of realism. The more they plug away at it – the more high-resolution their human characters become – the deeper they'll trudge into the Uncanny Valley.[14]

Possibly the most quoted example of 'Uncanny Valley' in the games arena is the much-distributed promotional trailer for Quantic Dream's *Heavy Rain*.[15] Its cinematic pretensions and handheld camcorder look, bolstered by a thoroughly motion captured character, 'Mary Smith' – holds a morbid fascination as we zoom in on dead eyes and waxen features. It's almost there. Almost. The lights are on, but there's no one home. However, crucially (and this is a telling point, reflecting Clive Thompson's earlier comments) early reviews by games insiders didn't seem to notice anything was wrong! 'The really intriguing thing about the *Heavy Rain* demo is that purportedly, the whole thing was running in real-time. Real-time facial expressions, real-time tears, real-time everything', gushed the UK Gamespot website review.[16]

After years of claiming that the 'Uncanny Valley' effect could be solved by throwing more pixels at the problem, there are signs that the 3D technologists seem to have had a re-think. The 'Uncanny Valley' concept is now fully recognized within Games circles and the industry has developed new strategies to deal with it. One is to claim graphics are secondary, like the Nintendo Wii, and that immersion in the game-play is heightened not by greater detail, but by less. Shawn White compares the aforementioned *Heavy Rain* character to the Wii's lower resolution character Link from the *Zelda* game:

> Mary is very photo-realistic; Link is not. My subconscious mind is not attached to the woman, since she is not an extension of me, but another person entirely...All in all, Mary's realism creeps me out too much to notice her emotions. But Link's lack of total photo-realism allows me to focus on his emotional response, which heightens my own emotional response, which enforces the bond between player and character.[17]

Glenn Entis, Chief Technical Officer with EA, one of the largest games publishers in the world, told a packed 'SIGGRAPH 2007' audience that games makers had to stop focusing purely on a photoreal look: 'When a character's visual appearance creates the expectation of life and it falls short your brain is going to reject that...Just adding polygons makes it worse.'[18] Entis's answer seems to be to combine motion capture with other artistic tools, and he's not alone.

What the technological evangelists saw as an ultimate destination may be becoming just another option, like hyperrealism in the world of painting. Like Entis and EA, leading Games developer Ubisoft's promo for the game *Assassin's Creed* seems to exhibit sensitivity to the dangers of the 'Uncanny Valley' concept.[19] Animation project manager, Elspeth Tory, cites the 'Uncanny Valley' as a hurdle in achieving realism, but makes a distinction between reality and believability: 'A character that's *realistic* will seem to have ticked off a checklist of human characteristics, but a *believable* one will display nuances and subtleties that make them seem unique and alive.' Tory states that the interplay of weight and timing are some of the most important aspects that contribute to a character's believability. Note that these have always been the province of the animation artist.[20] Alex Drouin, an animation artistic director at Ubisoft adds: 'Everything was hand animated in *Prince of Persia*', their previous game. Would this have been highlighted a few years before, when the prevalent zeitgeist dictated you talked about how your clever software automated the production?

It could be said that Clive Thompson's comments earlier about game players essentially being acclimatized to the vacant characters they encounter or manipulate, fails to take into account that characters in games are there to fulfil the game's unfolding interactive experience, rather than to be passively viewed and consumed like in cinema.

How the game plays has always ranked higher than the graphics. So why do game developers bother to try to leapfrog the 'Uncanny Valley'? Firstly, the way you sell a game still depends on the potential buyer seeing stills in print to allure them. Selling a game through moving clips, on TV ads or websites, is problematic because it involves the potential purchaser as viewer, not do-er/player. Thus, the marketing reverts to spectacle, not game-play. Secondly, both games and film companies use the same software for building and animating increasingly converging worlds. The means of creation and interface pull the software user ever deeper into the mimetic, with physics based particles and dynamics, lighting and texturing. Film and games technologists are now talking about blending data with artistry. Ubisoft claims this approach is helping animators create a game that looks both believable and realistic, without getting mired in the 'Uncanny Valley'.

Motion capture technology is now used as a matter of course. Indeed, the blending of motion capture data[21] with other more craft based animation techniques seems to be one way of crossing the 'Valley', or maybe of forgetting about it altogether. As an example the makers of the much slated *Polar Express* came back with a new offering in 2006, Robert Zemeckis' *Monster House*,[22] but this time they had combined their motion capture techniques with old fashioned key-framing and stylized facial features. There's now a change of emphasis on the tools they use: 'To me, the motion capture represents live action reference', says Imageworks' animation supervisor on *Monster House*, Troy Saliba. 'We could use it to emulate reality or to add depth of performance and still go stylized and exaggerated.'[23] The terminology is being changed; the industry now talks of performance capture. Director Gil Kenan also points to the decline of the 3D technologist's agenda we have been charting. 'There's a veneer that exists from 3D renders that puts me at a distance. I like things to feel tangible. I like seeing hand-painted textures, thumbprints in things. I had to work very hard to create a system where I would feel excited by the result.'

'CG is beautiful', admits the film's visual effects supervisor Jay Redd, 'but we wanted the antithesis...To make the film feel tangible. I wanted it to look like it was made of something real.'

So capturing physical movement is now being relegated from an end in itself to a starting point for artistic expression. Jay Redd's, 'something real' is essentially motion capture data heavily mediated by artists, and not left unadorned as one might expect. So are we seeing the collapse of a 3D photoreal agenda, or its redeployment to new areas? In *Sin City* and *300* we see heavily stylized, technologically mediated visions, but these are primarily 2D flat visions; actors shot in front of blue screen. The 3D CGI is subordinate to the actor's performance in these films, often providing the *mise-en-scene*, or at most augmenting the actor's appearance. 3D CGI is not the actor, but the furniture.

Despite a welter of 3D CGI films in the last five years, none attempted a *Final Fantasy/Polar Express* type look again until 2007's *Beowulf*, which seems to show that at least one studio is still keeping a photoreal trajectory. As such, *Beowulf* has been seen by many media commentators as a useful indicator of how 3D technology has developed. The surprising corollary to this has been how the 'Uncanny Valley' concept is now fully nested into popular culture, and is quoted again and again in blogs and reviews.

Beowulf is another Zemeckis film, this time as director, for Sony Pictures Imageworks. On the film's credits there are lead software engineers and facial wranglers; new roles supporting this

Fig. 5: *Beowulf.*

re-working of an ancient epic tale. The cognitive dissonance and eeriness is still there, but maybe more to do with the fact that Ray Winstone and Anthony Hopkins are familiar to us, and Winstone's digital six-pack pulls us back from full immersion in a way an unknown actor might not.

It is easy when examining such films to talk in terms of technical fixes, indeed that seems to be the way the Sony Pictures Imageworks technologists like to frame these movies. This then becomes the agenda for any review of the film. *Empire* magazine's Tom Ambrose exclaims, 'you'll be glad to know that the creepy dead eyes thing has been fixed', in the second sentence of his review, as if the film is a new version of some software itself.[24] This refers to the technique whereby tracking muscle pulses from the eye and eyelids, more of the facial nuances could be digitized. Electro occulography is the technologist's new frontier. However, it is clear that the artistic expression of the actors, when converted to data is still imperfect.

At a recent CGI conference (with a themed day on the 'Uncanny Valley'), acting coach and author of *Acting for Animators*, Ed Hooks,[25] was a lone voice pointing out what we are losing with the reliance on data 'as' performance. Hooks pointed out that whilst on a traditional film set actors will act differently for a close-up or wide-angle, there are no such cues in motion capture. The director decides the framing of the shot later, with a virtual camera. Hooks also suggests that characters in *Beowulf* often blink in the wrong place. Having been manufactured or moved in time, blinks no longer 'punctuate thought'. If Hooks is right, then Sony Pictures Imageworks, with more than 14 terabytes of performance capture data to filter and tweak, are still missing the small things that cause the cognitive dissonance between Ray Winstone the actor, and Ray Winstone the data.

As Brad Bird, a traditional animator who went on to direct Pixar's *The Incredibles* said:

It's easy to blow up a city in CGI, but it's hard for a character to grab another character's shirt. You could have some really spectacular scene, and [the animation staff] would just go, 'No problem. How many of those do you need?' But one character touching another character's hair: 'Aaah! No! Isn't there anything else you could do?' I mean, I had to budget shirt-grabs.[26]

This is the looking-glass world of 3D animation technology.

So whether motion capture is a live action reference and starting point for the creative animator and film-maker, or whether animators are merely appropriated to use their art to paper over holes in the data is a moot point. The technologists that CGI has brought into the film world are collecting more and more data of real performances, with new hybrid mixes of sensors and cameras but at the moment, the equation that will rid them of the 'Uncanny Valley' is still not complete.

 Pre-millennial chatter about replacing actors with 3D 'synthespians' or 'vactors' (virtual actors) seems to have dried up, but the 3D photoreal agenda winds its way onwards. Actors are being replaced, but with data from their own performances. The software will always make it tempting to add gratuitous blinks or embellish, thus ringing alarm bells in our cerebral cortex, but each film provides succour for the 3D technology zealots now occupying Hollywood.

With the arrival of new digital film formats and high definition TV we have ever-greater arrays of pixels to depict the worlds we want to tell stories about. Someone, somewhere is developing new software, which will change the way we create animation. The temptation to describe the human form and physical objects with oppressive levels of detail will always be there, but might in the end be kept in check by folk memories of huge losses and critical maulings, rather than concern about the effects of the 'Uncanny Valley'.

But for now another interesting question poses itself; if we are going to jettison the quest for the photoreal in CGI, what ARE we going to do with all those surplus pixels?

Notes

1. Central Processing Units and Command Line Interfaces
2. Gordon Moore co-founded Intel in 1968, and is widely known for expounding 'Moore's Law' in 1965, in which he predicted that the number of components the industry would be able to place on a computer chip would double every year. In 1975, he updated his prediction to once every two years. Essentially, this is popularly read as meaning the computer doubles in capacity every year or two. Source: http://www.intel.com/pressroom/kits/bios/moore.htm
3. Named after Pierre Bezier, an engineer who worked at Renault, who needed a way of economically describing curves mathematically. As is usual, and as another feather in the cap of French automobile design, it appears that he was actually beaten to the application of polynomial curves and surfaces by Paul De Casteljau, who worked at rivals Citroen in 1959. However, De Casteljau never published his invention, so Bezier got this now indispensable equation for curves named after himself. See also, Vince, J. (2005), *Mathematics for Computer Graphics*, Springer, p. 152.

4. Commodore International introduced the Amiga computer to the market in 1985. Let's leave aside the significance that the name Amiga is Spanish for 'female friend' and was selected by the developers themselves, who then, maybe showing a lack of awareness of Iberian names, code-named the first model Lorraine.The Amiga was the first accessible personal computer with an emphasis on graphics and sound capabilities with a GUI environment. This meant you didn't need to be a programmer to create animations. It got me started.

5. In many 3D programs you could call up a rather incongruent model of a 3D teapot as a standard reference. This seemed odd to the casual user because there were no other models available apart from what are called primitives; cones, spheres, cubes, tubes and a torus. The original data model was created by Martin Newell, a computer graphics researcher at the University of Utah in 1975, who needed a mathematical model of a familiar object. His wife suggested the tea service at home. At work he used Bezier Curves to design the model. He made the model publicly available, so it was adopted by many software makers. It became an icon or an in-joke depending on your perspective. It is said that there was also a mathematical model of a milk jug, but this is now lost to eternity. Like a saint's relics, the actual physical Melitta teapot that Newell copied now resides in the Computer History Museum, Mountain View, California.

6. Mori, Masahiro (1970), *Bukimi no tani: The uncanny valley*, MacDorman, K.F., Minato, T., (trans.) *Energy*, 7(4), pp. 33–5. Originally in Japanese.

7. *Final Fantasy:The Spirits Within* (2001) ,Dir: Hironobu Sakaguchi, Moto Sakakibara (co-director) UK Release: August 2001 Dist: Columbia Pictures

8. Plantec, Peter, 'Crossing the Great Uncanny Valley', http://vfxworld.com/?atype=articles&id=3494

9. 'Is It Fake or Foto?' http://www.autodesk.com/eng/etc/fake_or_foto/quiz.html

10. French, Philip (2004), *Polar Express* review, *Observer*, 5 December. http://film.guardian.co.uk/News_Story/Critic_Review/Observer_review/0,,1366496,00.html

11. Papamichael, Stella (2004), *Polar Express* review, 9 December. http://www.bbc.co.uk/films/2004/11/30/the_polar_express_2004_review.shtml

12. Arendt, Paul (2006), *A Scanner Darkly* review, 17 August. http://www.bbc.co.uk/films/2006/08/08/a_scanner_darkly_2006_review.shtml

13. French, Philip (2006), *A Scanner Darkly* review, *The Observer*, 20 August. http://film.guardian.co.uk/News_Story/Critic_Review/Guardian_review/0,,1855109,00.html

14. Thompson, Clive (2004),'The Undead Zone: why realistic graphics make humans look creepy', *Slate Online Magazine*, posted 9 June. http://www.slate.com/id/2102086

15. Quantic Dream's *Heavy Rain*. This game developed for the Sony PS3 is scheduled to be released in late 2008. It achieved notoriety within the pantheon of 'Uncanny Valley' when an excerpt entitled *The Casting* was presented to the media and general public at the Games Trade Show E3 in 2006. You can see the video trailer at http://video.google.com/videoplay?docid=136645717206489131

16. Gamespot review of *Heavy Rain*. http://uk.gamespot.com/ps3/adventure/heavyrain/news.html?sid=6150666&om_act=convert&om_clk=newsfeatures&tag=newsfeatures;title;2

17. White, Shawn (2006), 'The Uncanny Valley and Wii', from Wiire, the first site dedicated to Nintendo's newest gaming console, Wii. http://www.thewiire.com/features/149/1/The_Uncanny_Valley_and_Wii

18. 'SIGGRAPH 2007' Held in San Diego, SIGGRAPH is the world's leading computer graphics conference. There were 24,083 attendees in 2007. http://www.siggraph.org/s2007/main.php?f=attendees&p=featured&s=index

19. *Assassins Creed,* http://assassinscreed.uk.ubi.com/experience/ At the time of writing *Assassins Creed* is available from November 2007 on the Xbox 360.

20. Gouskos, Carrie (2006),'The Depths of the Uncanny Valley', 8 July, http://uk.gamespot.com/features/6153667/

21. This is the name for a range of techniques whereby the human performer wears markers near each joint to identify the motion and positions of their body in physical space. These are fed in real time into a computer, and can, with a little work, be applied to a computer 3D model. A famous example that brought this technique to the public consciousness would be Gollum in the film *Lord of the Rings.*

22. *Monster House* (2006), animated film, Dir: Gil Kenan Dist: Sony Pictures Entertainment (SPE).

23. Robertson, Barbara (2006),'Risky Business: CG Society Production Focus', 11 August, http://features.cgsociety.org/story_custom.php?story_id=3695&page=2

24. *Empire* magazine review, Tom Ambrose, December 2007. http://www.empireonline.com/reviews/reviewcomplete.asp?FID=11012

25. Hooks, Ed (2007),'Performance Animation', SAND Conference, Swansea, Wales, 27 November. Ed Hooks teaches Acting For Animators internationally, including workshops for PDI, Tippett Studio, Wild Brain, OddWorld Inhabitants, Lucas Learning, Electronic Arts (LA), Will Vinton Studios, and Valve Software.

26. Brad Bird interviewed by Tasha Robinson, 3 November 2004. www.avclub.com/content/node/23273

3

SPECTATORSHIP AND ACTION RESEARCH PERFORMANCE MODELS

Lizbeth Goodman, Esther MacCallum-Stewart and Vicki Munsell

This chapter argues that active spectatorship by young people in the age of new technology and the web 2.0 generation is best informed and framed by consideration of user-generated content models that build on lessons learned from early work by innovators of a previous era – specifically, from theatre and performance artwork made by women in the 1960s–1980s, when the aim was to encourage a reframing of the gaze on active and largely positive images of women in society, to more recent interactive media projects that have given skills training to previously disenfranchised groups so that they can make a real and lasting impact in the images created of the societies in which they live. The major case study discussed is ClubTech: a comprehensive technology programme to a very substantial test group of over five million young people at risk over a seven year period. Through the investment of over $150 million (from 2000–2008) in cash and software by the Microsoft CSR (Corporate Social Responsibility) programme, ClubTech was able to initiate a project that provided software, hardware, programme content, training and learning tools based in the real and digital arts, within the vast and growing network of physical safe spaces provided by the Boys and Girls Clubs of America. The project was an early pioneer of implementing digital technology programmes within communities through arts programmes, which developed on a massive scale, and which had significant social impact in local communities and in global discussions of 'accessible technology for youth at risk'. This attempt to address the digital divide remains one of the only cohesive provision programmes in the world with this level of success across such a wide geographical span and time-frame. This chapter examines the impact of the Digital Arts Suite that the ClubTech programme initiated, and its effects on young people's awareness of the potential of informed spectatorship and active participatory performance in the arts and in community engagement throughout the programme.

In the 1960s-1970s, critical attention was re-framed on women and their potential to retell their stories and re-frame their own lives with the aid of performance on stage and screen. The age of the active female spectator empowered by the ability to re-frame the gaze away from her body and surface image, and to direct the camera and then, in the 1980–1990s, on the increasingly powerful range of new media tools and online content systems, led to a new generation of women (and men) more comfortable in their own bodies and also more willing and able to make the next step to experimentation with the possibilities of virtual worlds and alternative forms of embodiment and self-representation, live and online.[1]

This chapter argues in brief that the twenty-first century heralded the century of Youth, empowered with tools and skills and a mentor network and community support system to enable active spectatorship and engaged participation in both the making and consumption of new media arts.

'Hope and opportunity comes in with technology...' Jasper Lamar Watts: Coordinator for YouthNet BGCA: 2005.[2]

For most people in the western world, access to IT is now commonplace both at home and in the workplace. However, this assertion masks the difficulties inherent in both gaining regular access to this technology and the ability to use it for productive purposes. By 2003, the American census showed that only 54 per cent of homes owned computers,[3] and in 2004, only 30.4 per cent of American homes had access to the Internet.[4] Whilst these numbers represent a significant proportion of the population – a number that is still rising – they are also directly related to income. Even in 2008, the computer is still an expensive, maintenance-heavy tool despite its widespread use. Thus, even in present times, what is known as the 'digital divide' remains a pressing concern both across nations and internationally.

> Universal access to computers and the Internet is considered necessary to avoid social divisions and offer opportunities for all by ensuring that future 'knowledge economies' include everyone [...] Failure to bridge the divide may result in powerful digital communication tools exacerbating and entrenching societal disparities.[5]

In 2000, this divide was far greater. Access to digital technology was already recognized as an undeniable facet in developing employment, education, communication and literacy. For young people entering a world where the use of technology was becoming increasingly important, making sure that they had equal provision and access to digital technology was becoming an especially pressing issue. Young people were also an obvious group for concern, since it was becoming obvious that their careers and life experiences were going to have more contact with computers and IT than their predecessors. Allowing children access to digital technology where it might not have been previously possible was identified by SMARTlab and the ClubTech programme as an essential part of their *modus operandi*. As has been argued by leading policy institutes and government agencies, including BECTA, the digital divide was one that also affected a student's ability to approach digital learning tools in the classroom:

> The proliferation of ICT in education and the expansion of Internet-based information and services further amplify the chasm between the information 'haves' and 'have nots'. Those on the wrong side of the divide(s) may have less opportunity to participate and engage with both formal and informal education, training and information.[6]

SMARTlab[7] was therefore keen to augment a programme to address these issues. The organization's long-term research and production experience with disenfranchised groups including women, youth at risk and people with disabilities worldwide informs the approach taken to the ClubTech review and expansion processed in recent years. The SMARTlab ethos to encourage social change and to effectively provide knowledge transfer in disenfranchised communities made a good fit with the emerging concerns of young people's access to digital technology. SMARTlab was commissioned to review the first five years of the ClubTech programme in the United States[8] on the basis of our work on the ground in shelters and community centres for youth at risk and survivors of abusive (domestic, ethnic, political and economic) regimes worldwide, in our SafetyNET, TRUST[9], and InterFACES[10] projects, wherein we spent some 15 years responding to invitations from communities to live and work with them to help to address complex social issues of deprivation and abuse whilst emphasizing the power of positive innovation, creative arts for personal expression and technologies as empowerment tools. Because the SMARTlab team never simply 'lands' in a culture or community uninvited, but rather engages in projects where our expertise has been sought out and where trust has been established through repeated visits and personal/professional collaborations, we did not offer to work on the ClubTech project until we had seen enough of the ground-up achievements to ascertain the ethical, social, cultural and creative aspects of the work to be undertaken:

> SMARTlab's ethos is simple: we begin our research on each and every project by 'landing' in a community, culture or research environment, and then spend time getting to know the local people, issues, concerns and needs, before we form teams of artists, computer scientists, medical and social care experts, educators, and scholars. Each team then tackles a given issue and attempts to invent new technology tools with real social impact, whether for individuals, for groups, or for wider international aims.[11]

The core tenets of the project also coincide with the ideas of stealth learning[12] – appreciating that in the field of digital learning, objectives need not always be fully visible in order to provide a strong platform in which to gain knowledge, and that producing a set of tools in which users have free agency to develop their own projects can produce unexpected learning outcomes. The ClubTech programme therefore aimed primarily to teach ICT usage through its Digital Arts packages. The Digital Arts Suite, provided by the project, led to a number of performance related outcomes, namely vigorous competition in Digital Arts Festivals and a plethora of performance pieces all produced by members of the BGCA.

Perhaps most importantly in this regard, the SMARTlab history of engagement with live performance and the creative arts in both analogue (real space) and digital forms, enabled the research and production teams to engage with core research objectives of long standing, while collaborating on a new documentary video and interactive review. This entailed working with thousands of young people and hundreds of their mentors, teachers, facilitators and parents, throughout a nine-month on-the-ground study of the project, and was conducted by Lizbeth Goodman with Jana Riedel, Taey Kim et al in 2004. This detailed documentation project informed the report that suggested re-funding the project for a further three years. This has since underpinned the creation of a new ClubTech project for Europe, starting in East London and reaching out to underserved communities throughout the United Kingdom and Europe, with a further roll out to the EMEA (Europe, Middle East and Africa) region now underway as well. To move this new phase of the project forward, Microsoft funded Goodman in 2006–10 to hire a post-doctoral researcher (MacCallum-Stewart) and a practice-based PhD candidate (Munsell) to conduct the investigations, further case studies and publications. MacCallum-Stewart's expertise in online game worlds and Munsell's unique experience as the original leader of the YouthNet initiative for BGCA made them ideal collaborators to work closely with Goodman, and also, with Akhtar Badshah and his team within Microsoft headquarters.

The role of spectatorship forms the key to this active research plan, which re-focuses the lens of the argument about 'corporate social responsibility' to show now only the most effective ways of enabling youth at risk to demonstrate and nurture their own creativity using user-generated content and accessible technology platforms. However, that further encouraged youth to engage in community projects that are transformative at a deeper level, in terms of self-respect and the positive images that can be created and shared when young people begin to see themselves as creative artists, with the tools of new technology in their own hands.

Boys and Girls Clubs of America: a short history

Boys and Girls Clubs of America began in 1860 when several women from Hartford, Connecticut organized a club for boys in an attempt to give them a positive alternative to roaming the streets. The group grew steadily until 1906 when several such organizations decided to affiliate. The Federated Boys Club in Boston was formed as a direct result of this, with 53 member organizations, marking the start of a nationwide movement. In 1931, the Boys Club Federation of America became Boys Clubs of America and in 1956, Boys Clubs of America celebrated its 50th anniversary and received a US Congressional Charter. In 1990, the organization changed its name to Boys and Girls Clubs of America to recognize that girls were also part of the group's cause, and Congress accordingly amended and renewed the Charter. In 2006, at the centenary of the BGCA, there were over 4,000 clubs, and 4.6 million boys and girls had been served by the movement. The organization has several notable alumni, including Jennifer Lopez, Michael Jordan, Edward James Olmos and Denzel Washington.

The BGCA cites the following membership statistics:

- 64 per cent are from minority families
- 11 per cent are less than 7 years old
- 26 per cent are 7-9 years old
- 30 per cent are 10-12 years old
- 21 per cent are 13-15 years old
- 10 per cent are 16-18 years old
- 2 per cent are more than 18 years old
- 55 per cent are male
- 45 per cent are female[13]

The BGCA has distinct aims, specifically through its Mission Statement, which aims 'To enable all young people, especially those who need us most, to reach their full potential as productive, caring, responsible citizens'.[14] With all of these facets in mind, the clubs represented an established organization with a long tradition of helping children across America gain access, not only to a club that provides them with a safe environment, but also to a range of facilities, information, and support networks with which they could engage. The club's emphasis on motivational learning through 'opportunity', expertise in working with youth, and ability to implement programmes on a large scale also made it a perfect place to instigate a large-scale introduction of technology.

Overview: ClubTech

In 2000, Microsoft pledged to donate $100 million in cash and software to the BGCA to create and provide ongoing support to the ClubTech programme for five years. The intention was to initiate a national deployment of digital technology resources into the BGCA, providing a comprehensive and sustainable programme, which would align with existing BGCA programmes and transform the clubs and the club structure from the ground up.

Although the original idea began at the BGCA, the local offices then leveraged the Microsoft funding and used the Microsoft name in order to gain additional support. Microsoft Community Affairs made the decision to provide ICT curriculum, software and training. This was particularly important as it provided cohesive content across all spectrums of ICT learning – the artefacts, the software to run on the systems, and the training to use them – not simply one aspect in isolation. Therefore, the funds available went towards all aspects of digital provision and learning, aiming to provide innovative content and best practice models as well as software and ICT related technology. Microsoft's donation enabled Boys and Girls Clubs of America to generate an additional $100 million in cash and in-kind support from public and private sources to support technology programme growth throughout the movement. The money donated by Microsoft, therefore, also leveraged additional corporate funding to support the project by association.

The bulk of the contribution was made in software: BGCA received a package of the latest Microsoft products for each participating club. However, the difference in the ClubTech programme was the additional provision of $12.3 million in cash. This was used to develop technology programmes around the software, intended to give members basic computer skills through the Skill Tech curriculum; to introduce them to digital movie making, music making, digital photography, graphic design and web development through the Digital Arts Suite; and to guide staff in using technology to enhance all programme offerings. ClubTech included extensive curriculum and technology training opportunities for Club staff at all professional levels, and training within the Skill Tech and Digital Arts Suites for BGCA members. At the end of this period, a review decided that the project should continue in the long term, and that rollouts across the United Kingdom, Canada and Europe were also appropriate. The scheme continues to develop at present.

Objectives

The ClubTech programme aimed to integrate technology into every aspect of each club; from overall management to core programmes, including education and career development; the arts; sports, fitness and recreation; health and life skills; and character and leadership development. The programme also has a strong emphasis on Internet safety and ethics. This was a deliberate correlation with BGCA's aims to teach citizenship, health and education to its members. In many ways this implementation was also intended to be an 'upgrade' for the clubs themselves, moving them away from the perception that BGCA was simply a 'swim and gym' club and making both clubs and their users part of the digital age.

As an addendum to this, because BGCA operate in the after-school space, they faced the additional challenge of making learning fun, since attendance or participation in the programme is voluntary. This is a unique component compared to the formal educational setting. By using clubs as their focus, ClubTech enabled youth professional staff to implement ICT knowledge that was needed for general usage, as well as what was simply required in an educational context, on a greater scale. The national focus of the clubs allowed diverse communities to be reached, and the emphasis on minority families that the clubs already possessed also meant that target groups for the project – those falling below the national average – could be reached more effectively. Finally, the Boys and Girls Clubs of America provided a place where children could feel they had their own agency[15] in the projects they took part in, and thus would provide somewhere where learning could be construed by users as 'fun' rather than 'necessary'. As a result of this, performance pieces created through digital media were considered a core part of the project, as they presented an ongoing objective that does not superficially appear to be learning orientated. In fact, the technology needed to produce music, performance, digital recordings, short films, animations and artwork is of course significant, and requires knowledge across multiple fields of ICT expertise.

ClubTech's strength came from the cohesive nature of the information and resources it provided to club staff and club members. Both groups were targeted as potential effective technology users, and the supporting educational packages contained insight into using computers both as resources and as practical, physical objects in themselves. To support this, each initiative emphasized community mobilization and collaborative learning as strategies, rather than a tiered system of learning (teacher – pupil). Familiarization with the technology on all levels was an essential part of this. So in the ClubTech system, all staff, as well as the club members, were targeted as learners, and all learners at all levels were encouraged to learn in non-judgemental environments. This was intended to remove the alienation and doubt many users experience when confronted by a non-intuitive system – such as the computer itself, or the learning packages associated with it:

> Just typing something doesn't necessarily help you but if you know how you can type it, where you can type it, it will help you at home, in your studies, in a later career, all of those things help our kids and they realise that just through experience as part of the programme, as they use it, they learn, 'oh this makes my life much easier'.[16]

At the same time, the learning was directed towards a creative outcome via the Digital Arts Suite, rather than obvious educational gain. This also made the learning agenda more intuitive. If users were learning in order to reach a different objective (for example, if they were learning to attach documents to e-mails so that they could send pictures they had created to each other), the learning agenda was also associated with the social usefulness of passing on something that the user had created.

As one ClubTech coordinator[17] pointed out, most students are expected to use computers in schools, but often only gain individual occasions to use them for very brief amounts of time. The provision of computers through the ClubTech system meant that fewer users had to share machines between many, and therefore had more time to play, learn and explore on their own for extended periods of time. The ClubTech programme intended that all users should be hands-on, so that members of BGCA gained access to learning tools about the computer or equipment they were using, rather than becoming spectators over a demonstration tool that they subsequently could not operate themselves. The ClubTech system also allowed users to learn in a way that they perceived as less pressured (less competition to use the machine), and as a 'cool' activity rather than with the ennui that often comes from 'edutainment' packages (which often have a clearly didactic viewpoint or emphasis placed on them).

In 2000, less than 100 BGCA clubs had Internet access, and what computers there were, were used in sporadic ways, primarily for educational gaming or simply non-networked gaming. Computer usage of this kind was causing concern – was the technological potential computers could provide being squandered through poor or low usage with inadequate software? There was no cohesive network between the many clubs, despite the community atmosphere that BGCA wished to promote. The ClubTech programme aimed to remedy this by introducing the use of computers in meaningful, positive and safe ways. After the project was initiated, there was access to the Internet, as well as digital facilities in 3,700 clubs in all 50 American states and on US military bases overseas. By 2004, the project had already reached 4.4 million young people, but just as importantly, it had allowed these children to meet each other and share their own work creatively.

From simple programmes such as learning to use the computer, to complex tutorials allowing users to gain better access and create their own work, ClubTech provided a series of packages and courses, which culminated in participation in the Digital Arts Suite programmes at the top of each tier. Additionally, the comprehensive nature of the package was intended to cover all aspects of computer usage; courses at many clubs included maintenance as well as usage, so that if a computer broke, staff or students would know how to repair and maintain it. This structure therefore comprised several different aspects of tutoring that were cohesively meant to present a structured curriculum but at the same time were carefully tailored so that progression 'doesn't feel like work'. The tangible product of this learning was their participation in the various digital arts projects, and their production of performances through this technology.

ClubTech basics

Before an overview of the Digital Arts Suite programme is presented, it is first necessary to contextualize it within each section of the ClubTech programme, giving a general idea of what the project aimed to teach at ground level. Many of these ideas have subsequently been used in the digital arts performance projects, including the sizeable contribution by BGCA members to the ClubTech Review[18] that was produced in 2005, where members created most of the audio, visual and digital footage shown on the accompanying CD. The multifaceted nature of the project also means that many of its aspects blend into the formation of the Digital Arts Suite, and are intended to be accommodated through each programme.

Ethics, Internet/computer safety and 'basic' learning

> They teach us about Internet safety, they show us what websites not to go on. They protect us, they have a server protection now up here, so if a website looks inappropriate they won't let us go on it, it blocks it. If there is something you need on that website, they have a password they can type in.[19]

The basic elements of the ClubTech programme are deceptively simple, allowing students to access basic learning tools when using computers or other electronic equipment. This ranges from learning how to use the machine and its peripherals (mouse, USB cable, modem) to learning simple tasks involving access and manipulation of the interface. This develops steadily through usage of the various design packages in the Digital Arts Suite, which comes with the hardware provided. There is also a tiered system of programmes that users can complete, designed to accommodate different age groups. Younger users engage with more short-term games and tasks, which teach them the basics of net safety, interface usage and application, and navigation around a computer's software, whereas the various 'Tech' programmes (see below) engage older users with more complex, creative tasks. Throughout the programme, the emphasis on Internet and computer safety and ethics remained a priority.

In interviews about the projects, club members cite some of the following achievements as things they have learnt. The diversity of these answers – from very specific situations to broad, interpersonal issues such as learning together – demonstrates how the tools in the programme functioned on a wide scale, and how users responded to individual elements of the programme by making small-scale, personal identifications with what they were doing:

- how to send e-mails
- how to use PowerPoint to make slides
- using the 'ctrl-alt-delete' function
- not to click 'yes' on pop-up advertizements
- where to download music legally
- not to send out personal addresses on forums
- how to save documents on disk, or on a cd if too large for a disk
- how to use Adobe to manipulate images.
- how to loop music streams on Music Tech
- how to work towards shared goals (one student had taken the Music Tech programme, the
- other had taken advice from others as well as teaching himself; both were working together to make a 'spooky' music soundtrack)
- how to 'research' by using web pages to help with homework

Overall, the sense is clearly conveyed of using hands-on tools – often very basic ones that might otherwise be overlooked – in order to understand and learn digital literacy. The emphasis of the replies given by ClubTech members is also on 'fun' activities – very few of the members interviewed specifically identify traditional patterns of learning in their answers, although many acknowledge instead/as well that they have previously used computers at school in order to engage directly in the learning process. This process of response is typical of the stealth learning approach – students may have assimilated a vast number of learning objectives, but they will often resist defining these as educational, even when specifically challenged. Instead, users quantify what they have done in terms of achievement, enjoyment or simply detailed descriptions of their ICT knowledge. This sort of response is ideal to stealth learning objectives in ICT, as it shows that learners have not only assimilated what they need to, but are specifically applying it outside 'straight' learning criteria.

YouthNet[20]

> YouthNet has made an impact in the sense that it has allowed our members really to learn to communicate; to understand that there is a broader community of Boys and Girls Clubs out there. Before, members were very much focused on their club as would be expected. This really broadens that horizon, gives them the chance to communicate with a broader segment of other teens and to really raise issues, to become involved in projects and in other kinds of ways of communicating. So the impact really has been to help teens draw together to understand that there is a broader Boys and Girls Club movement, that there are other teens doing the same things they are and really kind of reinforces the skills that Boys and Girls Club tries to impart to our members.[21]

YouthNet is the online aspect of the ClubTech programme. It is a regulated web space that was initially only available to BGCA club members, before it was opened up in August 2005 to all youth users on the Internet. The site operates as the central portal for members to communicate with each other. It is moderated by adults, but the content is primarily written and provided by club members. This programme has since evolved to become a portal for programme content for youth and teens. While the clubs still have the ability to host interactive chats, as was initially intended, this is no longer a focus of YouthNet, partially as web 2.0 has made this type of communication far easier and has allowed sideways development through creativity and performance. YouthNet developed in 2003–6 as a peer-produced (and adult moderated) site, with the members contributing the majority of articles, downloads and discussion, as well as interacting actively with the 'Digital Arts Festival', where entries of best practice creativity in digital media are showcased through the website across the BGCA network, ending with an annual national competition and awards ceremony. As noted in the team's recent research into the impact of the programme on the workforce initiative for retraining and skills provision for youth at risk, however, the YouthNet site eventually became too large and too difficult to keep up to date, in the face of the unprecedented growth of social network sites including Facebook, Myspace, Youtube et al.. In 2007, YouthNet was thus reframed as an online portal for the ClubTech programme, where participating youth can still provide content but are no longer entirely responsible for generating all of the site's content.

The initial target group for YouthNet was children with limited computer access – again spotlighting the significant percentage of low-income families in America that did not have regular access to the Internet. In the long run, it was also an important tool in bringing BGCA together, allowing members to communicate across the world with one another and share their experiences:

> Through the Internet and through chat the youth are able to connect with other youth throughout the country to share their experiences, to just make new friends in other places that they might not have thought about: 'hey look I am talking to someone in Oregon, where is Oregon?' – 'Well let's get out the map and find out where Oregon is'. So it is able to expand their sense of connectiveness and know that there are people like them everywhere.[22]

Whilst the project fostered a safe space for children to enter, within this space members were encouraged to explore, develop their ideas and learn from each other. Overall the atmosphere created was intended to produce a common ground where children could communicate with each other safely with as little adult intervention as possible. YouthNet's increased communication through the relative anonymity of chat-rooms allowed children to share ideas, thoughts and dreams more easily – and to learn about each other. This openness also meant that children could express themselves and learn on a level playing field – YouthNet was an area of peer learning and an area of self-moderation for the participants.

YouthNet had a major focus on Internet safety and ethics. The project was initiated at a point when Internet safety was a big issue (and regulation of the Internet as a space was very low), and when people were becoming increasingly aware of how vulnerable young users could be.

YouthNet, therefore, encouraged communication and sharing, whilst at the same time keeping an eye on its users and steering them in the right direction in a positive sense. The programme brought together diverse communities (children from reservations, children from inner cities, children from American military bases around the world), and allowed them to share ideas. Although it might appear at first to be merely the provision of a safe space online, the intention of YouthNet was to unlock the potential of communities and the learning of individuals (the feeling that it was a group effort where everyone could express themselves) in line with the rest of the ClubTech programme.

The Digital Arts Suite

Combining technology and the arts, the Digital Arts Suite (available in English and Spanish) is an engaging suite of five web-based programmes for members of all ages and technical abilities. Digital Arts Suite provides participants with skills in various Microsoft software programs such as Microsoft Publisher, Microsoft FrontPage, Microsoft Movie Maker, and Microsoft Digital Image Pro, while exposing them to new, creative uses for technology, including areas of potential career interest. The five programme areas include:

Web Tech – teaches the basics of creating websites, advancing to more advanced sites that include page links, graphics, text and sound, learning important design lessons along the way.

Design Tech – teaches artistic concepts and technology skills that allow students to create professional-quality print materials and animation, including logos and posters.

Photo Tech – explores the photographic composition of digital photos and the effects of distance and angle. Participants then learn how to use photo-editing software, from completing basic tasks such as cropping and colour and light adjustment, to taking on advanced projects that use image filters and layering.

Music Tech – explores a variety of digital music software applications and basic music theory where members learn to mix musical loops and compose and record original songs.

Movie Tech – helps members learn how to write screenplays, film their own movies, and edit their raw footage into a finished piece.

The Digital Arts Suite curriculum teaches users how to make websites, music, images, animations and videos. The programmes are designed to be stand-alone as well as to work in combination, and each aspect is initiated at a different point in the year, allowing members to join the programme at any point, and catching new members who may not have been in the club at the commencement of each arm. The programmes are also designed to work without extensive recourse to the Internet, although networking the skills learned has become an important part of the programme as web 2.0 has developed.

The projects were aimed at children of 10 years of age and older, although they still encoded the ideas of web safety and ethics (for example, interviewees reported that whilst completing Music Tech, they were also instructed on how to download music legally), as well as the basics of computer usage:

> The Digital Arts Suite is a comprehensive package of software that has been donated to us by Microsoft. One of the things that we did was called Photo Tech, which involved giving the kids digital cameras, which they had to learn how to use before they could do anything else. Then we showed them: 'this is how you import the pictures using a USB cable.' – 'What is this cable called again?' – 'USB cable!' You have got the kids to learn the terminology about what it is they are using. Once they have learned the hardware stuff then we delve into the software stuff. ...We have a goose skiing. We have so many wonderful pictures, you have to see it...But these pictures allowed us to see how far creatively can a kid go.[23]

The culmination of each package is the production by club members of creative pieces of work, which are then submitted to the annual Digital Arts Festivals (see below).

The emphasis on the arts in this section – involving users in the total design of performance and arts pieces – engages users on an extremely complex level with ICT. The skills needed to create a video or animation, with all the accompanying design, sound, coding and performance, is a significantly large achievement. The resultant pieces of work are specifically meant to be joint collaborations (although members may also produce their own individual work), thus also encouraging the concomitant skills of leadership, social behaviour, teamwork, cooperation and delegation at the same time as teaching arts skills and ICT.

In 2008, SMARTlab has launched a new phase of the project, which is adding new tools and applications to the Digital Arts Suite, including wearable technology and fashion skills training, robotics for girls and boys, accessible interfaces for people with disabilities and multi-lingual translation through the Microsoft Digital Literary programme link. Also, a hands-on MAGICbox toolkit for 2d-3d design and rapid prototyping, to show young people how their ideas can be transformed into real world prototypes and tools for use in business development and young people's social entrepreneurship initiatives.

The focus on the new ClubTech for the EMEA region is on user-generated content and the role that young people can play in empowered citizen journalism, creative expression and community engagement. This work is being developed alongside other SMARTlab initiatives including the SafetyNET[24] media skills for women's survival stories project, and the Youth Academy for Peace linked to the United Nations.

The Digital Arts Festival
The Digital Arts Festival celebrates club members' creativity. Each festival is held at the culmination of one of the five technology and arts programmes within the Digital Arts Suite. Festival winners and participants are recognized at local, regional, and national levels.

Fig. 6: The winning entry from Briana Hill (aged 10) for the PhotoTech Competition (2006–7).

Fig. 7: *Sophisticated Teen*, Regional Winner of the Graphic Design Section: Boys and Girls Clubs of Milwaukee, 16–18.

The first Digital Arts Festival held in 2004–5, for instance, had 515 music entries submitted, and the Festival has steadily grown in size and popularity ever since. In 2006–2007 alone, 799 individuals from 478 clubs submitted entries in the competition. Since its inception, the Digital Arts Festival has had Club members submit 5,654 pieces of digital artwork. This should give an example of the success and scale of the project. Winning results have been exhibited nationally and in a more permanent form online.

All the winners are exhibited online at http://www.bgcadigitalarts.com/ and were also physically represented in Seattle alongside the Regional and National Finalists of all categories.

I did Hurricane Katrina because it made me express my feelings about those people trapped in the flooding. It made me think about if I was with them. It would be horrible for the people. I just wanted other people to know, and to think of the people who were there, and to realize that you could be one of those people at any time.[25]

Conclusion

In this room it is all about imagination; it is all about creativity. And that is what we have to stress; it is originality and creative thought.[26]

The ClubTech programme used creativity, performance and innovation as a springboard for ICT learning. By couching a learning agenda within a series of arts-related training programmes, the project allowed literally millions of ClubTech members to experience ICT outside the context of formal education, but within an environment that fostered learning. By submerging this within the auspices of the Digital Arts Suite, members learned transferable skills under the principles of a stealth learning agenda – teaching them valuable techniques without appearing to do so. The competition created by the Digital Arts Festivals results in a positive conclusion to each project – one which has seen considerable success and which grows in participatory numbers every year. At the same time, the Digital Arts Suite allows children to gain essential skills in the field of ICT, as well as providing a mouthpiece for expression, sharing and communication across the YouthNet network.

Whilst the Microsoft and Boys and Girls Clubs of America ClubTech programme is a success, it remains one of the only such projects of its kind. The implementation across the board of digital technology and the knowledge to use this technology has positively affected literally millions of lives and is a bench-mark for future projects. It is the cohesive nature of the project, supplying all aspects of technology as well as teaching the usage of it along the principles of stealth learning – providing users with one agenda whilst at the same time producing additional educational outcomes as they achieve it – which still makes it stand apart from other endeavours. It is this aspect that can provide a strong best practice model for future developments. At the same time, rapid development, and advances such as the use of web 2.0 all point towards the tremendous increases that digital technology has made since the project began.

The digital divide is still an issue, which needs to be continually addressed, in new and increasingly inventive ways, with emergent media forms and user-generated content models, especially as technology continues to develop rapidly and is characterized in the development of a digital dividend for youth in the new millennium. The ClubTech programme demonstrates that digital arts and performance are accessible entry points to creative expression, and therefore function as a way in which to provide universal points of reference that also keep young technology users within a contemporary framework. As young people engage with ClubTech, they encounter and evolve increasingly sophisticated skills in the use of role-play and movement in performance, and also learn to engage with digital tools that have been designed with youth at risk in mind. The programme thus encourages active embodied and responsible learning about social and cultural issues, developing in line with technological progress. The exposure that the ClubTech and YouthNet programmes give young people to role models, ways of seeing and involvement in community engagement, and ways of taking control of and responsibility for their own digital dividends in learning and career development have a spin-off impact on the engagement of these young people in their local (and global) communities as empowered citizens.

In early 2008, a research and evaluation summit at Microsoft Headquarters in Redmond, United States, was followed by a lecture tour about the project to the Gulf region of the Middle East. Between these two radically different geographical and political spheres, with all the many and varied levels of computer literacy and all the wide range of social issues that emerge in and between them, one common agreement was made: ClubTech is to be updated and revised. This will be with additional tools and a customized curriculum added, for a re-branded set of pilot SMARTclubs to be rolled out in Europe in 2008–2009, and then in the EMEA region (Europe, Middle East and Africa) in stages from 2009. This major new phase of the project is already underway, and is focusing on youth empowerment and skills development: on how young people can reframe their own images and use user-generated content models and web 2.0 capabilities to their own advantage, and to the advantage of a more informed and more equally empowered digital, and real world community. The research for this new phase of engagement activity is based on decades of study. In particular on the impact that other marginalized or under-represented groups at risk in previous eras (such as women in the early years of the twentieth century women's theatre movement) had, in adapting tools and methods to empower their own active gaze at culture, and at their own roles within their own lives and communities.

The digital dividends of this newest and rapidly evolving age of active spectatorship are yet to be captured, but they already look set to extend well beyond the frame of any one project, or any one way of viewing the triple bottom line of social, environmental and economic sustainability for generations to come.

Notes

1. Goodman, L., (ed.) (1999), *Mythic Women/Real Women: Plays and Performance Pieces by Women*, London: Faber and Faber, May; Goodman, L., (ed.) (1998), *The Routledge Reader in Gender and Performance*, London and New York: Routledge; Goodman, L. (1993), *Contemporary Feminist Theatres: To Each Her Own*, London and New York: Routledge, translated into Chinese and Japanese,

1997. Goodman, Williams, Coe BBC (1997), 'Creative Imagination and Media-Assisted Learning', *Literary and Linguistic Computing*, Oxford University Press, print and electronic forms, Nov; Goodman, L., (ed.) (1996), *Feminist Stages: Interviews with Women in Contemporary British Theatre*, London and New York: Harwood Academic Publishers; Goodman, Kueppers (2001), 'Audience Architectures, Extended Bodies and Virtual Interactive Puppetry (VIP): Towards a Portable Software for Empowering Performance Interactions', in *Leonardo*, MIT Press. http://mitpress2.mit.edu/e-journals/LEA/TEXT/lea9-4.txt- for the *Leonardo Electronic Almanac*, Volume 9, No. 4, April, 2001.

2. Lamar Watts, Jasper, 22 February 2005. ClubTech interviews cited all recorded by the SMARTlab team on video, in the Clubtech archives and transcribed for purposes of this publication.

3. US Census, 2003.

4. World Summit on the Information Society 2005, 'The digital divide at a glance' , available at http://www.itu.int/wsis/tunis/newsroom/stats/

5. BECTA (2003), p. 2.

6. Damarin, S. (2000), in BECTA, 2003: 2. Damarin, S. (2000), 'The "digital divide" versus digital differences: Principles for equitable use of technology in education', *Educational Technology*, Vol 40, No. 4, July–August 2000, pp. 17–21.

7. SMARTlab, (2007), 'About the SMARTlab'. Available at http://www.smartlab.uk.com/1about/index.htm

8. Goodman, MacCallum-Stewart, Munsell (2008), 'Skilling Up: The Workforce Agenda & the Club Tech Contribution to Youth at Risk', forthcoming in the special issue on 'ICT goes to work: Skills and economic opportunities for marginalized groups', *The Journal of Information Technologies and International Development*, MIT Press.

9. Duffy, Goodman, Price, Eaton, Riedel, Sudol, O'Hare (2005), 'The TRUST Project: Immersive Play for Children in Hospitals and Rehabilitation', 4th IEEE Chapter Conference on Applied Cybernetics 2005, 7–8 September, 2005, City University, London, United Kingdom; SafetyNET, 2008, www.safespaces.net. Goodman. L, with Duffy, Brian , Sudol, Jeremi, Price, Marc et al. (2007) 'TRUST: robotics and haptics for extreme interaction and universal design', *Leonardo* MIT Press, special issue – 'Mutamorphosis', November 2007.

10. Goodman with Donegan, Palmer-Brown, Kennedy, Zhang (2008), 'InterFACES: Affective Interactive Virtual Learning Environments for People with Cognitive & Physical Disabilities', forthcoming in *Leonardo*, MIT Press, special issue – 'Mutamorphosis Online', 2008.

11. SMARTlab (2007), 'About the SMARTlab', available at http://www.smartlab.uk.com/1about/index.htm

12. Badshah, Goodman, MacCallum-Stewart (2009), *Stealth Learning and the Digital Divide*, in the Emergenc(i)es Series, (ed.) Goodman, L., Massachusetts: MIT Press, forthcoming 2009; MacCallum-Stewart, E. (2008), 'Stealth Learning in Massive Multiplayer Online Games' in De Frietas et al., *Learning Through Play* in the Emergenc(i)es Series, (ed.) Goodman, L., Massachusetts: MIT Press, forthcoming 2008.

13. Boys and Girls Clubs of America 'Who we are: The Facts', available at 'http://www.bgca.org/whoweare/facts.asp

14. Boys and Girls Clubs of America, 'Who we are: Our Mission', available at http://www.bgca.org/whoweare/mission.asp

15. For further discussions on agency within ICT environments, see Murray, Janet (1998), *Hamlet on the Holodeck*, Massachusetts, MIT Press; Parsler, Justin, (2008–present), *A Taxonomy of Agency*, unpublished thesis, The University of Brunel. Murray and Parsler's ongoing work on the way that players interact with games in meaningful ways and are given the relative ability to do so through game dynamics and play. In short, agency is a Games Studies term that is used throughout this paper to mean the relative ability players have to gain control of their digital environments.

16. Amanda Lavoe: BGCA – Mary Ryan Club, Milwaukee: 2005. ClubTech Interviews cited all recorded by the SMARTlab team on video, in the ClubTech archives and transcribed for purposes of this publication.

17. Jurkiewicz (2005). ClubTech Interviews cited all recorded by the SMARTlab team on video, in the ClubTech archives and transcribed for purposes of this publication.

18. www.microsoft.com/about/corporatecitizenship/citizenship/giving/programs/up/casestudies/clubtech.mspx

19. Miguel Santiago – Club Member, Woburn, Massachusetts: 2005. ClubTech Interviews cited all recorded by the SMARTlab team on video, in the ClubTech archives and transcribed for purposes of this publication.

20. Ynet Kids Village (2006), available at http://ynetkids.bgcaYouthNet.org/YNetKids06/splash.html. YouthNet (2000–present), available at http://www.bgcaYouthNet.org

21. Dan Rauzi, Senior Director for technology programmes for training for Boys and Girls Clubs of America, 2005. ClubTech Interviews cited all recorded by the SMARTlab team on video, in the ClubTech archives and transcribed for purposes of this publication.

22. Chris Roberts, Programme Director of Fairfax County Boys and Girls Club, the Boys and Girls Clubs of Greater Washington, 2005.

23. Roger Ortiz, Director of Technology at the Boys and Girls Club of Wayne, New Jersey, 2005.

24. SafetyNET (2008), www.safespaces.net

25. Hill, Briana (2007) (interview), 'Putting Youth Creativity on Display', Microsoft, http://www.microsoft.com/presspass/features/2007/jul07/07-19clubtech.mspx

26. Roger Ortiz, Director of Technology, Boys and Girls Club of Wayne, New Jersey, 2005. From interview transcript, as above.

PART TWO: IMAGINATIVE ESCAPE

4

THE ACTIVE AUDIENCE: THE NETWORK AS A PERFORMANCE ENVIRONMENT

Gregory Sporton

Creative practice through web-based technologies is developing a distinctive character of its own. This encounter often begins in new media versions of old media style practices, but the environment of the Internet can do unusual things to resources offered to it. This chapter argues that the distinctions between producer and consumer in the 'spectating relationship' break down in the context of the web, presenting new challenges for creative practice there. The supporting technologies of the Internet enable us to ask questions about the effect of releasing work on it, and how the creative relationship changes when the medium is more 'pull' than 'push'.

In September 2006, the research group I lead in the Department of Art at the Birmingham Institute of Art and Design were working on a film project. In fact, it had begun life as a potential live performance project that we were to present in an exhibition in early October. We had, however, waited far too long to get everyone organized to be in the same place at the same time. So, after considerable discussion amongst ourselves, and bearing in mind who was available and when, we decided to film the work we had already made and to make a further assessment of the 'results' after that. Those 'results' steered our way of thinking about what and how changes have manifested in the relationship between an audience and an idea. As it happened, much of the impact of our work turned out to be beyond our control, pointing towards a different set of relationships that were emerging between performer and audience when the complex and unpredictable network is used as a performing environment. Making the film turned out to be only the first stage of the evolution of the work.

The Visualisation Research Unit (VRU) at Birmingham City University had already been in operation for about a year or so, and had been generously funded with every kind of high level digital technology that could be imagined, from motion capture equipment to supercomputing. This particular project, however, suggested to us a slightly different approach, the low-tech route, could be possible. We had been approached by the Archive of the Birmingham Institute of Art & Design to create some work that responded to material we could find there. Looking through their suggestions of useful material, our interest was aroused by the documents the archive held about the early twentieth century crank (or visionary depending on your disposition) Sanford Bennett. Discussions with the archivist suggested that no one knew exactly why the photographs and books of his unusual system of physical movement and fitness programme were there. However, it was clear from the archive that the original inhabitants of the College of Art at Birmingham were far from conservative and were happy to entertain a number of possibilities about how life might be lived. The material we decided to use for our inspiration was a poster of still photographs giving instruction about movements that could be performed under the bedclothes. The rationale for this eccentric approach was set out in Bennett's accompanying book, also available in the Archives, and to which colleagues became accustomed to reading the confident aphorisms of a man confident that he had solved the riddle of eternal youth.[1]

Bennett had developed his movement system after becoming, at the age of 50, an old man. Indeed, the photographs in his book, *Old Age, its Cause and Prevention*, illustrate the journey back to youth, undertaken after he found himself 'wrinkled, partly bald, cheeks sunken, face drawn and haggard, muscles atrophied, and thirty years of chronic dyspepsia finally resulted in catarrah (sic) of the stomach, with acid rheumatism periodically adding its agonies'.[2] Bennett began to see the drugs, medicines and chemical treatments on which he had previously relied as a mendacity on the part of the drug manufacturers, and was equally concerned that his family's habits were probably contributing to their shortened lives.[3] For Bennett, it seemed there was a possibility of a much longer life expectancy if only we could imagine it, if we only would formulate a programme of natural living where adequate helpings of 'sunlight, pure air, pure water, cleanliness and exercise' were available.[4] Indeed, like Descartes, he suspected that we die because we assume we will, and that it might be the failure of the imagination rather than of the body that brings us mortality. His own case, he believed, was quite unique. He had, by the age of 72, the body of 'an athlete in training',[5] the physique of a man apparently half his age, who proudly subjected himself to any amount of testing by prominent physicians to prove his point.

As Bennett's book was his testament to the theory that all humans can rediscover their natural opportunity to live healthily (and potentially for a very long time),[6] and given my background with dance and the body, we began to look closely at the actions as they were presented on the poster. This enabled us to work out what it was exactly Bennett was doing to rejuvenate himself. Bennett's *Thirty Exercises* are coyly described as being performed 'under the bedclothes', though the photographs show Bennett in his underpants being photographed against a straw mat. Reconstructing the movements is complicated by the fact that so much rests on the description rather than the illustration. Each exercise has only a single frame to show it, and relies on a description about the action and the number of repetitions. Having created some approximations of the exercises, we filmed them, though this too demanded a specific decision. Rather than the full colours of high definition television, we chose one of the lowest resolution cameras in the cupboard, a Sanyo C5, designed as a hand-held pocket-style video camera. Bennett's photographs are old, black and white of course, but in 16:9 ratios that show the full length of the body when outstretched and not much else in the surrounding room. Our straightforward reconstruction of archive material would give life to the photographs by emulating them as closely as we could with live action. Our grainy camera would capture the essence of the original photographs, and we could reframe the video in Final Cut Pro to give the slightly panoramic effect of the source material. There was one further discovery in the shooting stage. Bennett's exercises, whilst working different parts of the body, were fairly even in duration if the subject followed Bennett's instructions about the number of repetitions. For me, as the man doing the exercises, it turned out to be about thirty seconds.[7]

Once the definitive take of each exercise was shaved to about this length, we thought we should add music of a similar period and looked for something equally enigmatic. Matching Bennett in tone, radicalism and time period was Schoenberg, and we used the editing process to splice his *Six Little Pieces for Piano*[8] into randomized thirty second sections which we arbitrarily applied to the video. The first version of this was predicated on the accuracy and similarity of the timing mechanism in the two programmes we used to do the editing. It turns out that what is thirty seconds to Final Cut Pro is not the same duration as Max/MSP.[9]

We presented this work as part of the 'Nature-Inspired Creative Design' exhibition in Birmingham in September 2006, and felt we had done some justice to Bennett and created an interesting little video. The exhibition was probably seen by about 200 people over the course of three days, and at its conclusion we were ready to file our DVD in the very archive that had inspired it. At this point someone suggested that we mount it on YouTube. In September 2006, YouTube was rapidly developing into the phenomena that would attract lawsuits from international entertainment companies angry that their intellectual property rights were being flouted by the site's users, but it was still something of a mystery to us until we checked it out. It seemed an excellent place to record and store a copy of our work, with the assumption that we would probably be the only visitors, and it would enable us to refer people to something else online if they wanted an example of the sort of work we were doing. The job complete, we forgot all about it after the initial excitement of searching for ourselves in the YouTube database and visiting our film.[10]

A random Google search of our names some four months later turned up some surprising results. As YouTube has the ability to embed video into other websites, we discovered our video offered as content for up to half a dozen other sites. These, it turned out, were mostly about French dance and theatre, and they had gone to the trouble of translating our brief paragraphs about Bennett. We also found ourselves added to sites about exercise in general, content sharing sites, video collections of 'spiritual' movements, and even in a site dedicated to 'extreme videos'.[11] In addition, we found people making occasional comments of all sorts, congratulatory, insulting, accusations about our motivations and even advertizements for things that were totally unconnected with us. These were immediately available to any viewer before they clicked the arrow to start the ten-minute film of randomized exercises done to Schoenberg.

What the example and experience of *Thirty Exercises* did for us as a group was to turn the conventions of spectatorship on their head, and connect our work with what we used to call an 'audience' in a surprisingly original way. There appeared to us to be several issues involved with the distribution method we had accidentally discovered, and this changed the direction of much of our practical work as a means of trying to address those issues. That the usage and interest in the material wasn't anything like what the creators had intended or anticipated is a long standing issue in cultural production, though it should be recalled that we looked upon YouTube as a storage mechanism and it was chosen as a platform for that reason, rather than as a distribution channel. The network and its functionality assisted the user community to pull the original material into new contexts quite autonomously from us, and forced on us a series of reassessments about the use of the web as a platform for creative exploration and engagement. How do people come across this work, when it is taken out of the physical environment of a traditional exhibition? What properties does the network have as a performance environment? Were we thinking in 'old' new media ways by presenting work on it and simply expecting it to be taken at face value? This chapter is about how the network itself suggested different possibilities as a performance context, and how the development of creative interactions with a networked audience changes the assumptions about the development of content and the methods through which it can be received. The dynamism of this relationship offers significant challenges to those trained in the assumptions about art as the expression of individual vision, and to the idea that art has a definite and finished state.

Shortly before this encounter with the web, I had been reviewing a series of dance films and installations that had been specifically placed in art galleries.[12] What struck me at the time was the inappropriateness of the material being offered, given the presentation context of an art gallery. Choreographers and film-makers had assumed that an art gallery was merely another theatre space, and didn't appear to have distinguished in their work or their presentation of it between theatre, cinema or gallery. The consequence of this was work that had the aesthetic and feel of massed concentration, the demand for hundreds of eyes trained directly and immediately in a specific place. The content developed as if the gallery visitor had the same lack of choice and fixed perspective of the theatregoer, invariably narrative in structure and sequential in development. However, the dynamics of a gallery are the inverse of the dark, artificially lit spaces of the theatre where people sit fixed in seats for a predetermined duration. The gallery visitor has far more discretion to be engaged or to ignore as they perambulate around white-painted rooms on pine floorboards. The viewing conditions and conventions at galleries are significantly different, and as such require different treatment from the mass, simultaneous event that accompanies an evening at the theatre. The mismatch between work being offered by the choreographers and the context that was provided in which to view them brought this argument into sharp relief. Few, if any, of the artists had thought through the context for spectatorship and accommodated or consciously worked the potential of the encounter between one sort of spectating tradition and another. That the interaction with artwork in gallery spaces is invariably social, with their obsession with viewing conditions, the permission to stroll about the collections at leisure, long opening hours and expectation of sharing the experience of looking at the art in the presence of a few others, was ignored as a context. The conventions of the theatre, with its manipulation of lighting, the accompanying expectation of audience silence and direct attention on the action tends to make it a solitary experience carried out jointly rather than a social one contextualized by the presence of others. The visual arts are a category about which we can argue in the presence of them: this is rare in the theatre, where we do our arguing afterwards. In the context of presenting a dance work in this way, it becomes necessary to think about the material differently, acknowledging that with the growth of moving image practice in gallery contexts, there 'are' moments when people can be expected to stop and watch, rather than look. This has significant impact for the experience of art, and for the judgement required in order to draw attention to the work in its context. In other words, creative practice is never context free, but the complexity of that context depends on the received understanding of the environment and the dynamics generated by the presence (or absence) of art. A theatre space requires a different treatment to a film. A film shown on a big screen requires a different treatment to one for the Internet. The dynamics of the latter are only beginning to emerge, but considerations of necessity include download speeds, compromising audio and visual quality for accessibility, flexibility of media to work with existing media players and the conventions and practices of consumers using the Internet. All these determine the impact of the work, but none more so than the judgement about the suitability of the environment for the presentation of this particular set of ideas. Conscious control and judgement of the medium through which an experience is offered is part of the artist's task as the conduit of mediation.

Having established this principle, that there are specific qualities and properties of the spaces in which we experience and appreciate creative practice, it is worth looking more closely at the difference between our existing assumptions about the platform that is the Internet and how it differs from the meditative technologies of the relatively recent past as a medium for spectatorship. Both the notion of authorship, as understood as the presentation or publication of work by a single author, and the question of the spectator as a by-standing consumer of cultural production, come under significant pressure in the exploitation of new technologies. Our previous certainty about a division of labour between producers and consumers is put into play. The celebration of choice, which made early Internet surfing something of a qualitative gamble in terms of page design, is now less prominent than the pooling together of resources into a creative playground, where distinctions between creator and audience are far less clear. Any understanding of this new sphere of cultural production and new type of creative activity requires the acceptance of a mode of thinking beyond the models that were so dominant in the discourse of cultural production in the twentieth century.

The now conventionalized distinction between earlier forms of cultural production and those specifically for the Internet was identified by Naughton[13] who differentiated between technologies by noting their respective natures in the handling of content as either 'push' or 'pull'. This useful dichotomy defines the means of communication in terms of the underlying technology that delivers it yet, as will be noted, the function of the technologies is dependent on an operating principle. This comes to the fore when the style and purpose of the content refers itself to the technological framing in which it is presented. According to Naughton, traditional mass media, like broadcast television and radio, 'pushed' stuff at a viewer or listener, within a narrow range of options. From the outset, this was a governing principle of its technological development and implementation. Viewers or listeners could simply take or leave the channel (or channels) of unrelated stuff emerging from the devices in their homes. The broadcaster on the other hand focussed on having a steady stream of material available for as much of the time as possible. The only real-time options for the audience were the use of a tuner or channel selector or an off switch. For the broadcaster, most of their assumptions relied on guesswork that might be confirmed by ratings surveys released long after the event that were used as evidence to attract more advertizers.

The economics of this system were perfectly adequate, and allowed a small number of producers access to a market with a vast number of consumers, usually to a prescribed and published timetable. The potential size of the audience could tempt advertizers to fund production and the lack of choice was begrudgingly tolerated, despite the poverty of televisual quality once the box in the corner of the room acquired the same domestic centrality as the fire once possessed. With the development of an industry that could reach into people's home, came regulation of output, but television as part of the broadcasting system became 'a licence to print money'.[14] The regularity of availability and the mild variation in types of content on it always implied an understanding by the producer that there were different types of consumers they were pushing at, and also provided the pretext for long broadcasting hours to meet the multiplicity of demand, within a regulatory framework meant to protect the passive consumer.

The Internet, from the very beginning, had a very different character. In his account of its development, Naughton cites Kuhn's theory of paradigmatic shift.[15] For the executives at AT&T (American Telephone and Telegraph) who, in the form of the telephone system, had been in charge of the creation of the largest communication network yet known, the idea that a technology could split things up and would use a variety of routes to reconstruct them was beyond their imagination. It required the acceptance of too many counter-intuitive proposals, especially the necessity for sharing of intellectual property in an unregulated and irretrievable way. It took the Networking Working Group, a group of graduate students set up in 1969 by web pioneers Advance Research Projects Agency (ARPA), to design the protocols for connecting computers together. Naughton claims the methods they used to develop their recommendations were as influential as the results in determining the nature of future use of the Internet, in addition to resolving the technical difficulties. Indeed, for Naughton, this relationship was symbiotic and continues to configure the use and the application of the Internet: 'The fundamental ethos of the Net was laid down in the deliberations of the Network Working Group. It was an ethos that assumed nothing was secret, that problems existed to be solved collaboratively, that solutions emerged iteratively, and that everything that was produced should be in the public domain.'[16]

Thus, the Internet as a basic environment for communication contained an inherently different value system to the communications technologies that preceded it. It had required a fresh look at the problems by those without vested interests in the existing systems of what were called mass communication, but were inherently dominating monologues. It was these new values that determined the development of the Internet into a 'pull' medium. Users could pull material towards them without reference to the organizing principles of the producer in terms of time or opportunity of access, after the computer time-sharing model rather than the broadcasting model. Naughton's formulation remains broadly correct, though the changes in usage and functionality of the Internet from a time when a 24.4 kbps modem was considered the height of technology are considerable. The development of content has required an equally fresh look at the purposes and context of the Internet. We also have far more by way of custom and practice to inform us about how the Internet connects us than Naughton possessed before the turn of the millennium.

The development of 'pull' technologies was originally based on how much they had adapted existing broadcast strategies. By working from forms that people could easily recognize, the first generation of pull technologies, those using the limited functionality of slow connection speeds and limited graphics, permitted by the then ubiquitous browser Netscape, meant that the early experience of using the web was like flicking through models of graphic design samplers, all begging to catch the eye. This also required a great deal of producers' time and energy spent registering a site on various search engines to make it available to the consumer who searched for particular concerns on particular sites. In this, it remained broadly similar to existing outlets for print media, like a big magazine interconnected through the hyperlink. By adopting forms that people could already recognize, the pull technologies developed an audience whose participation in a new experience was based around old principles. New forms of passivity developed, like 'lurking', (when a non-participant monitors the development of a site or discussion thread without contributing to it), or staged forms of interaction were emphasized because of the difficulty of establishing the identity of anyone posting or contributing to a website. Despite Naughton's assumption that the 'pull' character of the Internet would be its chief and most interesting feature, there turns out to be a different dynamic affecting the relationship between a producer and their audience, and one just as related to the basic technological disposition of the Internet.

Alvin Toffler[17] had foreseen what he described as 'narrow-casting' as the alternative to broadcasting in a world where so few producers controlled the output compared with the vast numbers of viewers or listeners. However, where narrow-casting has emerged, it has done so in the form of cable television (as Toffler predicted), rather than networking computing, because it requires a change in demand rather than a change in approach. Push technologies are broadcast, and as such are largely dependent on static hardware and static relationships. The offerings from the broadcasters are fixed, with controlled and mediated access to the means of production. Whatever ingenious ruses the broadcasters produce to convince their audiences that the choices are in their hands, the basic arrangement of a producer who pushes onto a passive viewer remains. The selective technologies of network computing, on the other hand, have introduced a greater range of behaviour and content that can be developed by the users of any particular site. The significant difference is being network based, and is therefore dependent on interaction as determined by users for validation. This marks a significant shift in the application of technology, though the result is less democratic than is often claimed. The rights in cyberspace belong to those with the technological savvy, which does not always equate with a richness of ideas.

At this point, it is worth making a distinction between new media practice and the kind of network-based art practice that is of interest here. Digital technology as a medium for artistic exploration ought not to be confused with creative practice in networking, though there are clearly times when the networking component is an important aspect of the experience of the work. Dixon[18] has presented a handsome collection of digital media experiments, presenting a history of new media as interpreted through the analogue forms of theatre, dance and installation art. The attraction to digital technologies of practitioners in these fields is presented as inherently new, but though the collection is vast, the newness of the approaches remains less convincing and more rhetorical. Invariably, the role of digital technology is as an enhancement of existing theatre or performance practice, a shiny gloss to dazzle the jaded spectator. As such, the work painstakingly chronicled by Dixon often presents itself as having all the qualities of dazzle, in that we cannot quite see the substantive or qualitative point of the work. Given the distracting power of technology to deliver a diversion, the substance of new media approaches are often difficult to identify. Vacuous and expensive embellishments justified by sheer novelty become more important than the light shed on the human condition through the practice of art. The digital technologies themselves do not decide the work; they only determine the constraints of the content. As such, this approach risks two interesting features emerging all too rapidly in the creative process. The first is the breathtaking speed with which cutting edge technologies acquire bluntness in a rapidly changing technological environment. The second is the dependence, indeed the divorce, of the creative practitioner from the technologies (with a few distinguished examples of what might now properly be described as the craft practice of creative computing). To consider Stelarc's use of prosthetics as 'rendering the body "absent" or "obsolete"'[19] is to make spectators into slaves. Of course, he does nothing of the sort, only asserts a confused claim that augmenting the body makes us inhuman at the same time as directing our attention to his humanity through his nakedness, whether semi or complete. As a sensationalist, he is persuasive, but like most digital art in this vein, he mistakes his own wonder, for deep insights into the human condition. To attract attention he must create outrage, but the nature of his performances retain and reinforce the old media relations between artist and spectator, however stunning the performance of the technology may be.[20] Dixon's catalogue is fleshed out with minor, marginal events that often fall between practices, and whilst the assertion that they represent significant change in some established practices (for example, Cunningham's *Hand-drawn Spaces* (1997) stands out as a genuine attempt to create work differently), the technologically enhanced performance does little to change the spectator's perspective. Nor does it transform the ideas we have about creativity through the technological enhancements that accompany it. This becomes a one-sided discussion for artist alone to ponder.

Equally, there are times when the 'pull' technology of the Internet is used as if the network was simply another narrow-casting opportunity. The flexibility of the technology and potential as a delivery system make this all too tempting, though the result is invariably tempered by the tendency of the Internet to make use of the resources that are uploaded to it. Focussing on the possibility that the technology can apparently democratize access to an audience suggests an as yet unfinished agenda relating to broadcast. The dominance of the push media in the second half of the twentieth century in determining the story of contemporary life almost certainly distorted the perceptions of the people to whom they were pushing their stuff, as well as marginalizing a large range of voices and talent with another version of events that struggled to be heard. The emergence of a technology that would allow alternative voices and ideas to be presented in the public domain appears inevitable in retrospect, given the fear of governments and citizens alike of the power of broadcasting to determine the public mind. The reality of narrow-casting through the Internet is that it invariably replicates the structures and techniques of broadcasting, permitting the peripheral to be addressed on the same terms as mainstream broadcast media, but only by pushing at a segmented target group. Rather than democratizing, this approach to the technology risks creating closed circles of self-referential discourse, using the low costs of production and distribution as a means of empowering the self without creating anything like a new way of encountering ideas, experiences or art, or exploiting new technology to do more than resolve a long-standing difference with the old ones.

For Grau, this change in spectating and spectatorship is the result of a combination of developments in art, science and technology, intensified by their interaction.[21] The result of these developments is a new medium that appears to be both threatening in its destruction of old media, and promising in the creative horizons it might develop. In this context, Grau is often found compounding technologies together, like an outsider looking at what appears a coherent system, when closer inspection suggests the interactions are invariably unplanned, accidental and short lived. Distinction in creative terms is best served by identifying subject matter rather than technological media, setting aside McLuhan's famous injunction about television. The extent to which variation and texture can be found in Grau's formulation of the inter-capitalized media art diminishes the strength of an argument about coherence, either in medium or in message. The effort, however, is in pursuit of an explanation of the radical effect technology has had on creative practice. Both Grau and Dixon point to a vast catalogue of practical examples, though it is often difficult to determine either what is new in them or what they have in common. I want to focus here on the spectating relationship, noting that for both of these authors the features of technology are not necessarily redefining art but the use made of them by artists. In this, too, they often prefer an implicit similarity to the historical model of artistic practice. So, films become the expression of their directors according to a convention developed in the fifties as a means to argue the value of film as an art form.[22]

The promise I have made for the technology is that it can offer new forms of creative practice and in particular those forms will depend on the collaboration of the web community to produce them. This development of the web as a creative environment is usually referred to today as 'web 2.0'. The term was coined by Tim O'Reilly and associates after the dot.com collapse, initially as a method to signify the changes in the way software designers and users interacted with each other and with the web.[23] It marks a distinction between the first iteration of web-based activity, generally thought to have shaken out the application of web-based services and their supporting technologies. By making clear which types of application worked, in the sense of using the web's functionality to its best advantage, web 2.0 is less interested in the creative and economic models of broadcast, and more in the potential of the technologies to deliver something different, shifting creative practice from the individual producer into dynamic interplay between broad user communities.

This promise is based on significant differences in the way the web operates as a technological platform, including how some unique features can be exploited creatively by a broader community of creative practitioners than might have been traditionally allowed or defined as such. Digital technology depends on creating traces of activity that can be tracked and recovered in order to reproduce it. The consistency of digitized resources means that they are not reproduced so much as reactivated. Beyond the simulacrum, the digital process produces originals rather than perfect copies. This in turn creates the possibility that the underlying data can be reformulated, metamorphosing into different forms using the same basic digital information; a sound can be used to make an image, usage statistics can become compositional components, or an image re-contextualized, embedded in a new visual environment without ever taking it out of its old one. Refined through techniques like tagging as a means of flagging up for interested parties the main features of a digital resource, the potential for the use of resources from sharing to stealing has not been lost on the user community. The semantic web, where software agents can find, share and integrate data, information and knowledge exchange still remains a long way off, but Berners-Lee's dream of intelligent data has found intelligent agents through human users. The web 2.0 applications spawned by this process are based on the principles of social networking as a creative practice, making the web a collaborative space in which users can share resources, sometimes wittingly, sometimes not, as in the case of the Bennett video discussed above. The context of the appropriation provides a new filter through which the work can be seen, often tapping into a new community of interest beyond the initial inspiration for the work or the community for whom it was made. The social networking principles of web 2.0 put creative work into a state of potential flux. If enough people can be attracted to the resource, it becomes caught in a tidal flow of use and counter-use, giving it life and meaning unimagined at its origin. The Internet frees us from having to present the final say about anything, indeed makes such a proposal impossible given that once the source material enters cyberspace, it need have no final destination.

Under these conditions, the network becomes an important new performance space. The artist becomes a collaborator in the formulation and reformulation of work that has no final form. The creative process is distributed across geography, time and is filtered through the hands and minds of those curious enough or lucky enough to come across the work, either by design or by accident. As a pull technology, the Internet leaves the power in the hands of the user, who is at liberty to press the back button at any time. The interaction across the network can bring together vast numbers of collaborators who are all free to form the material as they choose, rather than to accept the structure of the presentation they are offered.

With this comes the development of a new craft practice for working with computers. To extract the potential of web 2.0 as a creative experience, the formerly passive spectators of the broadcast age are replaced by technologically skilled creative partners. When Wordpress, a popular blogging site, includes the phrase 'Code is Poetry' as its slogan, and explains that it has a mission to combine 'aesthetics, web standards, and usability',[24] an impression of the way a craft practice is emerging becomes possible to form. Like any serious creative endeavour, it requires a commitment to the development of skill, but the knowledge of context is what distinguishes the best from the mediocre. The opportunity for artists is to accept the idiosyncrasies and parameters of the form and to use them to create new forms that are able to use the web's best features.

What is at stake here is a redefinition of how to be creative and what creativity looks like in the context of the Internet. The network uses resources differently, by emphasizing collaboration and reformulation rather than originality. It includes a deep craft that demands respect, especially given the potential for creating art that engages an international community generated from an inexpensive laptop connected from anywhere in the world. The results can be surprising, and their unpredictability reflects the current instability of our creative enterprise. In the Internet, the locus of creativity shifts from the individual and their work to the tidal flow of the user community it can find. As Naughton has asserted about the technological processes of the Internet, the creative ones also seem on the verge of a Kuhnian-style paradigm shift. This depends on an active and participating audience, who become partners in the creative process by contributing to it. In this sense, the Internet is unique in granting the opportunity to participate in a creative enterprise simply by being interested in it.

Notes

1. Bennett, S. (1912), *Old Age, Its Cause and Prevention The Story of an Old Body and Face Made Young*, New York: The Physical Culture Publishing Company.
2. ibid., p. 18.
3. In this Bennett was adumbrating the chemist and medical sociologist L.J. Henderson's view that, 'prior to 1912, a random patient with a random disease had chances no better than 50:50 of benefiting from a consultation with a random physician.' See Holloway, S. W. F. (2000), 'The Year 1000: Pharmacy at the Turn of the First Millenium', *The Pharmaceutical Journal'*, vol. 264, no. 7077, pp. 32–4.
4. ibid., p. 19.
5. ibid., p. 17.
6. Bennett lived until his mid-80s when he was apparently killed in a car accident.
7. There was a lot of interest from colleagues about the effects of the exercises. Basically, they are isometrics, and work mostly on developing core stability alternating with gentle stretching, not dissimilar to Pilates.
8. Schoenberg, A. (1911), *Six Little Pieces for Piano*, Opus 19, Ref. Type: Music Score.

9. A graphical environment for music and multimedia.

10. It remains available on YouTube at http://www.youtube.com/watch?v=yaPFDKKXX_8 for those interested.

11. 'VideoCarnage' (http://www.videocarnage.com/index.php?search=movements) describes itself as 'videos to the extreme', where 'you will find an awesome collection of funny videos, wild videos, or any video you can think of!', including, apparently, ours.

12. See Sporton, G. (2006), 'Capturing the Space', Body, Space, Technology Journal, vol. 6, no.1. http://people.brunel.ac.uk/bst/vol06/home.html

13. Naughton, J. (1999), A Brief History of the Future, London: Weidenfeld & Nicolson Limited.

14. This phrase is attributed to Roy Thomson, then head of Scottish Television, in describing the value of an ITV franchise. See Braddon, R. (1965), Roy Thomson of Fleet Street – and How to Get There, London: Collins.

15. Naughton, p.110. See Kuhn, T. S. (1962), The Structure of Scientific Revolutions, Chicago: University of Chicago Press.

16. Naughton, p.138.

17. Toffler, A. (1970), Future Shock, New York: Random House Publishing.

18. Dixon, S. (2007), Digital Performance, London, Cambridge Mass: The MIT Press.

19. ibid., p.316.

20. It is worth noting that none of Stelarc's prosthetics would ever find themselves in serious use given they fail too many basic principles of usability. They cannot be considered as serious propositions in this regard, only as theatrical spectacle.

21. Grau, O. (2007), MediaArtHistories, London, Cambridge Mass: The MIT Press, p. 1.

22. See Sarris, A. (1968), The American Cinema: Directors and Directions 1929–1968, New York: E.P. Dutton.

23. See http://www.oreillynet.com/pub/a/oreilly/tim/news/2005/09/30/what-is-web-20.html for a comprehensive account of this process.

24. See http://wordpress.org/ for further details.

5

THE AUDIENCE IN SECOND LIFE: THOUGHTS ON THE VIRTUAL SPECTATOR

Dan Zellner

This chapter focuses on the virtual world of Second Life and the role of the audience within it. My frame of reference is primarily improvisational theatre as practiced in Chicago with reference to one of its historic predecessors, the Commedia dell'Arte. While the focus, Second Life and a regional version of improvisational theatre, may seem very narrow, I hope to draw from this analysis some observations that have a general application beyond Second Life and the approaches to improvisational theatre described in this chapter.

 In writing this chapter I find my approach similar to the construct that Viola Spolin (one of the famous proponents of improvisational theatre) used in setting up the structure of one of her improvisational theatre games: identify the problem ('point of focus'), have the participants directly engage in solving the problem, and then evaluate. In this case, the reader will observe as I work to solve the problem of creating theatre for an audience in a virtual world. The reader can then evaluate the observations and approaches presented. Certainly, as Spolin observed, there is always more than one way to solve a problem and I state the nature of the audience in Second Life as a problem only because at this point, at least among theatre practitioners, there seems to be considerable experimentation and no established approaches.

One thing is certain, the direct transplant of the relationship between the theatre audience and performer as practised in the real world or first world (as some Second Life users prefer to say) is not vital and does not work in Second Life at this moment in time. Certainly, early experiments in any medium use approaches from an earlier form: one need only look at early television and film to observe this phenomenon. I should note that I will be using the term first world instead of real world or real life. I make this choice to emphasize that actions that take place in Second Life have an effect and a form of existence in the real world. It is also important to mention that the two worlds are not mutually exclusive and that there is certainly some overlap. That being said, I use the term first world to provide a quick comparison between the two worlds when needed. A very exciting and challenging element of approaching any new venture of this sort is that it requires you to look at the very fundamentals of your work in a new way. In this spirit, I investigate the nature of the audience in Second Life.

The point of focus – Second Life

Second Life is an online-networked environment created by Linden Labs. Its appeal is its relative ease of access and the capability to connect with people from various locations in a 3D environment that is dynamic: elements of the environment can be modified, changed and can react to users. Philip Rosedale (the founder of Linden Labs and one of the creators of Second Life) expresses one of his objectives for Second Life as follows:

> One of the things I'd always been interested in, ever since I was a young boy, was how we manipulate the world around us. The world has so much stuff in it; there was always something I wanted to change, something I wanted to add, something I wanted to build

Fig. 8: Basic improvisational theatre game with ball.

out of the things I saw around me. That, to me, was magical; seeing the world change in response to the ideas in my head. One of the things I wanted to do when we started developing Second Life almost a decade ago was to give anyone a chance to work the same magic.[1]

Second Life is not a narrative driven game (many contend that it is not a game at all), however, due to its structure it does have an implicit narrative. This implicit narrative and its implications could be the subject of an entire book. For the purpose of this chapter, the focus will be on the structure of the user experience in Second Life. We will focus on this structure in order to figure out possibilities for the theatre audience in this virtual world.

As I see it, there are five key characteristics of the Second Life user experience that influence the nature of an audience in Second Life. These characteristics are as follows: Second Life is a mediated experience; its space is mutable; it uses an objective perspective; it is asynchronous; and it is iterative. I will now examine these characteristics and their implications for theatre artists and audiences.

This game was played at the 'Symposium on Second Life in Creativity' (New Media Consortium), 16 August, 2007. The purpose of this game is to establish a basic connection between all participants in the virtual space.

1. The mediated experience
Fundamental to Second Life is the avatar – the representation of the user in this virtual world – a world that is viewed on the user's computer screen. An avatar, at present, is controlled by the user's keyboard and mouse. These fundamental, and perhaps mundane, facts create an extremely important relationship between the user and any potential performance. The fact is that the user, in essence, is connected to his/her virtual body through movement and 'use' of the avatar. An avatar that is not in action creates a disconnect between the user and the virtual world. It seems to me then that it is not reasonable or engaging to have a Second Life (virtual) audience sit in virtual chairs and remain static for an entire performance. This is equivalent to giving a speech before an audience in a computer lab. The situation presents a tension between an audience sitting in front of computers and the presenter. The speech is in the wrong venue. Likewise, there is in the Second Life (virtual) audience an irresistible and understandable desire/ need to use the keyboard and mouse.

Antonio Fava, one of the premier contemporary Commedia dell'Arte artists, writes in his book, *The Comic Mask in the Commedia dell'Arte*, 'devoid of dynamism, the mask becomes empty. The art of the mask is an art of movement in space and time, of movement as the sign of spirit in anything, even in that which appears static'.[2] In Second Life, the avatar is the user's mask: it must be in action in order to exist. This action can be characterized by movement but could also be manifested in camera movement – a change of the user's view or perspective. It should also be noted that in the Commedia dell'Arte the term 'mask' has several meanings including the object worn by the actor as well as the complete character including gesture and psychology.

Spolin states quite emphatically that, 'all those involved in the theater should have personal freedom to experience, this must include the audience'.[3] Interestingly both improvisational theatre as practiced in Chicago and the Commedia dell'Arte do not use the convention of the fourth wall. Direct contact with the audience is part and parcel of the show.

If the audience needs to move, to be in action, to experience, this then prompts the next logical question: Is the spectator an actor? It's possible to actually make the audience actors during select portions of the show. At this point one has to mention Augusto Boal, the famous Brazilian theatre artist and founder of Theatre of the Oppressed, and his 'SpectActor'. In Boal's theatre, the ability for an audience member to assume one of the roles of the actors onstage is essential.[4] It empowers the audience and provides a method for all to solve the problem being addressed in the play. In Chicago style improvisation, it is not unusual for a member of the audience to be included in a scene or for the audience member to provide material for the scene. In Commedia, a lucky spectator may be included in a 'lazzo' or comic routine/action. In Second Life, one could provide an opportunity for the audience to try out a situation or help create the situation. There are any number of ways that spectators can become involved or have a choice. For example, the show can incorporate the audience as a character by simply adapting the narrative – a classic example: a press conference in which the audience becomes reporters. Also in Second Life, the act of looking at something requires a fairly high level engagement. Consequently, a show could require that the audience engage in very active spectating (that is, change viewing perspectives frequently in order to fully appreciate the performance).

Fig. 9: Author in virtual rehearsal space (New Media Consortium Virtual Campus).

Whatever the approach, the necessity to connect with the audience in an action-based context is crucial.

In addition to the options above, the tension between an avatar based audience and the performance may be resolved by having the show literally move. This movement could be created by either moving the audience (like an amusement ride) or by requiring that the audience move from location to location. During my improvisation workshops on the New Media Consortium Campus in Second Life, I learned that I could make a simple bench that seated several people. Much to my surprise, this bench (with several spectators on it) could be moved by a single actor. From this experience, I imagine that a seating area for 40 could be built and one actor could simply pass the audience to another! Conversely, audience members could pass the stage around. Having a show in multiple locations is certainly a well-established technique. In Second Life, one can teleport to many locations. I decided not to employ it because this sort of show (even in the virtual world of Second Life) involves a good deal of coordination and production time. In my work, I have opted to use one location in Second Life and move within it.

2. The mutable space

Christine White notes:

> Since the Renaissance the ability to change scenery and create spectacle for the audience has been a central feature of the theatre. It celebrates the ability of humanity and art to control its world, signifying the importance of transformation both politically and culturally. The delight of witnessing clever or spectacular transformations has always been a crowd pleaser...The ability of scenery and space to change has been one of the cornerstones of Scenography.[5]

Space in Second Life is highly mutable. In terms of a performance, this means that scene changes can be accomplished in the Second Life space much as in the first world but also these changes can be created to react to audience actions. As a matter of fact, the potential for dynamic scenic elements in Second Life far outstrips the capability for Second Life avatar movement.

In many cases, scenery in Second Life can be created and staged much faster than in first world situations. One major exception to this case is found in improvisational theatre. In many improv (improvisational theatre) shows the audience is asked to provide a location for the action of a scene. This location is called 'The Where'. In Spolin's work a basic premise is that, 'we know where we are by the physical objects around us',[6] and so, a sense of space is created by these objects in the immediate space. In the improvisational theatre, these objects and spaces are imaginary and mimed by the actors. This allows for extreme flexibility and for incredible transformations. Indeed, one of Spolin's basic games involves passing an imaginary object. Each player uses the object in its current manifestation and then transforms it into something else. In Second Life this level of spontaneous object manipulation is not possible. Additionally, in this virtual world imaginary or mimed objects are not the rule – the expectation is a realized object rendered in 3D or at the very least a wire frame or basic representational shape. At present, avatar movement in Second Life must be scripted and strung together like basic conversation in a foreign language. Subtlety of movement is very challenging. I mention objects in regard to space because so many spaces in Second Life resemble lifeless backdrops with no real sense of location, that is, interactive objects that are intrinsic to the 'where'.

In spite of these limitations, the virtual world of Second Life can benefit greatly from its similarities with the improvisational stage. On the most basic level, Second Life can adopt improvisational theatre's lack of the fourth wall. From my perspective, this performer/audience relationship is the most vital for Second Life theatre. We also learn from improvisational theatre that in choice comes connection. By giving the audience a choice, whether it is in the location of the scene or some other element of the show, for instance asking the audience for an object, a strong connection is established. In improvisational theatre, in order to help define the space, actors many times assume the role of objects or other scenic elements, improv groups can turn into just about anything, from animals to rainstorms to trees with serpents slithering through them. In Second Life this sort of 'people space' can also be accomplished. Avatars can change form quite easily so it is entirely possible to have a group of avatars change into trees if needed. Avatars can also assume a role similar to extras in a movie. They assist in creating the scene and the space. These extras could be actual avatars (Second Life players) or objects created to look like people with some preset scripts (robots). At present, robots are used in Second Life in bars as bartenders and in many other locations to assist in creating an atmosphere and sense of location. Many Second Life residents are offered money to simply be present at a certain location. This sort of job is known as 'camping' in the Second Life vernacular. All these techniques seek to establish a vibrant and dynamic environment, mise-en-scene, for the avatar comprised audience.

Beyond improvisational theatre, Second Life offers qualities of space that provide a unique experience whether it is scuba diving in the Caves of Rua or sky-diving. These direct experiences in which the user engages with the space and, for a moment, has to negotiate with it directly, provide an immediate and exhilarating sensation. These complete spatial experiences of, for example, swimming, falling or flying can be experienced in Second Life at a moment's notice. The give and take of control between the avatar and the environment is a key technique to engaging the audience and providing a truly exciting experience.

In the situation where the audience is choosing action and negotiating space, is the audience then an author? Yes, in this case the audience has a role in creating the story and a degree of authorship. Consequently, in Second Life a technique that could be used to retain the audience connection is a series of moments of audience authoring. Whether it is creating an environment which must be negotiated, filled with water or other media, soliciting suggestions, providing a moment in which the audience actually moves/views in one direction or another, or some other form of audience directed authoring (for example, selected audience members adding objects to a scene which the actors then incorporate), the need to keep the audience avatars engaged is critical. Of course, there will always be the option to simply watch and this option must be clearly delineated in the performance environment either through use of the space or other methods.

3. *Objective perspective*

In the first world an 'out of body experience' is considered something unusual or out of the ordinary although I must admit as time goes on I think this sort of experience will become less and less unusual. In Second Life, the default view for an avatar is called 'Guide View': a point of view that is outside of oneself. Guide View is an over-the-shoulder shot. Of course, in Second Life you can change your camera view or your perspective very easily. For example, one alternate perspective is 'Mouse Look'. When a Second Life user is in this mode, the camera is manipulated with the mouse hence the name 'Mouse Look'. 'Mouse Look' is equivalent to a POV (point of view) shot. Additionally, there are a number of map views to orientate oneself in the larger world of Second Life. As a result of all these different views in Second Life, a great deal of time is spent watching yourself. This happens when adjusting your appearance or simply when opting to view things from a different perspective. I have even watched myself watching a show! This perspective creates a different type of awareness in the audience. Rather than trying to limit the perspective of the audience to the typical first world experience, artists should consider utilizing and creating for first and third person perspectives. A different experience for different perspectives is certainly possible or a carefully choreographed movement through perspectives is another option. In any case, action that accommodates multiple perspectives is critical.

In conjunction with this very self-conscious state is an incredible flexibility of character. As mentioned earlier, one of the first things you do when you enter Second Life is create your avatar – your in-world being. This representation of you, and it doesn't necessarily have to look like you, is just a starting point for many more identities. A person in Second Life can have a whole repertoire of identities that can include human, animal and even alien beings. These identities can be changed at a moment's notice. This ability to adjust character makes it possible for a user to be unique or a group of people to create avatars that look identical, creating very interesting possibilities both onstage and off. With users of Second Life assuming various characters, acting has already begun. How then do you cope with an audience that can change its identity at any time? How do you perform to an audience that consists of all manner of beings, for example, animals, humans, aliens? One could conclude that the best model for performance or a theatrical style event would be an acting workshop since in these situations participants move between being actors and audience. Another option is a situation in which the audience could be asked to assume a group role as part of the performance or play a role at a certain moment in the show. Identities could be issued/given upon entering the show. The many options for viewing and the many possibilities for the identity of the audience (respective and collective) are some of the most difficult and yet most interesting challenges in creating a performance for a virtual world. As with the first world, the audience and its characteristics must be acknowledged.

4. Asynchronous

It is not unusual in Second Life to wander through many environments and not see a single person. When I have shown Second Life to colleagues and other interested parties a common question is: Where is everyone? Certainly there are places in Second Life with plenty of people and when one becomes more familiar with the world and its activities you can easily find a crowd. As much as real-time interaction is a major part of Second Life, another fundamental fact of Second Life is that it does involve an asynchronous element. Messages, objects and other artefacts are left for others to read and use at some other time.

It seems then reasonable and most effective to use these two elements (real-time and asynchronous interaction) in the design of a Second Life theatre piece. Put another way, a theatre artist should consider designing a show for two audiences: the real-time and the asynchronous. In this case, these two audiences will most likely have different experiences but hopefully the experiences will be equally as engaging. These two audiences will require what I call a live space. What I mean by live space is a space that can engage a solo visitor and a number of possibilities for action. It is a space that has an inherent narrative and it is a space that can function as a player on its own. The best analogy I can provide for this sort of space is a tennis court with a backboard. If one person comes to the court, she can use the backboard and play. If two people come to the court they can play a game. If three people come to the court all can play or two can play and one can watch. A number of play possibilities exist and the space invites all these possibilities. In the case of the solo player the space becomes the other player. This space stands at all times and provides a place for solo or group performances and, with the introduction of robots and playback options, multiple viewing options are also available.

5. Iteration

In first world theatre there is the run of the show. Each iteration of the play is just a little different and this spontaneity and difference makes each performance special. In the case of some improvisational theatre, this can involve multiple iterations of a form or game. An example of a long form improvisational game is 'The Harold'. This game creates an entire show based on a single suggestion from the audience.

Theatre in Second Life can also involve multiple iterations of a show. Similar to the first world, these possibilities can include multiple performances but also can involve additional elements. These additional elements can include digital capture of moments of play as well as the addition of digital objects that can be left behind for others to use and play with. In Chicago's improvisational theatre style there is a basic concept known as, 'Yes and...' The concept of 'Yes and...' is that in any situation the improviser accepts what is given to him/her and builds upon it. In this way, through collaboration and heightening, an engaging scene is created. In Second Life this concept of 'Yes and...' can be used to include recording moments of play, addition of objects, scenic elements and many other kinds of digital media. Additionally, players can lay down performance tracks much as musicians record individual tracks in a recording studio. These tracks can then be combined to create shows or used in part with live performers to create interesting mixes. This process of sampling, capturing and using other digital elements adds not only another element to the audience experience but the audience itself may be sampling parts of the performance to share, view later, or use! Ultimately, a feedback loop is created in which a very dynamic creative dialogue is established between performer and audience.

Time for the show

With these observations in mind, if someone asked me to create a show right now I would create a large scale, 'grand game'. The game is large in scale because within its system it consists of a number of games, similar to some forms of long form improvisational theatre. It is ongoing, and like a theatre space it accommodates a number of theatre projects or groups of artists. The game would leverage in its design the basic nature of Second Life utilizing elements of the improvisational theatre theory. Is this 'grand game' simply Second Life itself? Mick Napier,[7] a prominent figure in the Chicago improvisational theatre scene, describes the improvisational theatre as a 'closed system' in which there are inputs – one being the audience. 'The audience adds real energy with their sound of laughter, fueling the scene farther.' In Second Life, the theatre is a system with different parameters and inputs yet it still has its boundaries. It is a closed system. The space, and objects within, shapes the narrative and the game or collection of games within creates this system. The space leaves space for added content by players and also leaves room for solo or multiple play but guides this play in both concrete and content terms. Imagine a gymnasium with apparatus surrounding the room all linked to a theme yet independent. This is the closest analogy to the sort of show I would consider creating in Second Life.

I will now attempt to walk the reader through a general sketch of the game. An avatar enters the space at any time. In the space is an information kiosk or other sort of object/resource that provides show times, and also serves as a communication point for theatre artists and audiences. Communications may involve invitations to try certain games, to incorporate certain pre-recorded performance tracks, and also audience suggestions concerning new narratives. I also see a role for the moderator of the space who may leave messages for participants concerning new narratives for the space and other notes concerning the nature of the space and its content. If it is during a show the spectator observes some sort of pattern game in action – by observing they see both the pattern of the game and its inherent narrative; for example, Sisyphus and the rock. For a more complex game there may be the need to provide instructions or with some games participation may only be limited due to the amount of time and involvement of the current players. All of this depends on the author(s) of the game. This game is played, heightened and explored until it by nature transforms itself or, if it is a conducted game, it is ended by the game-leader. One can simply watch or participate or switch between the two modes. Some play, some watch, some record. As mentioned before these roles can be defined by the space: 'hot spots' where any avatar within this space will be involved in the performance and 'cold spots' where the avatar may simply observe. Certainly there will be seats for observers, a convention that makes it very easy to identify an audience space, but the seating area does not have to define the space; nor should it. I mention this because the mutable nature of the Second Life space can be limited by the overuse of audience seating. Actually this has a parallel to first world theatre in which many theatre artists prefer a black box theatre configuration because it allows for great flexibility in the audience/performer relationship. Beyond using the space to identify performer/spectator roles, as mentioned earlier, identification can be accomplished by other means such as clothing or objects. A great deal of care should be taken in not overburdening the initial setup of the game. If the audience member has to read three pages of instructions or notes in order to understand the nature of the game/performance then all the enjoyment and joy of discovery is gone. A huge disconnect has been established between the world of the performance and the potential audience member/participant. A number of possibilities are available for the solo visitor to the space. The solo visitor can play a game with the space, play in the space with a pre-recorded performance track, lay down a performance track, write a message for others or even compose a small script or scenario. The possibilities for performance are quite diverse involving variations from solo visitor to highly choreographed group shows/games. As with all theatre, the game is only as good as its players. This game, solo or group, can be played back and played against so there is a continual loop of play and developing play. In this sense, the show goes on and on in permutations and new and fascinating combinations like a folk story that is told and remembered and constantly adapted and developed. This is my vision of the grand game and a possibility for theatre in Second Life. As Viola Spolin notes: 'when our theatre training can enable the future playwrights, directors, and actors to think through the role of the audience as individuals and as part of the process called theater, each one with a right to a thoughtful and personal experience, is it not possible that a whole new form of theatre presentation will emerge?'[8] I have done my best to think through the role of the audience in a new space and from my observations I conclude that a new form of theatre is necessary for this virtual space. Whether this new form is simply a computer game with a theatre flavour or theatre that is influenced heavily by computer games is impossible to say at this stage.

Notes

1. Rymaszewski, M. (2007), *Second Life: The Official Guide*, Hoboken: J. Wiley, p. iv.
2. Fava, A. (2007), *The Comic Mask in the Commedia dell'Arte*, Evanston: Northwestern University Press, p. 18.
3. Spolin, V. (1999), *Improvisation for the Theatre*, 3rd edition, Evanston: Northwestern University Press, p. 13.
4. Boal, A. (1985), *Theatre of the Oppressed,* New York: Theater Communications Group.
5. White, C. (2006), 'Smart Laboratories', *The Potentials of Spaces*, (ed). Oddey, A., White, C., Bristol: Intellect, p.86.
6. Spolin, V. (1999), *Improvisation for the Theatre*, 3rd edition, Evanston: Northwestern University Press, p. 89.
7. Mick Napier, improvisation comedy director. Napier, M. (2004), *Improvise: Scene from the inside out*, Heinnman Drama.
8. Spolin, V. (1999).

6

CULTURAL USE OF CYBERSPACE: PARADIGMS OF DIGITAL REALITY

Iryna Kuksa

'Art, or the graphic translation of a culture, is shaped by the way space is perceived.'[1]

Society is facing a future in which technologies of computation will play an increasingly important role. In recent years, digital representation has become mainstream. It would be difficult, if not impossible, to identify precisely all the complex facets of this development, but all the available evidence suggests that computers are here to stay. They are diffusing into almost all other technologies employed in art, science and education, offering new opportunities to create, experiment and learn. Nowadays, a succession of technological advances has made it possible to express ideas, which used to be conceived as words, numbers, symbols, shapes, pictures, or sounds and which required a person to interpret them, in patterns that can be stored on digital media. This information can be easily, cheaply and rapidly reproduced, disseminated, and also manipulated by both machines and people. Another aspect of this rapid technological development is its influence on spectators' creativity and imagination. People are designing ways to socialize in new cities, communities and through new networks. They create novel modes to spread knowledge and information, resulting in a world-wide and rapid distribution of ideological, cultural and social messages.[2] However, this development does not imply that society necessarily foresaw all the consequences of accepting these technologies. Undoubtedly, new media have already become an integral part of our culture; however, the ethical, aesthetical, psychological and overall societal implications of this recent marriage remain to be explored.

Real or virtual? The 'realism' of digital reality
Digital techniques have made it possible to build upon the ability to construct realistic environments. A common misconception about the term 'virtual' is that it means 'not real', or

that it refers to something that exists in the spectator's imagination only. Certainly, virtual images are simulations that represent ideal or constructed rather than actual conditions; however, they are true in cyberspace. Pierre Levy characterizes the 'virtual' as being opposed to the 'actual' – not to the 'real'. He emphasizes that virtual objects have a real, or in other words, material existence, however, they differ in that their full potential has not yet been realized.[3] 'What is real?' asked the character of Morpheus in the blockbuster film *The Matrix*. The simple answer would be anything we can explore through our senses. However, remembering a simple experiment with a pencil and a glass of water during one of my physics lessons at school, I must disagree with the statement above. If you put a whole pencil in a transparent glass filled with water, it will appear to be broken, so it is obvious that our senses can deceive us and something that appears 'real' can be 'unreal' at the same time. This is obviously an 'old' discovery. About 55 B.C. a Roman philosopher Lucretius in his work *On the Nature of the Universe*, Book IV, 'Sensation and Sex' wrote:

> The nature of phenomena cannot be understood by the eyes. You must not hold them responsible for this fault of the mind...To landsmen ignorant of the sea, ships in harbour seem to be riding crippled on the waves, with their poops broken. So much of the oars as projects above the waterline is straight, and so is the upper part of the rudder. But all the submerged parts appear refracted and wrenched round in an upward direction and almost as though bent right back so as to float on the surface.[4]

There is little doubt that the relationship between human beings and visual imagery is deeply grounded in the art traditions of our society, however, for the last few decades the very idea of the image was irreversibly changed by interactive media. Virtual reality (VR) has recently become an inseparable part of this core relationship, transforming a picture into a multi-sensory interactive space of experience with a time frame.[5] Indeed, a virtual panoramic view with its sensorimotor exploration of an image space causes the effect of a 'living' and evolving environment, where the parameters of time can be deliberately modified. There is also a range of new options such as mixed realities, where images of the real world are blended with artificial images in a way that makes it very difficult, if not impossible, to distinguish between them. Therefore, it is not surprising that all these innovative applications raise an intriguing question about (artistic) originality or uniqueness. Digital images are stored in the form of binary codes, and their value is derived in part by their capacity to be easily accessed, downloaded, stored, manipulated and reproduced. For computer-generated environments the idea of the difference between a copy and an original is non-existent. Obviously, this is not the first ever attempt to 'fake' realism. The myth of photographic truth is one of these examples. In the past, the photo-camera was perceived as a visual medium, which was more accurate in recording reality than any of the other then available means, such as painting, drawing or sculpture. However, even in the early days, photographic techniques were employed to manipulate, more or less successfully, humans' perceptions of real events and environments. This was achieved through retouching, airbrushing, cutting-and-pasting, and also, re-photographing already existing photo-images. At the beginning, this manipulation of reality was very time-consuming, expensive and, furthermore, required a highly-skilled specialist to accomplish the task. Nowadays, every single desktop can function as publishing equipment, which can be used for scanning, editing and manipulating images. These technical specifications of a computer gave birth to a misapprehension of the modes used for the creation of virtual environments and imagery. One might believe that actual or representational images are produced through analog technologies; but virtual images, on the other hand, are only created through digital means and are specific to their era. In reality, however, virtual images are both analog and digital. They break with the convention of representing what is seen. A virtual image of a human body, for example, may represent no actual body in particular, but may be based on a composite or simulation of human bodies drawn from various sources.

Virtual reality is able to incorporate computer imaging, sound and sensory systems, in order to put the spectators in a direct feedback loop with the technology itself and the world it simulates. Rather than offering an environment to simply view and hear, like in traditional theatre or cinema space, VR attempts to create an experience, in which users feel as if they are physically involved in the world represented on all sensory levels. There are various external hardware and visualization systems that make interaction with virtual environments possible and achieve different levels of immersion. Virtual reality offers a three-dimensional experience where, with the help of various devices, such as head-mounted displays, data gloves, or body suits, users experience a VR world that appears to respond to the participants' actions.[6] Immersion within virtual environments acts as a replacement of the passive aspect of observing a computer monitor. It exists in parallel to our own reality and can be defined as augmented, partially immersive and fully immersive. VR systems enable their users to experience computer simulations of digital spaces that either have some correlation with the real world or which are completely imaginary. These environments are interactive, navigable in real time, and are not bound by any physical limitations. The decision process, in which participants distinguish between real, virtual, and imagined events is called virtual reality monitoring, where the quality of the involvement very much depends on the extent to which the spectators apply a willing suspension of disbelief.[7]

The ethical paradigm

The process of digitization created new dimensions of perception, which in turn led to some ethical considerations that have never previously occurred in our society. Obviously, virtual reality is a completely new environment, where its users can potentially find themselves under circumstances they have never encountered before. However, one might argue that the morality of cyberspace is based on the same codes of ethics, and that innovative VR practices only slightly transform the concept of truth and reality. This transformation only happens because of the roles, which are allocated or even forced on the participants, while interacting with or within virtual spaces.

> VR puts into question our traditional, western views of cosmology, epistemology and metaphysics by providing a perceptual construct of an alternate reality. This perceptual state is fundamentally different from our known, physical realm and our behaviors therein. Without this physical 'grounding' point from which to speak, it is difficult (or may

not even be applicable or possible) to establish a *singular*, rule-based way of being, or of meaning-making, or of clearly establishing 'right' from 'wrong'.[8]

All ethical norms are only relevant in connection with a belief system that indicates existing and non-existing things to assist a person in evaluating 'truth' or 'untruth'. Being 'true' is generally referred to as giving the true facts about something, as opposed to them being imagined or guessed. Although virtual environments bear a notion of reality, they are better described as an 'experience', not a 'place'.

The majority of ongoing experiments with VR in the field of computer sciences are concerned with the practice of imitating the action radius and the sensory experience of real environments in virtual worlds. Furthermore, it has become very popular to reconstruct the real conditions in virtual space, inhabited by avatars or representatives, who can be individually operated by a number of participants. A good example here is the Second Life project – http://secondlife. com – a 3D virtual community, which is built and owned by its 9,705,877 (and their number keep constantly growing) residents. There is little doubt that these practices successfully generate a genuine realm of possibilities and an accompanying range of options in cyberspace. However, VR desperately demands a plot motif to come into existence, in order to evoke a necessity to act. This need leads to various modes of behaviour and patterns of action that dramatically affect the truly autonomous interactivity of cyberspace. Some of them, however, could potentially disappear once the issues of authorship, regulations and the contextual environments come into existence.

Contemporary visual culture attempts to liberate itself from the technical and material restrictions of imaging technology, as well as from the repressive determinants of its social codes.[9] However, this claim can be challenged on the grounds that the continuous interaction between art, science and technology is constantly causing the emergence of new cultural forms, behaviours, values, and, as a result, a new set of social rules. For example, the person in cyberspace can be considered to be in two places simultaneously or, as one might argue, somewhere in between. The Internet gambling industry in the United States is a good example to support the above statement. In general, gambling is allowed only in some American states, while prohibited in the others. If gambling takes place online or, speaking figuratively, without geographic boundaries, the following question arises: if a gambling server set up in a state that allows this activity, was accessed in a state that does not, which state's law should apply to prosecute an illegal gambler?[10] There are many similar questions, which are still left without definite answers, because of the obvious duality of virtual environments. At present, cyberspace is an essential component of contemporary society's self-description and cultural change. Therefore, in order to define the use of technology in producing contemporary culture, it is necessary to introduce a new term – 'technoetic'[11] – that might be the key to explaining how our perceptions and knowledge of the real and virtual worlds around us evolve.

There is a tendency to regard digital media and especially virtual reality as an extension of our societal beliefs.[12] Indeed, they are constructed by people and thus utterly reflect human nature.

However, despite the fact that cyberspace is indeed a space for ethics, it is still uncertain how rule-and-value-systems can potentially evolve in virtual environments.

The aesthetical paradigm

The recent expansion of cyberspace has had a significant influence on contemporary visual culture and especially on its aesthetics. Aesthetics usually refers to philosophical notions of the perception of beauty and ugliness. The question as to whether such qualities are within the object itself, or exist solely within the spectator's mind, has been debated by numerous philosophers and artists for many centuries. One might argue that aesthetics in the new digital era is focusing on creating user-friendly software (that is, software aesthetics), and designing aesthetical computer interfaces including video games, online communities and also VR simulation. In this case, all these applications should also be considered as works of art and, consequently, aesthetic objects.

Currently, the dispute within the academic environment concerning whether virtual reality is an 'object' or a 'process' has generated strong polemics. Some argue that, 'virtual reality is not only a medium, like television or film, but is, like language, a medium that is able to reinvent itself...In it, the viewer may not only experience their own performance of the medium, but may witness the medium's capacity to perform itself'.[13] Others insist that virtual space is 'urban nomad, software engineering, the liquid architecture of the knowledge space',[14] which contributes to collaborative work-in-process. Furthermore, a small minority still believes that VR is a 'finite' environment. Here, I argue that despite being representational, virtual environments also possess an ability to be self-reflective, and to communicate knowledge. All these qualities are very specific to a process, rather than a restricted object.

From the 1960s onwards there have been numerous attempts, mostly made by installation and conceptual artists, to redefine traditionally defined aesthetic objects through applying various practical approaches.[15] In the digital era the illusionary symbiosis of spectator/participant and a work of art in a cyber-world represent a progression, where the interface, which is the key to any VR artwork (aesthetical object), can be understood as a form of interaction, representing, in a wider sense, a specific level of perception in virtual space. For example, there are some similarities between interacting with VR applications and watching a theatrical performance. A performance, both real and virtual, is a process, but at the same time a self-contained object, which is different each time a theatre audience perceives/interacts with it. This can be explained by the improvisational quality of theatrical space and also by the responsive nature of computer-generated environments.

There is little doubt that new technologies, centred upon digital micro-processing and computer programming, are transforming the nature of cultural production and perception. Communication is an attempt to transfer meaning; to share our emotional, visual, or aural experiences with other people. New computer-generated environments create a higher level of communication and information manipulation through combining text, images, and sounds and have the potential to further enhance the process of exchanging meanings. Nevertheless, even with the emergence and rapid development of such relatively new concepts as simulation, interactivity and immersion, digital media maintain a sense of multiplicity or hypermediacy that indicates the presence of previous means of communication and interaction.

The artwork, whether it is a painting, sculpture, or a performance, symbolizes a certain artistic view of reality. It has always been subject to historical change, where one form of art after obtaining the status of paradigm would be replaced by another. From the aesthetical viewpoint, the evolution of this term is particularly interesting in the context of digital reality. All digital images, in which the real and the imaginary are non-referential, categorically differ from traditional ones with their 'fixed' materiality. However, computer-generated or modified imagery represents truth, no more and no less than any other work of art. It has already been noted that the concept of the 'original', which is common in the traditional art world, is foreign to digital space. Obviously, the system is in charge of any kind of alteration; however, it is not able to guarantee any protection from copying the original artwork. Furthermore, the software and hardware devices can also be modified, in order to create mixed realities, where it is often impossible to distinguish between the unique and a simulation. As a result, the convergence of the work of art and technology into an inseparable whole could make the artwork (as an autonomous aesthetic object) disappear as such.[16]

One might argue that digital aesthetics are very much in charge of the present and the future of our ethical life in contemporary society. Although virtual art is no longer exclusive, in terms of creating aesthetic models of computer-generated worlds, there are some doubts that a common consensus on cyber-aesthetics can be reached today. In 1995, Lev Manovich predicted that instead of being charged for world-wide-web connection time, in the near future users might be asked to pay for visual aesthetics and the quality of the overall virtual experience: spatial resolution; number of colours; complexity of characters – both geometric and psychological. In fact, this is already happening in the industry of computer games and avatar communities, where animation quality at least partly determines retail prices.

The psychological paradigm

There is an immense compression ratio between digital information and human experiences. Thus, from behavioural and perceptual viewpoints, psychology serves to help us in creating, experiencing and inhabiting virtual worlds. It is the 'physics' of virtual reality that reflects upon the rules and constraints of computer-generated environments and where interaction is natural behaviour.[17] Our dependence on the internal state is obvious. Additionally, any interpretation of virtual involvement must also consider the external context – the environment. Cyber-worlds begin as emptiness and then introduce metaphysics or, literally, something, which is beyond the laws of physics, where computation becomes emotional by unifying analytic symbolism with audio-visual imagery.[18] As a result, the material no longer dominates the senses in virtual space. On the other hand, however, 'our conceptualization and reasoning are grounded in our embodiment, that is, in our bodily orientations, manipulations, and movements as we act in our world'.[19] 'In order to locate ourselves within spaces, we need to be able to take our bearings from the physical elements which serve as the coordinates defining and giving structure to the space, a portion of which we perceive ourselves to be in and occupying. In brief, we are spatially and temporally relational creatures.'[20] Indeed, VR experience may potentially cause a 'real' crisis of consciousness in an unprepared user. In order to avoid it, it is necessary to develop further our awareness of how valuable experience within and outside of cyberspace may be. Computer-generated reality is individually customized to the spectator's perspective and allows mutually inconsistent environments to co-exist without degradation.

One of the main goals of virtual reality, as stated by nearly all media researchers to date, is to provide spectators with the strongest possible impression of presence (or embodiment) and the maximum intensity of the transported message. Although the possibility of full immersion in VR space is still disputed, it is already more than simply a simulation of reality – everything is already 'real' in computer-generated environments. There is no doubt that it is quite complicated to simulate what one sees, but the creation of realism in cyberspace is not necessarily the primary objective. It is much more important to design virtual environments, so that they fulfill the existing practical, aesthetical, and psychological needs of their users. VR is a multi-sensorial space where all traditional media are united into a whole. It makes the participants a part of the virtual world, using immersion technologies, but at the same time keeps them quite separate from the virtual because of their ability to interact with VR environments.

There is the danger of the term 'interactivity' within digital environments being interpreted in a literal way, or, in other words, 'equating it with physical interaction between a user and a media object (pressing a button, choosing a link, moving the body), at the expense of psychological interaction'.[21] This view is probably the result of mistakenly discussing the concept of interactivity exclusively in relation to computer-based technologies. Obviously, all classical arts are interactive and employ numerous techniques to coordinate and focus the spectator's attention on different elements of the art-creation process. Contemporary art and modern media attempt to force these modes further, by placing new cognitive and physical demands on the viewers. For example, installation technologies often mobilize human emotions, in order to expand the limits of visualization and the possibilities of visual intelligence. This longing for transcending boundaries and abandoning the self is an integral part of any civilizing process.[22] One might argue that often, one of the main purposes of using computer technologies in art-creation is to make computation itself invisible. Indeed, design of the interface is gradually dissolving towards more transparent and intuitive forms, in order to avoid the psychological detachment of the viewer from the work of art. At the present state of technological development, the transparency of the medium is not quite possible and, I would like to point out, not ultimately crucial to achieve.

To some extent, computer technologies have become irreplaceable for us to perceive and co-create the real world. However, as Bertolt Brecht stated in his essay 'Theatre for Pleasure or Theatre for Instruction', 'when something seems "the most obvious thing in the world" it means that any attempt to understand the world has been given up'.[23] Indeed, technological innovations have already become rather 'obvious things' for many people. Nevertheless, there is still much left to explore and understand.

Art paradigm

One might argue that, at present, the traditional classification of arts seems dated. The common -isms of the nineteenth and twentieth centuries (for example, classicism, romanticism, cubism, surrealism, conceptualism) referred to intra-art practices, in which one movement naturally superseded the previous one, but these have not found a continuation in an era of digital art.[24] 'Supersede', however, is not the right verb to describe the evolution of the art styles – all of them naturally 'co-exist' with each other. It should be noted that to date there is no exact term that refers to computer-assisted imaging. The current expansion of multimedia technologies is now taking place on a much larger scale than in previous centuries; and their influence on the processes of art-creation and art theory is axiomatic. Nowadays, computer-based art and mediated performance have become one of the dominant art forms in our society, which includes a wide range of computer graphics and digitized images, animation, laser shows, cybernetic sculptures, interactive films, and telecommunication events. These new art forms often demand the involvement of the spectators to initiate the process of art-perception, enrich its content, and, eventually, finalize it. In the past, visual information was static and an image once created was fixed in its form or it was difficult, if not impossible, to change it. Once translated into digital language, every single element of the image can be manipulated and modified endlessly, because it becomes information stored in strings of binary code. This means that, in the contemporary art world, visual literacy is no longer limited to 'the object.'

Indeed, there is a strong connection between the evolution of art forms and technological progress. In the world of theatre, for example, the new technologies of stage lighting and sound reproduction in the early twentieth century encouraged the development of new scenographic forms. The artists often searched for inspiration looking to: 'the past, to primitive anthropological understandings and models, and at other times have pursued "human certainties" in attempts to analyze and define essential qualities of human perception within which a new, more universally accepted art might be created.'[25]

In an interview with the University of Warwick Research-TV in April 2005, Professor Richard Beacham further supports the above statement by describing the transformation of ancient Pompeian wall paintings into VR representations of Roman theatres:

> It's an interesting process because the ancients used a perspective technique which was similar to, but not exactly the same, as what we understand since the Renaissance, as perspective. And that meant that part of the project's tasks, one of the challenges of the project, has been to decode in fact ancient perspective technology and realize it and understand it and explore it by using modern perspective technology of the sort that we find in computer graphics.[26]

Although cyberspaces act as a present and future art medium, it is necessary to remember that they are also a means to understand and sometimes even rewrite our past. For example, the 'Set-SPECTRUM'[27] (Kuksa, 2007) project conceived by the author in 2006 proposes a new approach to designing digital educational packages applicable to the study of scenography

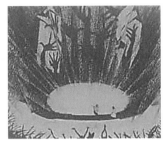

Fig. 10: Norman Bel Geddes, sketches for the production of *The Divine Comedy* by Dante Alighieri, 1921; high-resolution digital photographs of the originals.

in the twenty-first century and intends to provide a long-standing pedagogical impact. The Set-SPECTRUM aims to employ a new and useful vocabulary for learner-artefact interaction and creativity-training, providing greater knowledge of the use of new media technologies within the classroom and the potential to explore such difficult and sensitive subjects as, for example, Norman Bel Geddes'[28] 1921 presentation for Dante's *The Divine Comedy*[29] (Fig. 10 and 11). The 3D reconstruction (Fig. 12) of the original set-model, which was lost during the last century, facilitates academic research of the artefact and fills a gap in the history of western theatre design.

Today, there is a growing need to create more flexible educational structures and images, offering a variety of possible readings. These actions place the artefact-spectator relationship in a more behavioural context than in the past. The spectators began to participate actively not only in the act of creation, but also learning on all levels of experience – conceptual, emotional and physical. Virtual reality techniques simply enable this participation on a different, perhaps even higher, level. Computer-generated environments are a logical extension of arts integration and, furthermore, as some researchers argue, an ideal place for applying the existing knowledge

Fig. 11: Francis Bruguière's model photography for the production of *The Divine Comedy* by Dante Alighieri.

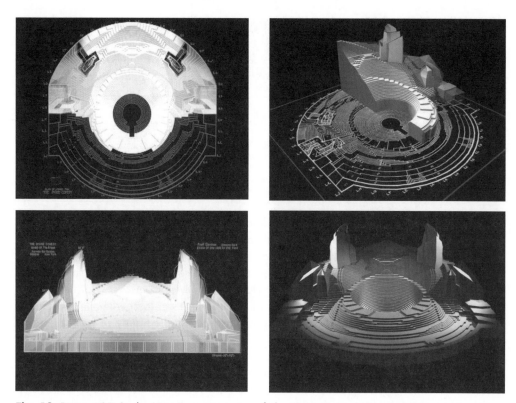

Fig. 12: Discreet 3D Studio Max 7 reconstruction of *The Divine Comedy* stage-model.

of human-computer interactivity.[30] Thus, virtual worlds should not be defined in the context of their intended interpretations, but rather by the artefacts left behind. The argument here is that VR is not only a means for reproducing existing art styles and artefacts for the purpose of storing or simply distributing them for mass-production, but also a platform for art-creation and knowledge transfer. Virtual space could also be considered as an art form in its own right.

The spectators' paradigm: applying a human-centred approach

Audiences, spectators and viewers are cultural phenomena, fully in charge of the status of any art event or theatrical performance. Since the 1980s, the further development of a theory of audiences has been strongly debated within various research disciplines. In the field of theatre studies, theorists (especially in North America) criticized heavily 'the devaluation, or even total rejection, of the text by performance artists'. They perceived this as 'the final straw in the alienation of audiences, sending them to the (culturally inferior) entertainments of cinema and television'.[31] On the other hand, Carlson emphasizes that 'generic expectations and relationships to other works (intertextuality) are clearly as relevant to theatre reception as to reading, and the juxtaposition of fiction and reality perhaps even more relevant, given the particularly central role played by mimesis and iconicity in the theatre.'[32]

Indeed, it can be argued that every live art performance is already some sort of reading, even without straightforward textual representation. Furthermore, some theatre researchers were fascinated by the idea of diluting the audience, as such, within theatrical space: 'from the unlocking of the theatre through costuming and make-up to the arrival of the regular time audience, and on to the clearing-up process and the final shutting of the theatre'.[33] There is little doubt that various experiments with audience participation can be highly successful; however, there are also many examples in the history of theatre when audience members responded to the performance (mostly experimental) in an unpredictable manner, which had not been foreseen by the creators of a theatrical event. The argument here is that even the abandonment of such a visible theatrical convention as the traditional stage-audience relationship does not necessarily mean that theatre loses its overall theatricality.

The relationships between the audience and live art are traditionally complex. The audience is a group of individuals, which implies that each spectator is a person with his/her own principles, experiences and attitudes, and, simultaneously, a member of a diverse group of people. Obviously, it is not always possible or even necessary to describe each individual response to a particular production. However, there is a need to study particular spectators in their social, material, and historical context. New media technologies can serve here as new tools to aid research and a deeper understanding of the production-reception dynamic of theatrical events. The ways the audience responds to a virtual performance is similarly important as in the 'real' theatre. However, there are some issues raised only in connection with virtual spectacles. For example, one might note that wearing devices, which are necessary for perceiving a VR show (i-glasses or head-mounted displays) can potentially cause the elimination of the spectators from the communal theatrical space. On the other hand, it can be argued that even while wearing these devices the audience is still able to see live on-stage action, computer graphics visualized on rear projection screens, and live video images projected within the HMDs.[34] Although by using these 'see-through' technologies, spectators can maintain a strong connection with a real-time live performance, it should be noted that the fluency of interaction between performers and the audiences at existing virtual reality venues is not yet equal to traditional theatre. Therefore, a VR show should not simply copy traditional spectacles, but rather emphasize its intrinsically different quality, in order to develop a unique impact on the audience members. Virtual environments offer an opportunity to create a new system of symbols, which is used for the better understanding of existing information and for building up new blocks of knowledge. By using these visual and auditory symbol systems of virtual space, there is a chance for audiences to re-estimate their perceptual, cognitive and emotional concepts and re-assess the issues of consciousness, community and connectedness in a social sense.

Multimedia technologies and virtual reality often serve as a means to help the spectators sacrifice realism for the sake of the live art experience. In terms of perceptual richness, however, VR goes at least one-step further than multimedia applications. The primary difference between the two is in intent – multimedia is simply a 'representation', whereas virtual reality is a 'simulation', whose intention is to deepen the suspension of disbelief even further.[35] Nevertheless, there are still many arguments about implementing advanced new media technologies in theatrical space, as well as using them as self-sufficient performance platforms. One of the reasons is the risk of socially excluding the members of the audience, as this can occur, if wearable technological devices conceal human aspects, by providing a buffer between actors, the spectators and the performance. Some researchers[36] are convinced that future interactions between theatrical images and their spectators will be characterized as 'bi-directional', where the audience transforms into a 'locally-based or net-controlled narrator'. Unfortunately, to date, there are no definite answers to these assumptions and fears.

There is little doubt that computer technologies and cyberspace play an important role in contemporary live art; and that by now they can be considered as an acknowledged vehicle for transmitting theatrical events to distant audiences. Virtual reality has had a deep impact on the interconnection between spectator, author and live action, greatly enhancing their relationship. However, there is a concern that, at present, the evolution of dramatic language sometimes seems to be more dependent 'on the speed of engineering, rather than on developing possible genres'.[37] This illustrates a constant need for creative practitioners to gain and implement new knowledge, whilst at the same time being aware of the possible detrimental effects of new media technologies on the modes of spectating.

It is fair to ask what new possibilities the digital era offers to the language of live art. Certainly, theatre is an ephemeral art, which happens in its time and of its time and it could be argued that trying to catch it in VR is anti-theatrical. Possibly, the whole VR movement in theatrical space is just a reflection of human culture, which keeps evolving, and sometimes enters a non-adaptive dead-end. Or maybe we are trying to adopt these technologies because they are there – not because they are suited for an application in theatre. Nevertheless, there is certainly no need to fit all these innovative techniques within conventional theatrical settings – perhaps this is the time to create a new form of theatre.

Conclusion

Virtual reality is invariably exploratory and seeks to reflect upon existing conventions, evolve new concepts, engage with experimental practice and draw freely on the widest range of references, influences and disciplines. It has been understood as an artistic, creative and presentational medium that is responsible for the origination of new modes of social engagement, employed by various museums, galleries, libraries, theatres and research centres. In the course of time its content has matured and created a new cultural dimension. It has provided valuable insights into the nature of creative interactions and contributed greatly in art, theatre and design, in a broader context. The advent of virtual reality creates an opportunity to redefine the boundaries of our cultural experience. Central issues such as scale, concreteness, abstraction, aesthetics and interface can be re-explored, and through the critical evaluation, receive new meanings in the virtual world.

It would be fair to say that our aesthetical and ethical choices are tangled in the digital realm. This raises the question of how cultural identities are being transformed in the digital age, in which we are living. The lines of investigation here are numerous – from addressing the ethical and legal issues of virtual communities, existing solely in the digital domain,[38] to exploring the aesthetic consequences of employing the computer as an active contributor to the creative process[39] or even re-defining what the aesthetics of the virtual world is. Some researchers argue that VR applications already affect the classical art world negatively, but does that mean we should actively refrain from using these technologies? It is difficult to control the work of art placed in virtual space – from how it was created to how it will or should be perceived by the audience. The notion of a unique image is rendered obsolete in digital worlds, thus the question here is how to define various artefacts, performances and characters once they are translated in digital language? It is a fact that the human perception of the difference between artificially constructed space and reality can be temporarily overwhelmed by using various images, that is the 'as if' effect.[40] Therefore, live art could be seen as relevant to electronic and digital media phenomena, because it encompasses such important questions as interaction, response, feedback, and the relationship with the spectators.[41]

There is no doubt that every medium and media event is integrated within social and economic environments[42] and cannot exist or work in isolation. However, the question here is how will copyright conventions be changed in the context of the digital realm, in order to regulate virtual culture? Furthermore, should the technological development and its implementation in art and theatre be guided? Or, on the contrary, should they be free of any kind of censorship and external guidance? It is obvious that such issues will require a long time before they settle down; however, it could be said already that the development of our culture, society, art, and theatre is and certainly will be, closely linked to the evolution of surveillance space. Some researchers[43] already fear that 'soon no aspect of our lives will remain untouched by these ubiquitous invisible forces', which certainly poses the question: if too much control is enforced would creativity suffer?

New media technologies refer to real actions, people and objects, increasing the communication bandwidth and enabling a smooth transition between real and virtual spaces, through developing various types of interfaces for face-to-face and remote communication. As a result, the intuitiveness of interaction is constantly increasing without the additional requirement for graphic renderings. There is little doubt that the relationship between digital technology, modern art and theatre has a considerable effect on how contemporary visual culture is experienced. Despite the fact that new media have already become an integral part of our everyday lives, it is not yet completely clear how our culture responds to these new virtual environments from ethical, aesthetic, psychological and overall cultural perspectives. Nevertheless, the most productive and dynamic work occurs when the technology-driven medium is found, or, to be more precise, when the artistic vision coincides with the existing technology.

Notes

1. McLuhan, M., Fiore, Q. (1967), *The Medium is the Message: An inventory of Effects*, New York: Bantam Books, p. 56.
2. Stoltermann, E., Schuler, D. (2000), *The Societal Design of a Societal Cyberspace*, Fairfax: Advanced Design Institute.

3. Packer, R., Jordan, K. (2001), *Multimedia: From Wagner to Virtual Reality*, New York: W.W. Norton & Co. Inc, pp. 335–44.

4. Lucretius, On the Nature of the Universe, translated by Latham, R. (1951), Harmondsworth: Penguin Books, pp. 142–4.

5. Grau, O. (2003), *Virtual Art: From Illusion to Immersion*, London: MIT Press.

6. Rush, M. (1999), *New Media in Late 20th Century Art*, London: Thames & Hudson.

7. Hoffman, H. G., Garcia-Palacios, A., Ayanna K., Thomas, A. K., Schmidt, A. (2001), 'Virtual Reality Monitoring: Phenomenal Characteristics of Real, Virtual, and False Memories', *CyberPsychology and Behaviour*, 4/5:10, pp. 565–72.

8. Osberg, K. (1997), 'But What's Behind Door Number 4???', *HITL Report TR-97-16*, pp. 9–10.

9. Weibel, P. (2002), 'Narrated Theory: Multiple Projection and Multiple Narration (Past and Future)', in Reiser, M., Zapp, A., eds., *New Screen Media:Cinema/Art/Narrative*, London: British Film Institute.

10. Adams, B., Beland, C., Lee, M., Crist, B., Mendrey, S., Rosenblatt, B. (1998), 'Towards a New Paradigm: Sovereignty on the Internet'. Available: http://swiss.csail.mit.edu/6095/admin/admin-1998/conf-details/topic9-sovereignty. html.

11. Jones, S. (2000), 'Towards a Philosophy of Virtual Reality: Issues Implicit in Consciousness Reframed', *Leonardo*, 33:2, pp. 125–32, p. 125.

12. Botler, D., Grusin, R. (1999), *Remediation: Understanding New Media*. London: The MIT Press.

13. Giannachi, G. (2004), *Virtual Theatres: An Introduction*, London: Routledge, p. 124.

14. Levy, P. (1994), 'The Art and Architecture of Cyberspace', in Packer, R., Jordan, K., (eds.) (2001), *From Wagner to Virtual Reality*, New York: W. W. Norton & Co, Inc., pp. 335–44, p. 338.

15. Manovich, L. (2001), *The Language of New Media*, Cambridge: The MIT Press, p. 163.

16. Grau, O., (2003), p. 349.

17. Bricken, W. (1990), 'Virtual Reality: Directions of Growth', notes from the *SIGGRAPH '90 Panel*, University of Washington Publications. Available: http://www.hitl.washington.edu/publications/

18. Bricken, W. (1990), 'Virtual Reality, as Unreal As It Gets', *Proceedings of DIAC-90*, pp. 265–7.

19. Johnson, M. (1999), 'Embodied Reason', in Weiss, G., Haber, H. (eds.) Perspectives on Embodiment, London: Routledge, pp. 81–102, p. 80.

20. Beacham, R. (2006), 'Making Space: Caught between the Monster and the Wall', presented at the *Making 3D visual Research Outcomes Transparent Symposium & Expert Seminar*, 23–25 February 2006. Forthcoming to be published by the AHRC ICT Methodologies Network, p. 6.

21. Manovich, L. (2001), p. 57.

22. Grau, O. (2003).

23. Willett, J., (ed.) (1957), *Brecht on Theatre: the Development of an Aesthetic*. New York: Hill and Wang, p. 71.

24. Rush, M. (1999), p. 168.

25. Baugh, C. (2005), *Theatre, Performance and Technology: The Development of Scenography in the Twentieth Century*, London: Palgrave Macmillan, p. 216.

26. *Available:* http://research-tv.warwick.ac.uk/stories/creative/theatron/transcript/

27. The Set-SPECTRUM project was conceived by the author over more than a year and a half-long period in the later stages of her PhD 2006–7. The project was structured after all the necessary research had been undertaken in the Harry Ransom Humanities Research Centre at the University of

Texas in Austin, and all crucial visual and textual materials had been discovered, evaluated, and analyzed.

28. Norman Bel Geddes (1893–1958) was a pioneer of American stage design. He was involved as author and/or designer in more than two hundred plays, theatrical performances and motion pictures. He was also a talented and successful industrial designer identified with the popular 1930s streamlining style in the United States. While scholars generally agree on the historical importance of Bel Geddes' industrial designs and widely criticize his architectural projects, his impact on theatre design seems largely overlooked, or as a minimum misjudged.

29. Norman Bel Geddes spent approximately two years developing a fully-functional model for *The Divine Comedy* production, which was lost during the last century. Currently, Bel Geddes' original idea exists only in the form of sketches, photographs, plans, and an annotated script, which are available for research at the Harry Ransom Humanities Research Centre at the University of Texas in Austin. Norman Bel Geddes' ambitious project was intended to mark the six hundredth anniversary of Dante's death, and the author aimed to stage the play in Madison Square Garden. Despite the fact that this imaginative design-concept was never produced, its historical importance for the development of the twentieth-century stage and lighting design remains unquestionable, although largely overlooked by the academic community.

30. Packer, R., Jordan, K. (2001).

31. Bennett, S. (1997), *Theatre Audiences: a Theory of Production and Reception*. London: Routledge, p. 14.

32. Carlson, M. (1989), 'Theatre Audiences and the Reading of Performance', in Postlewait, T., McConachie, B., (eds.), *Interpreting the Theatrical Past: Essays in the Historiography of Performance*, Iowa City: University of Iowa Press, pp. 82–98, p. 83.

33. Bennett, S. (1997), p. 11.

34. Reaney, M. (2000), 'Digital Scenography: Bringing the Theatre into the Information Age', *Art et Numerique*, Universite Paris, 1:1. Available: www.http.cc.ukans.edu/~mreaney/.

35. Osberg, K., (1997), p. 5.

36. Weibel, P. (2002), 'Narrated Theory: Multiple Projection and Multiple Narration (Past and Future)', in Rieser, M. Zapp A., (eds.), *New Screen Media: Cinema/Art/Narrative*, London: British Film Institute, pp. 42–53, p. 53.

37. Rieser, M., Zapp, A. (2002), (eds.), *New Screen Media: Cinema/Art/Narrative*, London: British Film Institute. Rieser, M., Zapp, A. (2002), p. xxvi.

38. Creed, B. (2000), 'The Cyberstar: Digital Pleasures and the End of the Unconscious', *Screen* 41/1, Spring 2000, pp. 79–86.

39. Youngblood, G. (1970), *Expanded Cinema*, New York: E.P. Dutton.

40. Grau, O. (2003), p. 17.

41. Gere, C. (2002), *Digital Culture*, London: Reaktion Books, p. 84.

42. Botler, D., Grusin, R. (1999), *Remediation: Understanding New Media,* London: The MIT Press.

43. Gere, C. (2002) p. 202.

7

Observing the Interactive Movie Experience: The Artist's Approach to Responsive Audience Interaction Design

Chris Hales

This chapter builds upon some of the author's findings from over a decade of work in the creation and public display of interactive films. A predominantly qualitative approach has been taken in which the artist/author spends as much time as possible attending his exhibition spaces, noting the minutiae of user activity at a touch-screen installation of his films and (where appropriate) recording video sequences of this. Recent work in which interactive films are presented as a live performance to audiences in a theatrical environment, a tradition dating back to the *Kinoautomat* of 1967, has lent itself more naturally to this approach.

Using this data has enabled new interactive films to be created, or existing ones to be iteratively improved, informed by findings from direct audience observation. A study of relevant literature demonstrates, however, that most artists working with interactive video sequences, or with interactive art in general, do not seem concerned with observing and documenting the quality of the user's experience. Most such studies are conducted by third-parties such as human-computer interaction (HCI) specialists and even by curators, despite the fact that the artist would seem to be the person best placed to conduct, judge and benefit from them.

As well as a review of artistic interest in the audience experience, and a brief summary of the author's work and observations, this chapter presents the methods used by the author to judge how and why an in situ interactive artwork can be deemed to 'engage' its audience. The parallel observations for theatre or live performance audiences are drawn as indicators of fields of future study.

All art is necessarily subjective and it would be a fool who believed that a systematic quantitative assessment of an artwork could report reliable results as to its creative impact and artistic value. If new artworks were created only as a result of user evaluations, then art (if that is what it might still be called) would be transformed for the poorer. Nevertheless not all art consists of self-expressive or conceptual 'fine art'. Elements of an artwork might be chosen by the artist quite systematically, so as to give an emotional (or other) effect in the viewer based on scientific study – a typical example of this can be seen in some of the work of Georges Seurat, who systematically used symbols in his paintings that had been shown to be associated with happiness or sadness. Interactive art, which emerged in the 1980s, broadly refers to a type of art practice that solicits some kind of physical response from a viewer or a group of viewers (often called users). Such works require technology, usually computers, and have been most often associated with gallery installations or live performances. Since the input-output system is probably controlled by a set of rules (for example, an algorithm) which can easily be modified, such an artwork might seem particularly suited to being adapted by the artist so as to elicit a desired response in its user. This response is no longer just in the imagination of the viewer since an actual physical activity is involved to effect the interaction (in almost all cases), hence it is, at the very least, an observable quantity. My work as an artist making interactive movies has undoubtedly benefited from a willingness to take into account my observations of the user's experience and to act upon them, and the results of this activity will be presented below. What has surprised me during my research is how so few enquiries into the response of the user to an interactive artwork, have been led by the artists themselves.

Inevitable issues arise around the definitions of terms that I and other writers use. For the purposes of this chapter, I define an interactive movie (my area of practice) broadly as 'a representation of primarily moving-image sequences, the display of which can be affected by the viewing audience.' Nevertheless, the intention here is not to develop new taxonomies[1] and terminologies – as Kuniavsky notes, even the key terms in this particular debate are open to multiple interpretations: '...defining "the user experience" is difficult since it can extend to nearly everything in someone's interaction with a product, from the text on a search button, to the colour scheme, to the associations it evokes, to the tone of the language used to describe it, to the customer support.'[2] Indeed, whether there is even any point in trying to evaluate the user's experience has itself been questioned, an argument most succinctly argued by Eric Paulus in his 2007 essay, 'HCI Cannot be Used to Evaluate Art', in which he writes: 'There is a major fundamental question that has yet to be addressed by the HCI community – why should there be user studies and evaluation techniques at all for interactive art?'[3] My personal experience suggests that benefits are possible, at least to offer guidance if not exact 'truths', and I am particularly interested in the artist's own interest in and reaction to audience interaction, rather than this activity being conducted by a third party.

Rethinking the interactive movie

The works that I create are, in physical terms, collections of organized and interlinked 'live-action' video clips (in my case stored on computer as Quicktime movies) under the control of some kind of software, the playout of which can be influenced or manipulated in some way by either a single user or a group audience. Films have always been displayed in the 'real' public domain, either as an interactive touch-screen installation usually displayed in art galleries (many different films can be displayed, accessed and interacted with on this installation), or presented to large groups of audience as a live event usually known as 'Cause and Effect'.[4] I categorize the latter as a performance because the format, a ninety minute show consisting of about eight different interactive films, requires the active contribution of a live actor/presenter as intermediary between audience and film: the audience's activity might also be considered to be part of the performance.

Fig. 13: Touch-screen installation on display at 'ARTEC95' in Japan.

Although my films show a wide variety of themes, structures and interaction systems, they are united under a common creative approach which I describe as 'movie as interface', referring to the design and creation of interactive movies which privilege the interactivity, beyond just being a final part of the production or post-production chain, to be at the top of the conceptual process itself. Generally speaking, the user's potential interaction is represented in the film frame itself, or in some way has a pre-planned integration with the type of story being told. This 'movie as interface' approach involves the invention of new types of interactive movie in which objects and items within the video scenes can have a particular narrative logic for being represented as so-called 'hotspots', or in which the filmic language or narrative of the represented film in some way integrates with the role of the interactivity. An early and successful example of the former is *The Twelve Loveliest Things I Know* from 1995, a poetic documentary inspired by images and commentaries from children, in which colourful and/or moving items portrayed in the film, such as a purple balloon or a kite in the sky, are spatio-temporal links to related video content and are activated if the viewer of the work touches (or in the CDROM version, clicks) such an item. An example of the latter is my 2003 film *Crescendo*, a fictional story without dialogue about a trainee opera singer who discovers she is able to break glass with her voice. Interaction is carried out through analyzing microphone input to the film: if the audience sing a powerful and sustained soprano note, the relevant items portrayed in the film (such as a glass of wine or a window) are shown to shatter – and the narrative is then able to continue.

Fig. 14: Five screenshots from *The Twelve Loveliest Things I Know*, 1995.

Crescendo has the additional characteristic that it is represented in a multi-screen format, with one central video scene displaying the central narrative of the film and (up to) five smaller video scenes around it. Although multi-screen is not unusual in traditional cinema (since it offers a way of simultaneously representing parallel aspects of a story such as characters or camera angles) it has only rarely been explored in an interactive video context. Not only is the multi-screen visual representation particularly appropriate for portraying certain types of story (for example in *Crescendo* the bottom right screen represents 'furthest' from the singer and the bottom left screen is 'nearest'), it also enables emergent behaviour

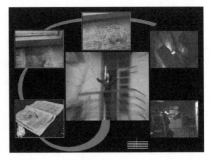

Fig. 15: A screenshot from *Crescendo*, 2003.

to arise from only a limited number of pre-recorded components. Since each element (for example, video screen) can have interactivity attached to it, the viewer might be offered multiple interaction possibilities throughout the play-out of the film from a surprisingly limited number of components, enriching and enlivening the potential experience obtained.

Performing the interactive movie

A third area of interest in my own practice is that of live performance of interactive movies to group audiences, primarily through the 'Cause and Effect' performances. In a historical context, the world's first substantial instance of an interactive film, *Kinoautomat*[5] (which was made in Czechoslovakia in 1967 – the same year in which the word 'interactive' was first used in a human-computer interaction context[6]), was created with 'dialogue gaps' in the film which were spoken by live actors on stage adjacent to (and even acting in front of) the main projected image. Hence this interactive film was *performed* to its audiences, and although live performance in front of audio-visual content has its own history (the *Kinoautomat* team were influenced by the 'Laterna Magika' performances, also created in Czechoslovakia, that were premiered at 'Expo58' in Brussels) this was the first time that affective audience activity became a part of the performance itself.

Given that *Kinoautomat* caused a sensation when it was shown at 'Expo67' in Montreal, there has been surprisingly little subsequent interest in this mode of presentation for interactive cinema with most artists and creators concentrating on installation, CDROM, DVDROM, or Internet based productions to display their interactive movies and to enable delivery to wider and more distributed audiences. After witnessing a *Kinoautomat* performance in 1992, Erkki Huhtamo suggested that the creators of these live cinematic events had a one dimensional view of the potential involvement of the interactivity: '...the "audience participation" still depends on majority decisions. It is difficult to introduce intelligent multi-person interactivity into a situation in which a traditional audience sits in an auditorium...The problem with multi-person interactive cinema is related to the very fact of combining it with a nineteenth century idea of public spectacle and the audience.'[7] The design of interactive films for live performance in my own practice can be seen as being inspired partly by the original *Kinoautomat* format itself and partly by the challenge laid down in Huhtamo's comments. In practical terms this becomes an extension of the 'movie as interface' concept to integrate with the various types of interaction mode available for the group situation. One way to counteract Huhtamo's objection is to emphasize the collaborative aspect of the group situation – Crescendo was in fact created for a group experience (with a microphone suspended over the audience) since it is difficult for a single viewer to sustain the power and duration of the required soprano note long enough to achieve the necessary task of breaking glass. Another method is to appeal to the curiosity and playfulness of the audience by constructing interactive movie experiences in which the audience are engaged by the manner of their interaction and its effect on the represented video, rather than concentrating on the complexities of a fictional story. Jochen Schmidt seems to concur with this approach, emphasizing the communal experience of the audience as a whole: 'Instead of concentrating on the narrative aspect on the screen, the interaction should be focused on the communicative aspect in the auditorium.'[8] 'Cause and Effect' has given 35 performances since it was premiered in 2002 and much has been learnt from observing its audiences, yet there seems to be little current interest by other creators in developing interactive cinema-shows as special location-based live events. Schmidt notes that 'up to now audience participation has been developed only in experimental forms on media art forums or special conventions', pointing out that the advent of digital technologies for cinematic display brings with it enhanced possibilities for audience interaction in future 'digital cinemas'. This makes the need for practical research into the performative aspect of interactive moving image even more pertinent at this particular moment in time.

Who cares about the audience?

All of my own experimentation with 'movie as interface' has been informed by the study of the presentation of the films in public settings – a discussion of my methodologies and observations follows later. But before detailing this, it is of interest to briefly review how other artists working in the interactive video domain have learnt from the study of their audiences. In fact, although it seems an obvious strategy to create more effective interactive works by observing how users act, surprisingly little published literature actually seems to concern itself with the user's experience of an interactive artwork – even though such artworks are the ones most suited to a user-centric approach.

In terms of published material dealing specifically with observations of audience interaction, the only closely related literature emanating from the artistic community seems to fall neatly into two categories. First of all there are writings by the artists/creators themselves presenting and enquiring upon their own works, although such writings are few and far between and almost never systematically presented or carried out. It is nevertheless my belief that this category can offer the most valuable resource on which to develop an effective methodology for studying user engagement with an in situ interactive artwork. The second category consists of papers by theorists and curators discussing a variety of interactive works from an external viewpoint. I do not deal here with the wider field of performance per se, considering only the situation in which an interactive product is presented as a live event to a group audience.

Although the approach of the HCI community cannot be totally ignored, this chapter is intended to focus on the approach of the artistic community towards observing the audiences of interactive artworks and movies. Eric Paulus puts the overall situation very bluntly: '...it is not constructive to evaluate interactive artwork under the same guidelines as traditional HCI work. There are often extremely divergent goals associated with artists and HCI researchers.'[9]

Beryl Graham also makes clear some of the difficulties in taking a third-party approach to analyzing the user's response to an artwork: 'Whilst the product designer tends to be bound to abide by the findings of user testing, the artist has more freedom to ignore, or selectively use these findings. The aim of an artwork, after all, may be to alienate or challenge, rather than to please, a certain target group, whilst seeking to please others.'[10]

Artists/creators writing about their own interactive works

If we look back to the *Kinoautomat* of 1967 we find that its makers were taken unawares by the audience reaction during the moments at which action was possible. The idea that the interactivity (audiences voted several times to determine the trajectory of the narrative) might influence the social dynamic of the event had not been anticipated whilst the project was being produced, as the inventor of *Kinoautomat*, Raduz Cincera, made clear in a contemporary newspaper interview: 'We did not anticipate that the moment when the viewers vote is another dramatic moment in the whole performance, that the sight of the film drama on screen and stage is combined with another drama which is taking part amongst the audience'.[11] Only after the first screenings was the importance of the audience response noticed and acted upon, the show being adapted so as to enhance the value of the interactive moments. An enlightened Cincera later explained to *Life* magazine: 'What we are doing here really is making a sociological and psychological study about group behaviour. It is fantastic. We are learning that people decide not on a moral code but on what they like to see'.[12] What Cincera and his team had discovered was the importance of studying – and learning from – the user's experience.

'Interactive art' is usually considered to have taken off in the early 1980s with the arrival of the personal computer and laserdisk technologies. One creator who took an active interest in the user's viewpoint relatively early in the history of interactive art is Paul Zelevansky, as detailed in his 'Crisscrossing the Interface: The Design, Display and Evaluation of an Interactive Computer Exhibit' from 1995. Zelevansky's paper in fact seems to be an exception – what is usually noticeable is that many interactive artists try to get into the mindset of the audience in quite general terms when creating and/or observing their works, rather than making any systematic and detailed enquiry. Ken Feingold, a pioneer of interactive art in the late 1980s and the 1990s, serves as a good example: although he has published several papers and articles, he makes only occasional and very general observations about how a user might approach an interactive artwork, concentrating on trying to understand and describe the user's mental processes:

> ...there is a desire for control, for mastery over the nonhuman entity. I also learned that it is a rare viewer who feels comfortable in the role of PUBLIC participant in an interactive work that has no clear goal. People always seem to ask the same questions when the

destination of an interaction is unclear: How is it structured? Is it random? How can I get what I want (to see what I want to see)? Am I doing it right? What will happen if I do this? These are big questions that, if taken in a larger context, bear a marked resemblance to questions regarding one's future in the life-world.[13]

Interestingly enough, Feingold (and others, such as George Legrady) seeks to understand the user's approach to his interactive artworks so as to deliberately frustrate and deny them the satisfaction of gaining control, as a means of provocation.

Judging by their published writings, most artists working with interactive media do not seem to consider the user at all, at least not in any analytical sense, and are concerned only with the artistic and intellectual process of creating their works. Bill Seaman, also an early pioneer of interactive art, published his findings in the 1999 PhD thesis 'Recombinant Poetics: Emergent Meaning as Examined and Explored Within a Specific Generative Virtual Environment' which presented the theoretical and historical standpoint for his art practice, as expressed in a culminatory interactive artwork entitled The World Generator. It is interesting to note that (although not a 'by practice' thesis) the 302 pages of this document contain only 28 pages that describe The World Generator itself and a total of zero that describe its reception by audiences.

More recently, this lack of interest in the user's experience was highlighted in Austin and Vogelsang's 2003 survey[14] of nineteen interactive art practitioners in which a series of questions were posed about the relationship of artist to user. In response to the question 'do you think about your audience as users and the ergonomic aspects of their interaction with your work?', my reported response (as one of the interviewed respondents) was that the 'work is entirely designed around the anticipated interaction modes of the audience.' This stands in contrast to the reported response of some other practitioners, such as successful media artist Simon Biggs, who seems to suggest that there are no special qualities to be taken into account when creating an interactive artwork: 'I do not think of my audience as users no more than a painter would think of their audience in such a manner.'[15] Austin and Vogelsang also posed the question, 'have you ever tested the usability of your work before or during exposure to an audience? In what way did you do that...?' Responses showed some artists showed no concern at all about their audience reaction, and others were so methodical as to employ trial users who give written feedback. Most artists, however, including myself, did seem to employ some kind of qualitative user testing, usually by public display of a modifiable 'work in progress'. Perhaps, therefore, this activity of audience observation takes place much more frequently than it is actually documented, by means of an informal and instinctive process rather than through a systematic approach.

Although the situation depends on the context and intention of a particular work as well as the individual artist concerned, there could be a case for arguing that a more formal interest in the user's experience is a relatively new phenomenon. Many of the earliest interactive artists drifted into the area from already established careers as fine artists or video artists and required teams of programmers and technicians to make their ideas reality. Once the field of interactive art became well established, a newer breed of creators, working at the crossover of art and technology, arrived on the scene with the ability to combine skills and sensibilities from both those fields. Chris Dodge, a successful media artist who fits such a profile, seems to have adopted a more user-centric approach to his work: 'It is my belief that good art arises from the artist possessing a keen understanding of the expectations of his/her audience, being able to instill a desire and then skilfully either fulfilling these wishes or denying them outright through surprise.'[16]

One might, therefore, extrapolate to suggest that current and future interactive art creation can only benefit from the artist taking a healthier interest in the user's experience than has been noticeable until now. Höök, Sengers and Andersson suggest indeed that a convergence is taking place, as interactive artworks become more sophisticated and computational and their creators become more multi-faceted: 'There is a conflicted convergence developing between human-computer interaction and interactive art. Artists are building interactive computational systems...that develop fresh new perspectives on interactive system design. HCI practitioners are adapting ideas from art practice to rethink fundamental problems in HCI.'[17]

Curators/theorists – discussing interactive artworks

Several published papers examine a broad range of interactive artworks from an external viewpoint, usually that of the curator, critic or media theorist. The benefit here is that the author is in a position to compare and contrast between a body of works from different creators, and takes the role of the user in order to experience a work. Back in 1995, in the catalogue to an exhibition of artist-CDROMs that he curated, Mike Leggett attempted to describe the process of 'uncovering the meaning', suggesting that a user gradually unveils four levels of meaning from an interactive artwork:

> Often no clue is given as to the consequence of making one choice or another. A first level of meaning is thus quickly established: that whilst sequences will have significance, a specified order will not – hence the narrative encountered will be the unique result of how an individual interacts with the work.

> The process of interacting by clicking on images or words is quickly learnt to influence progress, but is recognised as not necessarily having of 'control'. That becomes the second level of meaning.

> Now a process commences whereby the interacting subject attempts to delineate the furthest extent of each section of the work, clicking outwards in a conceptual circle, attempting to plot 'landmark' images along the way, before returning through the maze to the starting point, to then set out to test the path again before beginning again from another point. With so little to go on, the 'mazing' process itself offers the third level of meaning as the motivational drive changes into a pleasurable era of reflexivity...As mazing continues, 'control' is not wrested by the interactor but is at best shared.

A fourth level of meaning comes as the interactor invokes that familiar defuser of subversive strategies – interpretation. On what basis were these images/sounds/texts selected, created and combined? Does the interactive construction create space in the mind of the viewer to interrogate the images? What is the relationship between the structure of the work and its overt content?[18]

What is unusual in Leggett's analysis is the level of detail with which he attempts to document the user experience upon navigating an artist-CDROM, concentrating on internal processes of understanding rather than exterior technical data.

A thorough and very useful reference, indeed a landmark study, is Beryl Graham's 1997 PhD thesis 'A Study of Audience Relationships with Interactive Computer-Based Visual Artworks in Gallery Settings, through Observation, Art Practice, and Curation'. Graham develops a methodology to assess exhibited interactive works by a mixture of direct observation and audience questionnaires, and unusually (Graham is not recognized as an interactive artist) then attempts to create her own interactive work (Individual Fancies) into which her survey conclusions are incorporated. This experience subsequently feeds in to Graham's own curatorial policy, in which she appears to value a user-centric approach to creating an interactive artwork above all others: '...the extensive exploration of the ways in which the artwork might relate to the audience in turn made it very obvious how much the artists had considered the audience themselves, and artworks which showed clear evidence of this...were looked on more favourably.'[19]

As mentioned earlier, interactive art was still a relatively new field of practice in the late 1980s and early 1990s – although by the mid-1990s it had become a popular topic. But with specific regard to the user's experience, in 1997 Graham could only find tangential references in the literature survey to her PhD, stating that:

> With such a wide range of discourses informing the background to interactive computer-based art, the prospective audiences for the art may be arriving at a gallery with a very wide range of expectations, informed by games, education or fine art. The fragmented sets of literature existing presently do little to clarify 'good practice' in dealing with these disparate expectations, as the field is so much in development.[20]

The implication here is that others will soon fill the vacuum and contribute to the discourse. Certainly, Graham found a dearth of such material[21] emanating from artists up to 1997, reporting just two informal observations written by artists Jeffrey Shaw and David Rokeby.

Since that time, there has been significant growth in the field of curatorship for new media artworks, and a newer generation of curators working at the intersection of art, technology and science has come to the fore who are more actively involved in understanding (and potentially controlling) the user's experience of visiting an exhibition. One example is Lizzie Muller, currently researching a PhD on the audience experience of interactive art at the Creativity and

Cognition Studios at the University of Technology of Sydney. Muller also worked with Khut, Edmonds and Turner in studying audience reaction to various interface visualisations to the interactive artwork *Cardiomorphologies*, the findings of which were incorporated into an iterative design process. So perhaps here too, a more academically rigorous approach to audience observation and evaluation has recently come to the fore.

Personal approach

Having examined the background presented above, I can detail my personal approach to audience observation as a means of informing my own practice. The aim is to create public works that retain the attention of their audience and engage them in the process of interaction, but 'success' could be deemed to have been achieved if the audience seems to react to the work in the way that I intend. Although a strong emotional or intellectual response to the artistic message contained in the work is always sought, it seems a difficult task to gauge this reliably, even through direct observation, and achieving this has not been a benchmark for success. Others might have different criteria, for example, Beacham reports from Glorianna Davenport, head of MIT Medialab's 'Interactive Cinema' group for many years, that her measure of success is that 'In all these kinds of movies the issue is how participatory the audience is.'[22]

The retention of attention is a directly observable quality but one that could be interpreted in two ways. The first, which I consider a measure of success, is that the user is in some way enjoying or challenged by their experience, to the extent that they wish to prolong it, or even replay or revisit it. By careful direct observation it is possible to distinguish this from the unsuccessful situation in which the user is confused by inconsistencies in the interface or structure of the work (for example, a clumsy and badly made interface) and prolongs the experience simply in order to make sense of it.

Engagement, although somewhat subjective, suggests a psychological immersion in the experience of interacting with the movie. Insomuch as this can be measured, it might be done so through observation of recognizable expressions of surprise, pleasure, or concentration. In the 'live' presentation format of 'Cause and Effect', it is observable through the activity of audience members and their willingness to participate.

As mentioned earlier a useful reference to developing a suitable methodology for case studies of in situ interactive artworks was provided by Beryl Graham in her thesis,[23] although it should be emphasized that her study was based around quite general issues of overall patterns of audience behaviour (from a curatorial viewpoint) and did not consider specific production details within the artworks themselves. Some of Graham's methods seem flawed, for example, the time spent by users in front of an interactive work, which is one of Graham's numerical parameters to represent success, says nothing about the *quality* of the user's experience, as was explained above. Another of Graham's methods was the questionnaire, although her sample sets were small and the information gleaned from them seemed of limited value. When I attempted to use questionnaires the approach proved unsuccessful.

My own approach has been to use a variety of sources to obtain as much evidence as possible about the audience reaction to my work – but then to rely on my instincts as the creator of the work to act upon this data. In some cases the data is acted upon by a 'tweak' in the design or interface – changes can often be made very quickly to a particular aspect of an interactive movie, for example modifying an element of the audio, replacing a cursor, or making changes to video-to-video links. If a spatio-temporal link appears difficult or impossible for a user to find, it is generally a simple matter to widen the temporal window or enlarge the hotspot. In this way, numerous small modifications can be rapidly implemented with the potential to cause a fundamental improvement to the user's experience with the work, through a process of iteration: the product itself becomes a 'work in progress'. Kuniavsky states that 'iterative development is based on the idea of continual refinement through trial and error',[24] suggesting that not all modifications may be beneficial and that it may be some time before a definitive version of the work can be said to be completed. Although this can indeed be the case with any one-off product, previous experience becomes a significant factor in reducing the iteration cycle when a series of interrelated works with similar characteristics are produced over a period of many years.

In certain cases an observation of, or comment from, a user might open up a new line of enquiry as a new creative possibility is brought unexpectedly to the attention of the artist, supplementing that part of the creative development process which is inspired by the standard theoretical and historical contextual research activities. For this particular reason I consider it of great value for interactive artists to maintain a close connection to the point of contact between themselves and the audience. Visitors' books, informal discussion with users and direct observation have led me into new areas of interest, in particular with the visual display of audience interaction data (to 'prove' the film is reacting to the audience) and with my interest in multi-screen representation.

Questionnaire, visitors' book

Occasionally, I have attempted to obtain direct written feedback from audience members immediately after they have been involved in an interaction with my work – a process which is usually only applicable where the interaction takes place in a public display space such as an art gallery. Probably the most formal means of obtaining written commentary is by means of a questionnaire, a method which, I attempted on one occasion only, leaving A4 questionnaires adjacent to my installation in the Lethaby Gallery of Central St Martins College of Art and Design, London in 2002. This experiment proved unsuccessful. Visitors did not voluntarily complete the questionnaire, so I had to resort to waiting by the installation and accosting users when they finished interacting. Those few visitors who then filled in the questionnaire did so in the most cursory fashion, seemingly trying to 'escape' from the exhibition space as soon as possible and resenting my imposition. Questionnaire data was minimal and of little value, and I abandoned this method as being an unsuitable one.

Surprisingly more useful has been a 'visitors' book', placed by the side of the installation in the hope that constructive comments might be written. Visitors' books are not out of place in a gallery setting and are traditionally used for audience members to contact the artist (who might not be present) often with regard to future sales. In my case contributions were entirely optional and audience members were not required to write their personal details. Although the majority of written responses were trivial, some proved to be very useful to me in the development of future works and well worth the high 'failure rate' of this method.

Written material – after the event

By this I refer to the written, and usually published, comments of users who have experienced one or more of my interactive movies and after a period of reflection have written about their experience or in some way expressed critical analyses of the works themselves. This writing appears independently and usually without personal contact with myself. Examples are the discussions of some of my interactive movies that have appeared in critical texts, and the reviews of my exhibited work (and my 'Twelve' CDROM) that have been published in magazines and newspapers. Although artists are notoriously wary of their critics, these texts can be of value because in most cases the author is a specialist with a significant knowledge of comparable products and is therefore in a position to situate the work in a wider context. On the downside, this type of reporting is delayed whilst awaiting publication and hence its value to provide immediate feedback is minimal. Not all this material comes from publications, for example a 'Cause and Effect' show in Montreal was attended by a group of film students who were asked by their teacher to make a critical analysis of the performance. These responses were debated the next day in the company of myself, my colleague, the teacher and his students.

Direct observation of subject

This method is suitable for a public exhibition using the touch-screen installation, and for my live performance of interactive films such as with 'Cause and Effect'. It involves the presence of the

Fig. 16: The audience during a performance of 'Cause and Effect' in Tampere in 2006.

author in the presentation environment, observing at first hand (usually over extended periods of time) the user's actions, expressions, body language, and time spent in interaction with a film. Notes, if necessary, can be written, and sometimes video footage can be taken, but it is the intimacy of this study that is key. In my experience this is the essential method for an artist to learn from the audience, and there is a very clear parallel with the way in which a musician or theatre actor picks up the feeling of each audience and adapts every performance accordingly through a subjective assessment of the particular situation.

Video documentation of subject

This is a special case of direct observation, whereby the user or audience is filmed during interaction with the installation or during a live performance (taking into account ethical considerations where appropriate). This process has been in place since the first public exhibition of my film *The Twelve Loveliest Things I Know* in 1995. It has been carried out regularly, but not systematically, and the archived footage is preserved as a useful resource for deeper interpretation of the filmed actions and activities of the audience.

Conversation with subject

Occasionally, but not systematically, I have engaged an audience member in conversation about their experience after the event. It has proved of most value after the end of a 'Cause and Effect' performance when it is quite customary for audience members to voluntarily come to the front of the stage to offer comments or ask questions to myself and/or my colleagues. In this way there is no sense of coercion and information obtained has been, in general, most useful.

Analysis of numerical data

It is not a difficult task to modify the program controlling an interactive artwork (in my case these programs are Macromedia Director applications) so as to create an external text file of numerical data representing a user's activity with the film. In the case of the touch-screen, this would be limited to x and y coordinate data representing points of contact with the touch-screen and the times at which such contacts occurred. When a mouse is used, or (in the 'live' situation) a light is passed around by the audience to represent a mouse cursor, the entire pathway of mouse/light movement could be recorded. Depending on the film, it might also be possible to create a sequential list of video scenes viewed by a user. A trial was indeed carried out (with my film *Jinxed!*) which quickly resulted in the conclusion that such data did not add any additional dimension to the process of analysis to that which was possible through the actual observation of audiences. The use of this potential method of analysis was abandoned forthwith.

Actions, interactions and reactions

Without going into too much detail I will summarize some of the ways in which studying the actions, interactions and reactions of my audiences has contributed to the creation of more engaging interactive films. Back in 1995, when the idea of using coloured and/or moving items portrayed in the film as 'hotspots' started my interest in 'movie as interface', I was able to immediately notice that not only were the vast majority of audience members able to fully comprehend the concept, they were immersed deeply in the film by the need to concentrate on the rapidly changing visual content which offered only brief temporal windows of interaction opportunity. Parts of the film in which the concept was inconsistently applied caused almost universal confusion and frustration, and it was always found beneficial to create some kind of immediate feedback to any user action. Several subsequent works applied the same visual language (for example, items represented in the filmic representation can be clicked on as 'hotspots') very successfully before I started to

Fig. 17: A screenshot from *The Duel*, 2006.

look at multi-screen visual representation and at other interaction modes. The latter were developed mostly when I designed new films for the 'live' group situation since this allows greater variety than the tactile interaction possibilities necessary to interact with the touch-screen installation.

Audience reaction to the live screening of interactive films has been unpredictable and interesting. When no specific 'rules' are given to the audience it has been noticeable how collaboration, rather than competition, has emerged spontaneously out of the group experience. An example of this occurs during screenings of my recent film *The Duel* (2006), which paints the scenario of two enemies, Mr. Green and Mr. Blue, about to fight to the death on a barren icy plateau, and is controlled by tracking the position of a green light and a blue light as they are passed around by the audience. One of the two protagonists will indeed meet their demise at the climax to the film, but this is entirely dependent on the audience who can prolong the life of Mr. Green by manoeuvring the green light over his represented image – and vice versa for Mr. Blue. No teams are allocated amongst the audience, who seem to work together to extend the life of *both* protagonists, and seem noticeably saddened at the inevitable death of the 'weaker' contestant. A recent comment from an audience member that the entire show resembles 'group therapy' confirms the observation that interacting as a group towards a common goal becomes much more of a collaborative than a competitive experience.

As reported above, audience members have given useful feedback in informal conversation after screenings of 'Cause and Effect'. An example of this occurred when several audience members suggested that the films were only simulating the results of interaction and were not interactive at all. This surprising feedback opened my eyes to the fact that the audience approach the screening experience with a totally different mindset and knowledge base to that of the creator, and are very aware that computer systems are more than capable of deceit. From this point on I have chosen to explicitly display the audience-captured data on screen adjacent to the main film presentation in order to offer 'proof' that the system is really responding to the actions of the audience. Since that time no further comments have been received on this matter.

Related to both of the above phenomena is the deliberate attempt by certain audience members (who usually spontaneously form some sort of a collaborative subgroup) to 'sabotage' the trajectory of a film by interacting in an unexpected way. This behaviour at the simplest level might involve staying quiet for a film that depends on audio input, or hiding a light that is intended to be passed around the audience. This behaviour has now been incorporated into a new film, *Bad Education* (2007) in which an on-screen educational presentation becomes covered by the image of a face floating in a bath of water. The educational film can only be seen if enough audience members behave 'badly' by pushing the face under the water (this happens if a significant amount of the audience hold their hands towards the face portrayed on the screen) even though this can be seen and heard to cause anguish to the drowning person. It has already been noticeable that this film polarizes the audience between those who appear to object to pushing a person's face underwater (albeit a fictional character) and those who wish to remove the inconvenience so as to see more interesting content.

Conclusion

This chapter does not summarise all the findings of my research on how to create more engaging interactive films because the purpose here is to emphasize the potential value that a creator or artist of interactive art (and in particular interactive film) could obtain from a closer analysis of how and why the audience interacts. I have explained how my works have been designed for public display, either as an installation or live performance, and this close contact with the audience has enabled me to create more effective works. My own career experience has been one of only knowing what type of interactive film to make next as a result of audience feedback from previously made films: the audience have always shown me the way and have helped my work evolve.

Surprisingly, there seems to be little published material emanating from the artistic community (those who exhibit or perform using interactive media) pointing to any in-depth audience study of audience response. It is probable, however, that many artists do try to learn from observing their audiences, although they do not carry out this study in any formal way. Although such detailed analysis of the user has traditionally been associated with the HCI community, there seems to be a very recent emergence – and convergence – of newer artists more in touch with the demands of technology, curators more interested in the overall audience experience, and HCI specialists more sensitive to artistic endeavour.

My line of enquiry has taken the stance that the essence of a successful interactive movie is an integrated blend of interesting or challenging video content and a complementary user interface, with interactivity and narrative being intimately bound together in a product which the user approaches in a holistic way. This makes it inappropriate to assess the success of an interactive film purely on quantitative methods, since a substantial part of the experience is very subjective. I would claim that it is the artists themselves who are best situated to assess the audience response because a good artwork must have been created with a specific response in mind and the artist is the one most intimately linked to his or her audience.

My methodology has perhaps been somewhat subjective, serving to obtain as much empirical data as possible from all relevant sources and in particular by direct observation of the audience. Although it might lack scientific rigour, this process of analyzing the user(s) was invoked as a way of making more engaging interactive films and results have been acted upon directly and over a number of years through the modification of existing works and the creation of new ones. To this end it has been my hope that my detailed study of audience response might enable future makers to be clearer about the potential effects of interactive movies on their audiences, and to have a greater understanding of the role of the audience itself, both as a collective responsive group and as a gathering of responsive individual inter-actors. The potential applications of this research to the realm of theatre, or live performance more generally, is both obvious and intriguing to consider as a future field of study.

This chapter has been based around interactive artworks presented as in situ installations or as a live event. As trends and technologies shift the interest in interactive art away from the gallery and performance space to online and locative projects, there will be even less chance to study the user experience directly. The next stage of the debate will undoubtedly engage with the question of how to gauge user engagement with an online artwork, wherein most of the methods detailed here will no longer be applicable.

Notes

1. A useful taxonomy for classifying public interfaces was developed by Reeves, Benford, O'Malley and Fraser in their 2005 paper entitled 'Designing the Spectator Experience'.

2. Kuniavsky, M. (2003), *Observing the User Experience: a Practitioner's Guide to User Research*, San Francisco: Morgan Kaufmann, p. 43.

3. Paulus, E. (2007), *HCI Cannot be Used to Evaluate Art*, Workshop position paper for HCI and New Media Arts: Methodology and Evaluation, pg. 2. Last Accessed 8/8/07 from http://www.paulos. net/publications.html

4. 'Cause and Effect' is a format developed jointly by myself, Teijo Pellinen and Tomi Knuutila. A programme of short interactive films is shown to the audience with varying modes of interaction. Some, but not all, of the films are created by myself, specifically for this format. Further details can be found at http://www.causeandeffect.tk (last accessed 22/8/07) and in my 2003 article '"Cause and Effect": an experimental interactive cinema performance.'

5. Further details can be found at http://www.kinoautomat.org (last accessed 22/8/07) and in my 2005 article 'Cinematic Interaction: from Kinoautomat to Cause and Effect.' The system is known as the brainchild of Dr. Raduz Cincera, even though it was created by a large team of experts.

6. According to the Oxford English Dictionary.

7. Huhtamo, E. (1995), *Seeking Deeper Contact; Interactive Art as Metacommentary*. http://www. kenfeingold.com/seekingdeeper.html

8. Schmidt, J. (2005), 'Behind the Scenes – Before the Screens: Interactive Audience Participation in Digital Cinemas', In Bushoff, B., (ed.), *Sagasnet Reader: Developing Interactive Narrative Content*, Munich: HighText Verlag, pp. 322–43, p. 331.

9. Paulus, E. (2007), p. 1.

10. Graham, C.E.B. (1997), 'A Study of Audience Relationships with Interactive Computer-Based Visual Artworks' in *Gallery Settings, through Observation, Art Practice, and Curation*, Ph.D Thesis: University of Sunderland, p. 225.

11. Cincera, Raduz, contemporary newspaper.
12. ibid.
13. Feingold (1995), p. 401.
14. Austin, T., Vogelsang, A. (2004), *The Art Audience as User*, in Proceedings of the 'Pixelraiders 2' conference, Sheffield Hallam University, 2004.
15. I am not aware of the exact context of this comment: it maybe that Biggs is objecting to usage of the specific word 'user'.
16. Dodge (1997), p. 17.
17. Höök, K., Sengers, P., Andersson, G. (2003), *Sense and Sensibility: Evaluation and Interactive Art*, in Proceedings of 'Computer Human Interaction, CHI'2003', New York: ACM Press. pp. 241–8.
18. Leggett, M., (ed.) (1996), *Burning the Interface <International Artist's CD-ROM>*, Sydney: Museum of Contemporary Art, pp. 39–40.
19. Graham, C.E.B. (1997) p. 110.
20. ibid., p. 30.
21. ibid., pp. 54–5.
22. Beacham, (1995), p. 38.
23. Graham, C.E.B. (1997), pp. 49–59.
24. Kuniavsky, M. (2003), p. 28.

PART THREE: IDENTITY AND THE SELF-CONSCIOUS SPECTATOR

8

INTERIOR SPECTATING: VIEWING INNER IMAGERY IN PSYCHOTHERAPY

Valerie Thomas

This chapter explores the potential for theories of viewer reception to illuminate the practice of psychotherapy. To this end, a specific therapeutic practice of viewing inner imagery is examined through the lens of Bennett's theory of production and reception. Here, therapeutic imagery is re-visioned as an act of interior spectating, where the client is both creator and viewer of the image production. Pertinent aspects of Bennett's theory, such as the selection of the production and the social and cultural contexts mediating reception, are examined in relation to this therapeutic procedure. Bennett's idea of the double frame emerges as a particularly useful concept that allows imagery to be seen as a therapeutically purposeful process of production and reception placed within an outer conventional therapeutic frame. Within the inner frame, it is suggested that two types of gaze operate, the diagnostic and the reparative. Both types of gaze are explored through case vignettes of the internal representations of psychological structure produced by chaotic substance misusers detoxifying in a crisis intervention agency. This discussion shows how the type of gaze impacts on the reception of the image and, furthermore, raises the possibility that it may be mediating the nature of the image production. Based on this, the chapter concludes that spectating theory, with its inherent foregrounding of the viewer, has the capacity to disclose previously hidden aspects of therapeutic practice.

Introduction

The lights are dimmed. The spectator is ready. The production begins. The set is revealed. At first, just a large dark shape centre stage and then as the illumination increases giving it depth, clarity and colour – a little whitewashed country cottage made of stone with a thatched roof. But this building is in a state of disrepair – the door seems to be broken, there is a big hole in the roof. The front of the set opens up to reveal the interior – exposed to the elements, the core of the building has been badly damaged over time. The spectator walks into the set and takes an inventory. He points to the hole in the roof and calls urgently for a ladder and a tarpaulin. The first act is to temporarily secure the roof. There is no time to lose: any more water damage and the structure will be beyond repair.

What could be the start of an experimental interactive theatre production is, in fact, the beginning of a therapeutic imagery session with George, a client who is detoxing in a crisis intervention centre for substance misusers. He is visualizing a representation of his interior psychological structure in the form of a building and seeing how much damage his crack cocaine habit has inflicted (I will be returning to his story later on in this chapter.)

Of course, the similarities between what happens in the theatre and what occurs in a psychotherapy session revealed by the ambiguous description above were noticed very early on in the development of the profession. The therapeutic potential of drama has been acknowledged explicitly in approaches such as drama therapy,[1] and in a more general way, psychotherapists continue to exploit the rich seams of metaphorical allusion present in theatre practice.

But is there any more to this than a superficial likeness or is there a deeper level of commonality – one that would allow the theory making from one discipline to be applicable to the other? The purpose of this chapter is to explore this question by examining if recently emerging theories of spectating in theatre practice can tell us anything new about psychotherapy. In order to do this, I will be reframing a specific therapeutic practice of using interactive inner imagery as interior spectating and I will be viewing this through the lens of Bennett's theory of production and reception.[2]

Although there are a range of audiences for therapeutic imagery including the therapist who has an active spectating role, for the sake of brevity and clarity, the client in the therapeutic encounter is designated as the primary spectator, and, in the main, the discussion will be limited to this. Throughout this chapter, I shall be drawing on my own clinical experience in the substance misuse field to illustrate the discussion,[3] and all clients will be anonymized to protect their confidentiality.

Background

I have chosen to draw on Bennett's theory of production and reception because her specialism is theatre practice and, due to its potential for more active engagement with the performance, it would suggest more parallels with therapeutic practice and process. As Bennett points out: 'In much contemporary theatre the audience becomes a self-conscious co-creator of performance and enjoys a productive role which far exceeds anything demanded of the reader or cinema audience.'[4]

Bennett's theory of production and reception takes as its starting point the foregrounding of the spectator and situating the spectating act in a political/social/cultural context. It is partly informed by her critique of previous attempts to theorize reception. She states:

Neither theories of reading nor theatre semiotics, however, goes beyond the issues facing an apparently individual subjectivity. Neither takes much notice of reception as a politically implicated act. Indeed the relationship between production and reception, positioned within and against, cultural values goes largely uninvestigated. Yet all art forms rely on those cultural values for their existence and, among them, theatre is an obviously social phenomenon. It is an event which relies on the physical presence of an audience to confirm its cultural status.[5]

However, it is also important to note that her theory-making is also informed by the practice of experimental theatre, where a range of strategies is employed to subvert the normal passivity of the audience and to encourage its co-creation of a performance.

Bennett then goes on to identify and explore the constituent elements in the act of spectating a theatre production. She begins by examining the process whereby an audience member chooses to attend a particular performance, and she reads this as the relationship between production and reception. Although her main focus is on the spectator, she underscores the limitations imposed by wider cultural, social and economic forces on the range and availability of theatre productions. Thus, before the audience has even arrived at the theatre door some intervening aspects of production will have mediated their experience.

On the threshold of the theatre, other influential factors come into play. The way the theatre is designed and the type of production, for example, classical/formal or experimental/oppositional will impact on how the actors and audience relate. Other aspects of pre-production such as the nature of the information given in the theatre programme will all operate to a greater or lesser extent to limit or possibly even determine the interpretative strategies adopted by the audience.

Bennett has some pertinent points to make regarding the frame and her model posits two frames. The outer frame comprises the social/cultural/economic context of the event itself and this would include all the pre-production elements as well as culturally influenced expectations of the audience. The inner frame holds the particular dramatic performance. It is within this inner frame that the audience engages in one of the main functions of spectating; that is, interpreting or decoding the production.

Finally, Bennett examines theatrical practices that encourage more active audience participation and discusses how such practice impacts not only on the spectator but on the culture itself. She states:

In this way, the production-reception acts bi-directionally in broader cultural perspectives. Cultural systems, individual horizons of expectations, and accepted theatrical conventions all activate the decoding process for a specific production, but in turn, the direct experience of that production feeds back to revise a spectator's expectations, to establish or challenge conventions, and, occasionally, to reform the boundaries of the culture.[6]

In other words, the thrust of her theory-making is toward the emancipation of the spectator from a historically passive role, and she does this by foregrounding the spectator in the performance process.

Therapeutic imagery in psychotherapy

Before I explore the application of theories of spectating to working with inner imagery in therapy, it is important to briefly explain how this form of internal spectating operates in a therapeutic context. The capacity for imagery to act as a therapeutic tool both to diagnose and to effect change in peoples' physical, mental and emotional states has ancient roots.[7] Therefore, it is not surprising that over time there have been a wide range of applications in the field of psychotherapy that includes subjects such as the interpretation of dream imagery,[8] the exploration of archetypal symbols,[9] identifying subpersonalities,[10] exploring personal metaphor[11] and illuminating narrative.[12]

A simple explanation for the therapeutic efficacy of imagery lies in its capacity to operate as a direct channel of communication between the conscious and subconscious mind.[13] By the term subconscious I am referring to the much wider mind-body system that controls unconscious physiological processes as well as being the depository of all aspects of the person denied to conscious awareness; this could be past trauma, past conditioning, disowned aspects of the personality or positive potential of personality. The subconscious mind does not deliver its communications through a conceptual verbal language; instead it 'talks' through somatic and emotional states which can then be mediated through images and symbols. Thus, one way to facilitate a therapeutic dialogue between the conscious and subconscious mind is to communicate using imagery.

Furthermore, the bi-directional capacity of imagery as a language of communication permits it to be used in different ways.[14] Essentially there are three types of usage. The first type is directive. Here an image or a sequence of images is designed to depict a positive outcome or to evoke a desired positive state of being. This image or sequence is then summoned up, focused on and usually repeated over time in order to influence the working of the subconscious mind. An example that people would be familiar with is the visualization of a beautiful peaceful landscape in order to induce a sense of relaxation – guided imagery scripts for this purpose are a staple component of generic self help techniques.[15]

The second type is receptive. Here the conscious mind seeks information from the subconscious mind regarding, for example, a psychological problem or a physical symptom. This could happen through the conscious mind making a request for information stored in the subconscious about the presenting problem; a simple example would be the translation of a headache into a pictorial representation. The subconscious mind then responds with a package of information in the form of an image; this image is a container for the emotion, memories and physiological states associated with the presenting symptom. Ahsen[16] suggests this process is similar to opening up a computer file. As the contents of this subconscious message are assimilated, so the original physical symptom begins to change, and this will be reflected in corresponding changes in the representational image.

The third type is interactive imagery[17] or dialogic imagery,[18] which is effectively a combination of directive and receptive. Therapeutic imagery is interactive in type, and it is this form that I am using to illustrate this chapter. The therapeutic starting point might be directive when the conscious mind requests the subconscious mind to use a template; an example would be the use of a building to represent the structure of the person's psyche. Then, with the help of the therapist, the image is worked within a range of directive and receptive ways appropriate to the therapeutic requirements of the client. These ways comprise making sense of the image; making conscious directive changes to the image where possible in order to support a reparative process; and facilitating a positive unfolding of the image so that blocked material in the subconscious mind can be released and consciously integrated. The aim with interactive imagery is to establish a cooperative relationship between the conscious and subconscious mind; a creative and facilitative dialogue that promotes the therapeutic process.

Interior spectating

What happens when therapeutic imagery is viewed through the lens of Bennett's theory of production and reception? What aspects of her theory appear to be most applicable to this act of interior spectating? In both practices of theatre and psychotherapy there is a common element: this is, of course, the audience in the form of viewer or client. Thus, at its most basic level of application, the focus of spectating theory will remain the same; that is, the reception of the production. However, it is important to acknowledge, right from the outset, one obvious and fundamental difference between interior spectating and other spectating modes, particularly in relation to the nature of the audience; that the spectator is both viewer and creator of the image. Although I take Bennett's point when she states with regard to theatre audiences: 'Boundaries between the subjects, the creators and the receivers are no longer distinct and such a move signals the democratising of the arts',[19] interior spectating involves a more fundamental blurring of the boundaries as audience and creator are one individual. Production and reception are happening inside the spectator. This level of internal interactivity will have some impact on how spectating theory can be usefully applied.

The production

Bennett makes the point that the selection of a theatre production to be viewed by a spectator needs to be taken into account. The cultural/economic and social context will not only determine what productions are available but will also play a part in influencing, whether consciously or unconsciously, the spectator's choice. This idea of selection is a useful one to apply to interior spectating. The choice of imagery productions is not and can never be value free. In practice, it is tempting to collude with the illusion that this interior dialogue between the spectator and producer is unlimited in terms of content, but of course, this is not true. Cultural conventions influence a client's perception of what might be 'problematic' and thus important to resolve. He or she will need to work in co-operation with the therapist who also brings to bear his or her own repertoire on the therapeutic endeavour. The therapist can also be instrumental in shaping the spectator's attitude and expectations of the arising imagery productions through his/her introductory remarks and instructions initiating the act of interior spectating.[20]

It is important to examine the particular nature of image production in interior spectating. How is the viewed object brought into being? As the client closes his/her eyes and goes into a more deeply relaxed state, the way is cleared to begin to communicate with the subconscious mind.[21] The distractions of the external world are screened out and a conscious contemplative state encourages a move away from the surface chatter of the mind into a deeper reflection. A blank screen is created in the mind's eye. Then an image will be brought into being or summoned up. It is not quite accurate to state that seeing an internal image is the same as external sight. As indicated earlier, there are three general types of imagery when used for therapeutic purposes in internal spectating and each type has a particular mode of image production.

In directive imagery, probably the simplest form of image production, a pre-designed or pre-selected image is held in the mind's eye or projected onto the blank screen. An example of this might be an image of the self performing a desired action successfully.[22] Or the person might draw from a range of helpful symbols or images and insert one of these as a new element within an already existing picture, for example, visualizing a bandage being wrapped around a broken heart.[23] Receptive imagery, as its description suggests, implies a different kind of image production. This visual representation arising as a translation is made from one condition or state into its nearest pictorial equivalent. Quite often the mind, as it were, goes through a process of several versions of the image until it hits the right match. A simple example would be of getting an image of a headache; initially the picture might be a vague round reddish shape that fine-tunes itself into a glowing red piece of coal. Once the image feels 'right', then the person concentrates on it to bring it into sharper focus; as noted by Ahsen,[24] this process may well be accompanied by associated emotions, memories or physiological states.

How is this viewed object initially received by the spectator? This applies to receptive imagery when the conscious mind is the spectator viewing the productions of the subconscious mind. This will normally run along a resistance/acceptance continuum. Resistance is generated by disbelief in the validity or 'truth' of the production. At one end of this continuum the resistance is created by the belief that the image is being created by the wishes of the conscious mind and, therefore, it cannot be a vehicle for real information. This is often the case where the image produced by the subconscious mind contradicts a poor self-image held by the conscious mind. At the other end of the continuum the resistance is created by a belief that the image is being created by a hostile subconscious mind; the image cannot be accepted or owned because it is too alien. In the middle of the continuum lies acceptance; the image is both, to a certain degree, like and unlike the conscious mind's perspective. Clarifying and resolving this initial reception of the image is often the first task of the therapist and client.

The audience

Bennett's contention that the spectator is not a *tabula rasa* is a generally accepted understanding in psychotherapy – therapy is mediated through social and cultural conventions.[25] The client will arrive carrying his or her own cultural/gender/social agendas, both conscious and of course unconscious. A great deal of attention has been paid in recent years to the inter-subjective context of the psychotherapeutic project.[26] Each client arrives at the door of the counselling room with an already existing nexus of interpretative strategies and means of decoding not only the imagery productions but the whole experience of the therapeutic encounter. Lago and Smith summarize this understanding as:

> How and where we are raised, what stories and experiences we are exposed to – all are ingredients of the interconnectedness between the growing child, the immediate carers (most frequently the family) and key agents of socialization such as education, religion, health, politics, law and communicated messages embodied in the media. All have an (often unconscious) influence on our views of ourselves, of others and the world.[27]

However, I think it is correct to say that this particular audience engaging in interior spectating will also be characterized by a common expectation – one that is different to the viewing of an artistic production – an expectation that there will arise some kind of resolution or at least improvement in a presenting issue that is personal to them. This particular characteristic has important implications for the application of spectating theory to therapeutic practice, which will be explored in the following sections.

The frame

Beginning with Freud, psychotherapists have long recognized the usefulness of the idea of the frame and it is now a well-established concept particularly in the psychodynamic school.[28] In the therapeutic context the frame is understood to be the physical and psychological boundaries that are used to create a secure container for the therapeutic work to proceed. At the most basic level, the setting of the counselling room and the agreement to meet at regular intervals at the same time would set the boundary of the temporal/spatial frame; whereas the therapeutic contract regarding the limits to confidentiality and the therapeutic focus would comprise the psychological boundary. Any un-negotiated changes to any of these aspects could result in a breakage of the frame, and, particularly in psychodynamic theory, this would be seen as a potential threat to the maintenance of the therapeutic space.

However, as touched on briefly in an earlier section, it is interesting to note that Bennett posits two frames in her model of production and reception. I think that this notion of a double frame could be usefully applied to interior spectating although with a different understanding of the meaning of the inner and outer frame. Equating the outer frame with the cultural, social and economic context, although superficially attractive, does not mesh well with the particular psychotherapeutic understanding of the frame as something that can be broken. Other theoretical constructs are used to explain the impact of the wider context on therapeutic work. However, reserving the term of outer frame as the equivalent of the usual psychotherapeutic meaning of the term, that is the physical setting and contract, permits the possibility of another internal frame for the specific activity of interior spectating. This inner frame would demarcate the interior psychological space in which the spectator is viewing and interacting with his or her own productions. Perhaps a useful analogy might be of the theatrical device of a play within a play.

I believe that this elaboration upon the usual concept of a single frame in psychotherapy allows a much clearer definition and demarcation to emerge with regard to interior spectating. However, I think that it is important to fully clarify this inner frame and to identify how its boundaries are set. Otherwise, the whole range of a client's interior dialogue operating during a session would be included along with the specific act of engaging with therapeutic imagery. I would suggest, therefore, that a way of conceptualizing this inner frame would be to see it set by the particular purpose of this mode of spectating. The use of inner imagery in this context is an intentional act with a therapeutic goal, thus, it could be said, that interior spectating is framed by therapeutically purposeful reception and production.

Therapeutically purposeful production and reception

If interior spectating is framed as therapeutically purposeful production and reception, this clearly has implications for the way in which the spectator views the image. It would suggest that the viewing itself is different in some way to the spectating act of the audience at a theatre production. This is understandable at the basic level of the different purposes evident in going to see a play as compared with going to see a therapist. At a more subtle level, this raises very interesting questions about how the viewing purpose itself might operate to influence the process of production and reception in interior spectating.

In order to gain some more insight into this possibility, I think that it is important to unpack this concept of therapeutically purposeful production and reception a little further. If there is a different kind of viewing inherent in interior spectating, what might its specific characteristics be? I believe that Mulvey's seminal work on the nature of the gaze might be a useful starting point for such an enquiry.[29] At this stage, I would tentatively suggest that this form of spectating could be characterized by two types of viewing: a diagnostic gaze and a reparative gaze. In the following discussion, I aim to show how these designations are valid in this particular context.

The diagnostic gaze

Any act of viewing or spectating will involve the spectator making sense of the viewed object, and this will happen at both a conscious and unconscious level. As Bennett observes: 'Like the individual reader, the audience inevitably proceeds through the construction of hypotheses about the fictional world which are subsequently substantiated, revised or negated.'[30] Obviously, this is not limited to the realm of aesthetic judgement – it operates at a more fundamental level of perception itself and the general issue of how we decode sense data. This has been the subject of intensive research and discussion across many disciplines ranging from the physiological processes involved inside the brain,[31] through the phenomenological investigation into our experience of receiving the world,[32] right through to epistemological issues regarding the reliability of sense data as a basis for knowledge.[33] Furthermore, any audience will view an art production through its cultural and personal lens in order to frame an acceptable narrative or to engage in meaning-making of the viewed production. This will also happen when a client views a representation of an aspect of the self in therapy as illustrated in the following case vignette.

> James was a talented and articulate 40 year old white man who had been a heavy
> drinker and heroin user for the previous ten years. I worked with him over a period of

four months firstly in a crisis intervention unit and later at a residential rehab. He described his life as having been successful and exciting in his twenties when he worked as a musician. However, when he was thirty, his life had gone downhill after the ending of a long-term relationship. He wanted to get his life back on track and realise his potential. After he completed his detoxification programme he wanted some assistance with a nagging feeling of something big missing in his life, therefore, I suggested we could look at a representation of his inner psychological structure in the form of a building. He described this as an unfinished terraced house from the 1960s: the shell of the building was there but there were no doors or windows or interior rooms. He made the link between work stopping on the building and being sent into care as a young boy when his parents split up. He was very interested in this image of the incomplete house and said that he was ready to do the necessary psychological work to begin to complete it. I suggested a temporary site caravan as a dwelling place where he could imagine himself staying while he worked on the house, which would represent the temporary containment of a residential rehabilitation centre.

Here, clearly the client and therapist are engaged in constructing a meaningful narrative based on spectating this internal image. But, and this is an important divergence from the aesthetic perspective, in interior spectating this decoding function has a therapeutic focus. This is because the client coming to the therapy session brings a presenting issue or problem. Thus, this initial viewing of the image production will have a diagnostic objective. The following case vignette illustrates this more clearly. Here a client has a mistaken belief about the cause of a symptom that is revised by viewing the image representation.

Arthur, an intelligent, self-aware and articulate man in his early thirties from the north of England, was a long-term drug user and had spent many years in prison. He was detoxifying in the crisis centre from a recent heroin relapse and wanted some help with a common sensation that he had whenever he stopped using heroin; a cold shaky feeling as if his bones were rattling (a classic description of an opiate withdrawal symptom.)

However, as soon as Arthur began to focus on the rattling sensation that was particularly intense in his lower back, it became clear that this symptom was suggesting a different cause than physiological withdrawals. He reported a clear picture almost like an X-ray of his lower back revealing a missing gap where his spine failed to meet his pelvic girdle. This was an unusual response in that the procedure of therapeutic imagery is designed to elicit a non-literal image. I asked him to get some idea of how long this gap had been there and he was very clear that it had started when he was 5 years old. This was when a happy family atmosphere turned very sour when his father had an affair.

It was obvious to Arthur that the gap in the image needed mending but it was also clear that such a long-standing problem could not be resolved quickly. I understood the literal nature of the image a little more when he explained to me that he'd had serious physical problems with his legs when he was a boy and had been confined to a wheelchair. Although he had recovered the use of his legs and was, to all intents and purposes, physically recovered the image suggested that something remained unhealed in his lower back. Arthur realized he had misdiagnosed this unpleasant sensation as a withdrawal symptom when it had been, in fact, some information arising about a long-standing condition when he was in a physiologically sensitized state. This discovery allowed him to refocus his attention more productively onto longer-term recovery plans.

The reparative gaze

A client brings a presenting issue to therapy and then explores this in order to find some kind of resolution. Thus it is not enough for the gaze to be solely diagnostic. This would imply that there is another type of gaze operating in this process and I would like to suggest that this gaze is reparative in the widest possible sense. In fact, this idea is already acknowledged in psychotherapeutic theory and practice, but it is conceptualized from a slightly different perspective. This relates to the generally held understanding that the very act of bringing something into conscious awareness is, of itself, therapeutic. This is because something that has been outside conscious awareness now has the possibility of being processed and integrated. In other words, a process has begun. Wilber states regarding all therapeutic approaches:

> The curative catalyst, in every case, is bringing awareness or consciousness to bear on an area of experience that is (or has been) denied, distorted, falsified or ignored. Once that area enters (or re-enters) consciousness, then it can rejoin the ongoing flow of evolutionary unfolding, instead of remaining behind, stuck in a distorted or alienated loop and sending up painful symptoms (anxiety, depression, phobias) as the only indication of its imprisonment.[34]

Furthermore, the nature of interior spectating, that the viewer both produces and receives the image production, allows the reparative gaze to translate into the reparative act. This is because the spectator can begin to import new pictorial elements into the representation of damaged conditions that are designed to promote and support a movement towards repair.[35] This does not mean that the spectator can impose a new representation in place of the original one. This would be an expression of over-using the will and conscious use of directive intervention. Therapeutic processes, if they are to be successful, need to unfold organically through a sequence of stages. However, changes can be made to facilitate that process. In the following example, we return to the client whose story set the scene for this chapter to begin.

> George, an insightful West Country man in his early thirties, had been using heroin, crack and valium chaotically and had recently overdosed. He was referred to me for help with the disturbing mental states he was experiencing during the detoxification programme: he believed he was losing control over his mind. He told me that he recognized that he had reached a critical point in his life and was in danger of losing his wife and children. He had entered the crisis unit in order to detoxify and had decided he needed to go onto long-term rehabilitation.

> Due to his concerns about his psychological stability, I suggested that he represent his internal psychological structure in the form of a building. This took the form of a little

country house in a Cornish landscape. At first glance the structure looked reasonably sound but it was obviously neglected. The door appeared to be missing and the shutters on one of the windows were broken. However, on closer inspection George was concerned to discover a massive hole in the roof and a look through the windows revealed water damage that had rotted the middle of the house and the stairway. He was shaken by this discovery although it resonated with him. He made links between the rotting core of the house and his increasing sense that he was in danger of destroying his core values through his chaotic drug use. He was very keen to begin work on repairing the damage. It was obvious to him that the initial work was to temporarily cover the roof to halt the deterioration of the house. He imagined a ladder in a shed outside the house and he also created a tarpaulin, batons, hammer and nails. He secured the tarpaulin over the roof, making sure it was properly tied down and made weatherproof. George needed very little prompting from me as he had had actual experience as a roofer. He had a sense that it would take six to ten months to rebuild this roof and to replace the rotted central core of the house and this corresponded with the length of the programme at the rehabilitation centre he had applied to go to after completing his detoxification. As he reviewed the state of his house he realized that the front door was not missing as he had originally thought but in fact it was open, so he closed this. He left it at that point saying that he felt his house was temporarily secure and that he was clear what he had to do.

A few days later he reported that his mind felt much calmer and clearer and he had a sense of optimism and clarity about his immediate future.

Discussion

In general the focus in psychotherapy is on the client, the therapeutic relationship between the client and therapist, and the therapeutic process. Research has reflected these concerns through its tendency towards clarifying and developing our understanding of these three important aspects of psychotherapeutic practice.[36] Thus, in practices such as therapeutic imagery the actual act of producing and receiving the image is not fore-grounded. As would be expected, the focus is more on the content of the image and the interaction between the client and his or her internal imagery.[37]

This experiment of reframing therapeutic imagery as interior spectating allows a new perspective whereby the act of viewing becomes primary and the content of the viewing becomes secondary. As I have proposed in the previous section, applying Bennett's concept of the double frame (admittedly not quite in the way that Bennett originally defined it) permits a clearer demarcation of the internal viewing arena. This allows the spectating act to be seen as situated within a therapeutically purposeful inner frame. Such framing discloses a pre-existing bias to the act of viewing. This raises the interesting question as to whether the content of the image is influenced in some way by the functional bias of the spectating. In other words, does the diagnostic or reparative gaze predetermine the nature of the image? The fact that production and reception theory has the capacity to raise such fundamental questions concerning therapeutic imagery strongly suggests that this is a potentially fruitful line of further enquiry.

Furthermore, it is possible, at this early stage, to detect further applications of this theory to other therapeutic practices. The use of inner imagery is not the only procedure that involves acts of production and reception. A whole range of creative interventions are used, particularly in humanistic approaches such as *Gestalt*,[38] which involve the client creating and interacting with a production. One well-known example from *Gestalt* would be the practice of a client imagining a problematic aspect of himself or herself in an empty chair and then developing an interactive dialogue with it. The analogy of a play within a play is particularly resonant here. It occurs to me that the concept of an inner frame set by therapeutically purposeful production and reception would be just as applicable in these and other allied therapeutic practices.

Conclusion

I will conclude by returning to the question posed at the beginning of the chapter: are the similarities between a client using inner imagery in psychotherapy and a spectator viewing a theatre production superficial? Or do they share enough common ground for theory-making from theatre practice to be useful and productive when applied to the practice of psychotherapy? I think that, as this initial exploration suggests, I can assent most definitely to the latter. Recently emerging theories of production and reception when applied to the use of inner imagery in therapy appear to have the capacity to disclose aspects of this practice that were hitherto obscured. This would suggest that further collaborative enquiry that is grounded in an interdisciplinary approach may well be fertile territory for both practices. Having drawn so heavily on Bennett's work in this initial discussion it seems appropriate to end this chapter with her own acknowledgement of the potential for such cross-fertilization in theory-making: 'The interactivity that necessarily takes place between spectators as well as between spectators and actors suggests that the inquiries into drama's correlation with the social sciences are potentially fruitful.'[39]

Notes

1. Jones, P. (2007), *Drama as Therapy*, 2nd Edition, London: Sage.
2. Bennett, S. (1997), *Theatre Audiences*, 2nd Edition, London: Routledge.
3. Thomas, V. (2006), *Therapeutic Imagery with Substance Misusers: A Practitioner's Guide*, published on www.lulu.com; Thomas, V. (2007), 'Using Imagery with Substance Misusers', *Self & Society*, Vol. 34, No. 5.
4. Bennett, S. (1997), *Theatre Audiences*, 2nd Edition, p. 21.
5. ibid., p. 86.
6. ibid., p. 207.
7. Eliade, M. (1989), *Shamanism: Archaic Techniques of Ecstasy*, New York: Pantheon Bollingen Foundation.
8. Freud, S. (1900), *The Interpretation of Dreams*, Standard Edition 5, London: Hogarth Press.
9. Jung C.G. (1954), *The Archetypes and The Collective Unconscious, The Collected Works of C.G. Jung*, Vol. 9, New Jersey: Princeton University Press.
10. Rowan, J. (1990), *Subpersonalities:The People Inside Us*, London: Routledge.
11. Perls F.S. (1969), *Gestalt Therapy Verbatim*, New York: Bantam.
12. McLeod J. (1997), *Narrative and Psychotherapy*, London: Sage.
13. Achterberg J. (1985), *Imagery in Healing*, Boston: Shambala; Achterberg J., Dossey B., Kolkmeier L. (1994), *Rituals of Healing*, New York: Bantam.

14. Maier S.F., Watkins L.R. (1998), 'Cytokines for Psychologists: Implications of Bidirectional Immune-to-Brain Communication for Understanding Behaviour, Mood and Cognition', *Psychological Review*, 105, No. 1.

15. Brigham D.D. (1994), *Imagery for Getting Well: Clinical Applications for Behavioural Medicine*. New York: Norton.

16. Ahsen A. (1984), 'ISM: The Triple Code Model for Imagery and Psychophysiology', *Journal of Mental Imagery*, 8, No. 4.

17. Thomas, V. (2006), *Therapeutic Imagery with Substance Misusers: A Practitioner's Guide*, published on www.lulu.com, 2006.

18. Hall, E. et al. (2007), *Guided Imagery*, London: Sage.

19. Bennett, S. (1997), *Theatre Audiences*, 2nd Edition, p. 10.

20. Thomas, V. (2006), *Therapeutic Imagery with Substance Misusers: A Practitioner's Guide*.

21. Brigham D.D. (1994), *Imagery for Getting Well: Clinical Applications for Behavioural Medicine*, New York: Norton.

22. White D. J. (1988), 'Taming the Critic: Use of Imagery with Those Who Procrastinate', in *Journal of Mental Imagery*, 12, No. 1.

23. Thomas, V. (2006), *Therapeutic Imagery with Substance Misusers: A Practitioner's Guide*.

24. Ahsen A. (1984), 'ISM: The Triple Code Model for Imagery and Psychophysiology', *Journal of Mental Imagery*, 8, No. 4.

25. d'Ardenne, P., Mahtani, A. (1989), *Transcultural Counselling in Action*, London: Sage.

26. Moodley, R. (2003), 'Double, Triple, Multiple Jeopardy' in Lago, C., Smith, B., (eds.), *Anti-Discriminatory Counselling Practice*, London: Sage.

27. Lago, C., Smith, B. (2003), 'Ethical Practice and Best Practice', in Lago, C., Smith, B., (eds.), *Anti-Discriminatory Counselling Practice*, London: Sage, p. 4.

28. Gray, A. (1994), *An Introduction to the Therapeutic Frame*, London: Routledge.

29. Mulvey, L. (1975), 'Visual Pleasure and Narrative Cinema', *Screen*, 16.3.

30. Bennett, S. (1997), *Theatre Audiences*, 2nd Edition, p. 140.

31. Greenfield, S. (2000), *The Private Life of the Brain*, London: Penguin.

32. Spinelli, E. (1989), *The Interpreted World: An Introduction to Phenomenological Psychology*, London: Sage.

33. Audi, R. (1998), *Epistemology: A Contemporary Introduction to the Theory of Knowledge*, London: Routledge.

34. Wilber, K. (2003), *Integral Psychology*, Boston and London: Shambala, p. 99.

35. Thomas, V. (2006), *Therapeutic Imagery with Substance Misusers: A Practitioner's Guide*.

36. McLeod J. (1997), *Narrative and Psychotherapy*, London: Sage.

37. Thomas, V. (2006), *Therapeutic Imagery with Substance Misusers: A Practitioner's Guide*.

38. Perls, F.S. (1969), *Gestalt Therapy Verbatim*, New York: Bantam.

39. Bennett, S. (1997), *Theatre Audiences*, 2nd Edition, p. 211.

9

TUNING-IN TO SOUND AND SPACE: HEARING, VOICING AND WALKING

Alison Oddey

This chapter focuses on how the 'spectator-performer-protagonist's' body tunes-in to sound and space, listening to the atmosphere of the urban environment, the architecture of sound-scapes of urban drift and urban dream. What is it that makes us connect? This contribution to *Modes of Spectating* explores the interface of the walking spectator-performer and transportable technology, the interrelationship and interface of fragmentation, connectivity and the mobile phone. Using a 'hearing' based epistemology – how we think with our ears, how we know and experience the world through sound – I consider the significance of sound as a mode of spectating, performing and being. I look at the interrelationship of 'sound-scape' and performance, which begs questions about how to represent or notate the walker's sonic universe and the immediacy of the acoustic landscape. What compels me to speak as I walk? Is it the 'liveness' of connectivity with mobile space as contemporary performance space? Is it the 'live', heightened real-time encounter of the mediatized landscape of the city, which enhances the spectator-performer-protagonist's present life in the fragment of an engagement with the absent listener-spectator-viewer, who receives my picture and video messaging, texts, tones, and recordings? With the emphasis on visual culture, on looking and seeing, and the 'walk' enabling the viewer/listener/spectator/performer to intimately connect and interact with the city landscape, how do I listen and do I listen less?

The focus of my recent work in terms of the creation of a multimedia landscape through performance has been concerned with investigating the architecture of sound-scapes in urban environments and how within the art form of 'the walk', a solo 'spectator-performer-protagonist' emerges from the cityscape environment to interface with transportable technologies and the creation of a mobile creative aesthetic. I want to define the art form of 'the walk' in terms of both performance and installation work as the frame for reading this chapter, before examining the term 'sound-scape' and how it has previously been used. Walks involve the spectator making some kind of connection to the landscape, be it the urban city environment or the gallery space of the installation. It is the structure of the walk, which guides and enables the spectator to experience their surroundings imaginatively, via their unconsciousness, and through their sensory and cultural history connections to the particular environment. It is the spectator, who emerges as the protagonist of the walk, in their active self-reflexive narratives, made-up stories and poetics of art and everyday life. The walk invites the 'spectator-protagonist', to interact with the living environment surrounding them, to look at objects, to new modes of perception, which focus the spectator's memories of self and to think differently, walking across time. The place of performance resides within the spectator's senses and memories, engaging them in the live event of walking, whether as a constructed theatre-artwork or installation.

Murray Schafer, the Canadian composer, identified the term 'sound-scape' in his book, *The Tuning of the World* in 1977.[1] He 'began recording, observing, and acoustically analysing the sonic experience of space and place', and from this developed his definition of 'acoustic ecology', which Steven Feld states has not had great impact on ethnographers, 'who might study how people hear, respond to, and imagine place as sensually sonic.'[2]

Schafer has created numerous sound-scape projects, which pedagogically point us to how to listen to the world, 'Schafer's message is that we no longer "hear" the sounds of the natural world and that our leaders no longer "listen" to us.'[3] Bull and Black's description of the landscape as, 'a fluid and changing surface that is transformed as it is enveloped by different sounds'[4] begs questions about how to represent or notate the walker's sonic universe and the immediacy of the acoustic landscape. Listening to the landscape is different to the geographical concern with the visible world, exemplified in a static topography, which is mapped, drawn and/or visually symbolized.

Barry Blesser and Linda-Ruth Salter state that: 'Listening is more than hearing; it is more than sensing, detecting, and discriminating sounds. Listening is the act of making sense out of an aural experience by incorporating all that has been remembered from previous experiences.'[5] Blesser and Salter suggest that auditory intelligence is, 'distinct from visual, olfactory, and tactile',[6] a specific other intelligence. They put forward the idea that: 'A sound that is meaningful by definition, produces an emotional or affective response'[7] arguing that, '*feelings* are conscious awareness of the body's relationship to the environment, whereas *perceptions* are conscious awareness of the environment itself.'[8]

As a performer, I have considered a 'hearing' based epistemology – how we think with our ears, how we know and experience the world through sound – investigating Steven Feld's, 'primacy of sound as a modality of knowing and being in the world'.[9] He argues that:

Sound both emanates from and penetrates bodies; this reciprocity of reflection and absorption is a creative means of orientation – one that tunes bodies to places and times through their sounding potential. Hearing and producing sound are thus embodied competencies that situate actors and their agency in particular historical worlds. These competencies contribute to their distinct and shared ways of being human; they contribute to possibilities for and realizations of authority, understanding, reflexivity, compassion and identity.[10]

The meaning of Feld's definition of 'acoustemology' as, 'a union of acoustics and epistemology' is:

to explore the reflexive and historical relationships between hearing and speaking, listening and sounding. This reflexivity is embodied doubly: one hears oneself in the act of voicing, and one resonates the physicality of voicing in acts of hearing. Listening and voicing are in a deep reciprocity, an embodied dialogue of inner and outer sounding and resounding built from the historicization of experience.[11]

He suggests, therefore, that: 'The ongoing dialogue of self and self, self and other, of their interplay in action and reaction,' are 'sited at the sense of sound, absorbed and reflected, given and taken in constant exchange.'[12] Feld argues that:

The soundingness of hearing and voicing constitute an embodied sense of presence and memory. Voice then authorizes identities as identities authorize voice. Voice is evidence, embodied as experiential authority, performed to the exterior or interior as a subjectivity made public, mirrored in hearing as public made subjective.[13]

Therefore, in terms of a multi-site performance, who or what creates the sound-scape? How does the performance and sound-scape interrelate? It is the walker, as spectator-performer, in her listening, hearing and in being heard, that determines the relationship: 'Walking is a way of engaging and interacting with the world, providing the means of exposing oneself to new, changing perceptions and experiences and of acquiring an expanded awareness of our surroundings.'[14] The sound-scape is in the locality of the walking, which is about the movement of the body in space and time, across races, cultures and centuries, in the representation and evocation of the territory, geography and politics of the place, as well as in the walker-performer's imagination, drift and dream of the urban space.

However, it is the architecture of the city, the buildings that have been designed, constructed and aesthetically shaped by the architects, 'in structures that we see, hear and feel',[15] that the walker responds aurally. Blesser and Salter argue that it is not usual for architects to focus on the acoustic aspects of a building and that the, 'native ability of human beings to sense space by listening is rarely recognized'.[16] They state that, 'a rudimentary spatial ability is a hardwired part of our genetic inheritance',[17] explaining that: 'When our ability to decode spatial attributes is sufficiently developed using a wide range of acoustic cues, we can readily visualize objects and spatial geometry: we can "see" with our ears.'[18] Biologically, there is the 'hard-wired' structure of the external ear 'and its low-level neurological processing of sounds' and the 'soft-wired creative, cognitive, and perceptual structures',[19] which enable responses to the environment. Blesser and Salter suggest that, 'we have the hard-wired ability to fuse early sonic reflections with the direct sound' and 'the soft-wired ability to learn to hear space...'[20]

Blesser and Salter argue that, 'auditory spatial awareness must be considered the province of sensory anthropology'[21] and that,

> Hearing, together with its active complement, listening, is a means by which we sense the events of life, aurally visualize spatial geometry, propagate cultural symbols, stimulate emotions, communicate aural information, experience the movement of time, build social relationships, and retain a memory of experiences.[22]

They specifically define aural as 'the human *experience* of a sonic process', hearing as 'the detection of sound' and listening as the 'active attention or reaction to the meaning, emotions, and symbolism contained within sound.'[23] Therefore, their term 'aural architecture', 'refers to the properties of a space that can be *experienced* by listening'[24] and the belief that aural architecture is able to change 'the affective state of listeners, perhaps with only a subliminal shifting of mood, or perhaps with an overwhelming emotion.'[25]

As I walk down the urban street, it is sonically complex as every space I encounter has an aural architecture: 'The composite of numerous surfaces, objects and geometries in a complicated environment creates an *aural architecture*.'[26] Blesser and Salter suggest that, as I hear 'sounds from multiple sources interact with various spatial elements', that I am somehow transferring and entrusting 'an identifiable personality to the aural architecture'.[27] It is almost as if every building is a performer with a unique performing personality. I am responding and reacting to Blesser and Salter's 'aural architecture', whilst also reinforcing visual meanings, as I walk the city in terms of how my mood shifts, the associations I make in my mind and both the behavioural and emotional experience of space.

In walking the city, my sense is of some 'aural architecture' promoting my affective experience more than others, pushing individual, identifiable meanings, which only 'I' can know. My perception of the city is governed by my personal history, conveying and converting 'raw sensation into an awareness that has meaning'.[28] I am listening attentively to the sound-scape, which is filled with memories and emotions. It could be argued that I am perceiving a sonic event, that I am making some kind of intimate connection with all around me, which includes the 'aural architecture' of the city. Blesser and Salter suggest that, 'auditory memory plays a large role in acquiring the ability to hear space.'[29]

It is important to understand the acoustic complexity of walking an urban street as it is made-up of multiple sound sources and many objects within its sound field. My ability to hear space is not the same as each of the other walkers on the street: 'Hearing is the sensory means for receiving vocalised communications among conspecifics, and hearing is also the means for sensing the soundscape, which is composed of the physical environment and the sonic events contained therein.'[30] Each person's ears are sensing location in space differently. Auditory sensitivity and spatial awareness will vary greatly: 'Some listeners may be acutely aware of reverberation and enclosed volume of a space, whereas others may be aware of local objects and geometries in a navigational space.'[31] As a walker, I have learnt to hear space, which simply means that I become attentive to aural cues, which are proffered by spatial acoustics. I have an auditory spatial awareness, which is linking my own personal, internal experience and memory with what I observe around me. I acknowledge the spatial nature of sound and experience.

The sounds around me are embedded with both personal and cultural meanings, which make me examine and re-think my relational experience, that is, how I relate to others, myself, and the spaces and places we inhabit? Paul Moorhouse argues that such experiences provide 'a deeper understanding of the places we occupy',[32] and therefore, 'a better understanding of our own position in the world.'[33] With the emphasis on visual culture, on looking and seeing, and the 'walk' enabling the viewer/listener/spectator/ performer to intimately connect and interact with the city landscape, how do I listen and do I listen less? Paul Carter suggests that listening is 'engaged hearing',[34] is 'intentional hearing',[35] arguing that, 'Hearing remains monological, listening is always dialogical.'[36]

In 'The Art of Sound: Auditory Directions', Chapter 8 of my book, *Re-Framing the Theatrical, Interdisciplinary Landscapes for Performance*,[37] I wrote about how sound art and sound installation referred to the use of sound to articulate physical space, creating a proliferation of possibilities of forms of spatially-articulated sound. As an interdisciplinary art, the connections are evident between space and time, silence and noise, hearing and seeing, and object and sound, creating original forms of reception, tonal spaces and perceptual structures.[38]

Christina Kubisch's work, notably *Oasis 2000: Music for a Concrete Jungle*, which was designed for the front sculpture court at the Hayward Gallery in London in 2000, gave me a particular pleasure, enabling me to drift sonically in and out of reverie, to dream half-conscious in a state of being that was not real. Kubisch's work has often been described as 'the synthesis of arts', in her disclosing and exhibiting of acoustic space, as well as 'the dimension of time in the visual arts on the one hand, and a new relationship between material and form in music on the other.'[39]

In *Re-Framing the Theatrical*, I propose that 'the cross-over of poetics is in these "interrelationships", in the shifting perceptions and body of the spectator; in the complexity of their own composition of emotion, intellect and being', as well as in their 'everyday collision with the musical score of daily life.'[40] Therefore, the walker-performer 'encounters the interface of sound, as a subtle or intense sensory experience, and as a communicative, theatre tool, integrating and interacting to stimulate and inspire' their imagination.[41] David Toop's argument that media '...have fostered an image of a boundless ocean of signals'[42] supports my own practice-as-research experiments with the walker-performer's interface with the transportable technology and creative aesthetics of the mobile phone, interspersed with interruptions and infusions of listening, sound, observing, memories and the texts of audible mappings of the landscape.[43]

Being tuned in: how are the body, sound and space connected?

Feld suggests that: 'Because motion can draw upon the kinaesthetic interplay of tactile, sonic, and visual senses, emplacement always implicates the intertwined nature of sensual bodily presence and perceptual engagement.'[44] Bull and Black, however, argue that: 'It may be that within the registers of aural culture that memories are carried regardless of whether the bearers of such embodied traditions are aware of them.'[45] In terms of how sensory ratios change contextually with bodily emplacement, I am interrogating their interplay experientially through practice-as-research, how hearing and voicing bring together 'the felt sensations of sound and balance to those of physical and emotional presence.'[46]

In the public spaces of the urban city, the acoustic skyline is much greater than the visual or olfactory horizons. Therefore, the use of mobile technologies happens in the much broader space of general packet radio service (GPRS) and the sending of media and multimedia messages. This communicates an acoustic geography of the city with the sound-marks of various electronic signature tunes and music, replacing those of church bells ringing in a previous rural landscape,[47] rooting individual walkers within the cultural geography of contemporary city space.

I am using the mobile phone as a low-tech tool, so that the walker-spectator-performer can capture still and moving images, and make video calls. I am exploring sound as an integral part of my bodily experience of the world and how that is fundamentally different from understanding the world through a filtered visual frame. Sound tells us about what we cannot see, even though we may be viewing elsewhere. Sound is to signal connection, to provide networking, and to offer feedback. As Richard Long suggests, 'walking is also a way to find the beautiful landscapes of the planet...leaving traces which share the same place as other traces of animals...a record of all its human, animal and geographical history.'[48] In order to interrogate 'listening', Bull and Black suggest that: 'Thinking with our ears offers an opportunity to augment our critical imaginations, to comprehend our world and our encounters with it according to multiple registers of feeling.'[49] I am listening to everything that is audible; perceptually, I register every sound in the aural manifold. But am I filtering out what I don't want to hear and listening out for what I do? I am decoding sounds and interpreting them, furnishing my experience of these sounds with a concept. As I listen, can I be overtaken or even possessed by a sound-scape?

What happens to me – consciously – as I give in to this imperative to listen is that listening to music creates new possibilities of time, place and memory, and opportunities to consider issues of belonging, identity and history. As I listen in each particular environment of the city, sound gives me an immediate impression of the space that I inhabit. As the listener-spectator, I create an intimate, managed aestheticized space, which incorporates 'Happy Ride' from the Music

Player of my mobile phone's menu. My personalized sound-scape is reflected partly in the acoustic choices from the files of my audio databank on the phone. Jacques Attali suggests that: 'Listening to music is listening to all noise, realizing that its appropriation and control is a reflection of power, that is essentially political.'[50] Listening does demand practices of dialogue. It requires the establishment of my own performative, expressive territory through listening. I walk the city space (supporting Deleuze and Guattari's suggestion of such a territorialization[51]), tuning-in to sound, hearing, voicing and walking. It is sound that colours and interprets the city space in a similar manner to how light affects it; I am sensing with both ears and eyes, aware of how a particular environment changes the sound.

The mobile phone, fragmentation and connectivity

In making connections with people, as dialled or received, Caroline Bassett argues that the mobile functions as a 'mnemonic operator',[52] giving the walker-performer in this work, an inventory of the places and people s/he is connected to. It is how the walker's body interacts with the mobile phone's interface of the fourth screen, which creates an embodied technology, changing the walker's understanding of the sensory space. The walker gains a techno-sensual awareness in that his/her sensing body is technological, 'to produce an amplified, connected, expanded but also disequilibrated corporeality – a new sensorium.'[53] I am a digital flâneur with a technologized body, walking the city in aesthetic contemplation. I embody an experience which has negotiated with the mediated, which Caroline Jones argues, has always been mediated, ('Without the "medium" of air or water, the anthropoid ear finds it impossible to hear'[54]), and that it is our embodied experience through the senses that is how we think. This is further supported by Hillel Schwartz's arguments in 'The Indefensible Ear' that 'the ear, in addition to being a receiver and an amplifier, actually does broadcast sounds that, on occasion, others can hear.'[55]

I am currently researching how the auditory, as a site of embodied knowledge, manages my feelings, mood, sense of time and place, the city becoming what I want it to be. I am investigating how using the mobile phone as a portable creative tool, can enable dialectic between presence and absence through the performative aestheticization of the city space with and for the absent spectator-listener-viewer of the phone. This is particularly relevant as this technology is cheaply available and used in a variety of ways to capture life and share spectatorship, phone as both visual and audio recording device. In developing the art form of the walk, I have integrated the techno-human interface of the mobile phone to enhance my consciousness of self, via modes of hearing and thinking, as a creative tool, 'to amplify and accompany the self.'[56]

Jones argues that with new technologies, 'the simultaneous purification and de-corporealization of the body is instrumentalized to produce the contemplative conditions necessary for the self-reflexive modern subject to emerge.'[57] The auditory 'I' is always functioning within a mediated sensorium, so that 'hearing both enters and emanates from the body'.[58] 'Hearing, like seeing, has always been part of producing the self.'[59] I am experimenting and playing with stretching the viewer's range of experience of spectating, inviting them to participate in the subjectivating effects of the fourth screen employed. The mobile phone enables me to encourage or to cancel multiple subjectivities. It contributes to a creative dissociation, segmentation and re-assembling

Fig. 18: Visuals of cities: St Petersburg, St Marks' Venice, Helsinki, Washington, Grand Canal, Venice, and Rome.

of different sections of walking of the city, where the focus of my discourse changes from visual to verbal. This is a 'Visitextuality', which is an urban environment, 'a virtual experience, an aestheticized social exchange.'[60]

Fragment

I walk here...in the cities of St Petersburg, Venice, Washington, Helsinki and Rome. I listen there, in the virtual space of mobile connectivity, which takes me from and through the physical, spatial environment of Nevsky Prospekt, St Marks, the Mall, by the Grand Canal and the Kiasma at the same time as the auditory space, which opens up with the ringing of my phone. In an instant, my attention is taken from the visuality of the landscape and re-focused emotionally, intellectually and bodily to a space where I listen, hear and am heard. My physical, sensory everyday space is infiltrated and accessed by mobile telephony's ability to connect me to virtual spaces, and as Caroline Bassett argues in her essay 'How Many Movements?', 'Mobiles play a part in the production of contemporary space.'[61]

Therefore, as I walk, this mobile technology is contributing to how I speak, negotiate and agree new forms of subjectivity. As the emerging spectator-performer-protagonist tuning-in to sonic space, I am transformed in acts of hearing, voicing and moving. I am in De Certeau's spatial, narrative space[62] of this specific place and present time and I am connected to someone in a far away space. My mobile enables me to connect in diverse ways; to communicate through the processes of making or receiving calls. As long as I am switched on, there is always the possibility of 'remote intervention',[63] and therefore, the chance, the opportunity to shift or change perspectives and perceptions.

My identity is made more visible with mobile technology, with an always-on culture. It connects me to others in public spaces, acting as a tool towards the creation of a performing presence. I commune with the air, or so it seems, in the private space of the public space of the city. Sherry Turkle suggests that we are witnessing 'a new form of sociality in which the isolation of our physical bodies does not indicate our state of connectedness but may be its precondition.'[64] Turkle argues that the individual's 'state of connectedness is determined by our proximity to available communications technology'[65] and without our mobile phones, 'we feel disconnected, adrift.'[66]

I perform the appropriate role or aspect of my identity in relation to me. As I walk, 'the travelling body is in intensive contact with others, but spreads itself around the world.'[67] All that is on the mobile technology constitutes 'a projection of self in digital space',[68] which is stored, displayed and performed in the city. I am transmitting and receiving signals in some kind of e-space between urban drift and urban dream. In St Petersburg, I am distracted by looking for bands of gypsy children with mugging potential; in Venice, the flocks of pigeons crowding passers-by in the square; in Washington, the level of security around me; in Helsinki, the well-dressed shoppers; in Rome, the groups of visiting tourists. I am in a trance-like state, looking, embodying and visualising the place whilst speaking into the phone, the auditory space taking over and engulfing the spatial.[69] Research has shown how birds adopt auditory strategies: 'to optimize vocalization to the nuances of a habitat, individual birds learn the details of their songs rather than being born with a pre-defined song',[70] so that avian species pass on their 'oral-aural tradition of songs that are adapted to the acoustics of the environment.'[71] Urban birds, such as great tits, alter their singing to 'a higher pitch to attract a mate above the rumble of traffic',[72] changing their call sign in the wi-fi city sound-scape, whilst starlings in Copenhagen incorporate the sound of the ringing mobile phone into their own singing. Research indicates they favour the Nokia classic ringtone. The phone rings. I become consumed by voice, sound, and speech and everywhere the landscape is filled with infinite conversations of the everyday.

As Bassett suggests, 'mobile phones are at once a new symbol of a particular kind of contemporary freedom to move and act in multiple spaces, and a symbol of "always on" accountability/surveillance.'[73] Again, it is the possibility of connecting with someone somewhere else from the present place of Cambridge to Chicago, Zurich or Madrid...As the mobile-equipped walker, I am continually crossing the multi-blurred boundaries of GPRS space, communicating by satellite, tracked and surveilled over-head. This is the interface of one private, personal bodily world with other global, public cultural worlds.

As I walk, I can record my voice on the phone, speaking about the landscape, about both the visual and the embodiment of the space, and then, I can send this fragment of how I feel, what I hear and see, and what I think and experience to someone else. I can text the auditory and physical space of my environment, as I walk. As I move, I can take a photograph or capture a moving image of a moment of this experience with my mobile phone as camera. What compels me to speak as I walk? Is it (as Bassett suggests), a connection with mobile space being an experience 'as going "live"'?[74] It is the live real-time encounter in the mass-media marketing, advertising mediatised landscape of the city, an 'accelerated, intensified, sense of freedom and movement and of speed-up',[75] which enhances that fragmentary engagement with the absent listener-spectator-viewer, in the reception and receiving of texts, tones, images and recordings.

It is also the self-conscious feeling of the filmic, spectating the self in a fictitious sense. Not only in the chosen sound-scape of selected tracks, but in the performing of voicing, the style of standing and public presentation of the self. Turkle's concept of 'a tethered self',[76] where the mobile is always switched on, brings 'new behaviours. Each speaker talks out loud, often when walking, behaving as though no one around is listening.'[77] She states that they are, 'disembodied...with a certain suggested absence...Holding a cell phone (or the behaviour of "speaking into air" that indicates a cell phone with an earphone microphone) marks them as tethered. They are transported to the space of the new ether, 'T'-ethered, virtualized.'[78]

The 'tethered self' of the spectator realizes the ongoing opportunity of taking the world with them as they walk, the mobile phone always offering them the potential to capture another moment, to speak their mode of perception, to consider an alternative perspective. There is also the possibility of our whole lives becoming a landscape with a soundtrack, which develops a filmic sense of the world as we walk and pass through it. The spectator's emergence as protagonist of the walk, enables s/he to complete their own enclosure within their immediate personal sonic landscape. The walk serves as the interactive structure and potential for creative action for the spectator, whose personal sound-scape is constructed from the movement of walking the city as interface, so that the serendipity of everyday living and the personal experiences of the spectator's unexpected encounters or views, actively create and produce unfolding narratives and a new aesthetic practice.

The modality of sound is central to making sense as the spectator, to knowing and to an experiential truth of the city as a reverberant and reflective space. Mobile privatization is about the inhabitation of city spaces as I walk; a solitary, private and moving activity: 'Mobile privatization is about the desire for proximity, for a mediated presence that shrinks space into something manageable and habitable. Sound more than any other sense, appears to perform a largely utopian function in this desire for proximity and connectedness.'[79] I tune-in to urban sonic space, public and e-space, as I hear, voice and walk. I connect, am tethered (in Turkle's terms), to transportable technology: 'our devices have become more closely coupled to our sense of our bodies and increasingly feel like extensions of our minds.'[80]

I am virtual; I am always-on.

Notes

1. Schafer, M. (1977), *The Tuning of the World*, Random House.
2. Feld, S. (2005), 'Places Sensed, Senses Placed: Toward a Sensuous Epistemology of Environments', Howes, D., (ed.), *Empire of the Senses: The Sensual Culture Reader*, Oxford: Berg, p. 183.
3. Bull, M., Back, L., (eds.), *The Auditory Culture Reader*, Oxford: Berg, p. 21.
4. ibid., p. 11.
5. Blesser, B., Salter, L-R. (2007), *Spaces Speak, Are You Listening? Experiencing Aural Architecture*, Cambridge, Massachusetts and London, England: The MIT Press, p. 328.
6. ibid., p. 331.
7. ibid., p. 332.
8. ibid., p. 334.
9. Feld, S. (2003), 'A Rainforest Acoustemology', Bull, M., Back, L., (eds.), *The Auditory Culture Reader*, Oxford: Berg, p. 226.
10. ibid.
11. ibid.
12. ibid.
13. ibid., pp. 226–7.
14. Moorhouse, P. (2002), 'The Intricacy of the Skein, the Complexity of the Web: Richard Long's Art', in Long, R., *Walking the Line*, London:Thames & Hudson, p. 33.
15. Blesser, B., Salter, L-R. (2007), *Spaces Speak, Are You Listening? Experiencing Aural Architecture*, p. 1.
16. ibid.
17. ibid.
18. ibid., p. 2.
19. ibid., p. 319.
20. ibid., p. 320.
21. ibid., p. 3.
22. ibid., p. 4.
23. ibid., p. 5.
24. ibid.
25. ibid., p. 335.
26. ibid., p. 2.
27. ibid.
28. ibid., p. 13.
29. ibid., p.1 7.
30. ibid., p. 335.
31. ibid., p. 46.
32. Moorhouse, P. (2002), 'The Intricacy of the Skein, the Complexity of the Web: Richard Long's Art', in Long, R., *Walking the Line*, London: Thames & Hudson, p. 33.
33. ibid.
34. Carter, P. (2004), 'Ambiguous Traces, Mishearing, and Auditory Space', Erlmann, V. (ed.), *Hearing Cultures Essays on Sound, Listening and Modernity*, Oxford, New York: Berg, p. 43.
35. ibid., p. 44.

36. ibid.
37. Oddey, A. (2007), *Re-Framing the Theatrical, Interdisciplinary Landscapes for Performance*, Palgrave Macmillan.
38. ibid., p. 162.
39. www.discogs.com/artist/Christina+Kubisch
40. Oddey, A. (2007), p. 163.
41. ibid.
42. Toop, D. (2000), 'Sonic Boom', *Sonic Boom: The Art of Sound*, London: Hayward Gallery Publishing, p. 113.
43. ibid., p. 121.
44. Feld, S. (2005), 'Places Sensed, Senses Placed: Toward a Sensuous Epistemology of Environments', in Howes, D., (ed.), *Empire of the Senses: The Sensual Culture Reader*, Oxford: Berg, p. 181.
45. Bull and Black, p. 16.
46. Feld, p. 184.
47. See Corbin, A., *Village Bells: Sound and Meaning in the Nineteenth-Century French Countryside*, Translated, Thom, M., New York, Columbia University Press, 1998.
48. Fragments from 'A transcription of Richard Long's talk during a slide show given at the Naoshima Contemporary Art Museum, Japan, on May 25 1997', in Long, R., *Walking the Line*, Thames & Hudson, London, 2002, p. 146.
49. Bull, M., Back, L. (2003), p. 2.
50. Jones, C. (ed.) (2006), *Sensorium embodied experience, technology and contemporary art*, MIT Press, p. 24.
51. Deleuze, G., Guattari, F. (1987), *A Thousand Plateaus*, Minneapolis: University of Minnesota Press.
52. Bassett, C. (2003), 'How many Movements?', Bull, M., Back, L., (eds.), *The Auditory Culture Reader*, Oxford: Berg, p. 353.
53. Jones, C. (ed.) (2006), *Sensorium embodied experience, technology and contemporary art*, p. 2.
54. ibid., p. 5.
55. Schwartz, H. (2003), 'The Indefensible Ear', Bull, M., Back, L., (eds.), *The Auditory Culture Reader*, Oxford and New York: Berg, p. 500.
56. ibid., p. 17.
57. ibid., p. 27.
58. ibid., p. 30.
59. ibid.
60. ibid., p. 32.
61. Bassett, C. (2003), 'How many Movements?', Bull, M., Back, L., (eds.), *The Auditory Culture Reader*, p. 344.
62. de Certeau, M. (1984), *The Practice of Everyday Life*, Berkeley & London: University of California Press.
63. Bassett, C. (2003), p. 345.
64. Turkle, S. (2006), 'Tethering' in Jones, C., (ed.), *Sensorium embodied experience, technology and contemporary art*, p. 222.
65. ibid.

66. ibid.

67. ibid.

68. ibid., p. 223.

69. See Michael Bull re: modes of perception in relation to aural and visual.

70. Blesser, B., Salter, L-R. (2007), *Spaces Speak, Are You Listening? Experiencing Aural Architecture*, p. 339.

71. ibid., p. 352.

72. Briggs, H. (2003), 'Birds hit the high notes in cities', BBC NewsOnline Science, 16 July, http://news.bbc.co.uk/2/hi/science/nature/3068781.stm

73. Bassett, C. (2003), p. 345.

74. ibid., p. 350.

75. ibid.

76. Turkle, S. (2006), 'Tethering' in Jones, C. (ed.), *Sensorium embodied experience, technology and contemporary art*, p. 221.

77. ibid.

78. ibid.

79. Erlmann, V., (ed.) (2004), *Hearing Cultures: Essays on Sound, Listening and Modernity*, Oxford, New York: Berg, p. 177.

80. ibid, p. 225.

10

PICTURING MEN: PERFORMERS AND SPECTATORS

Jeremy Mulvey

This chapter looks at how images can help us to understand the nature of male identity and gives a variety of accounts of the key concepts of 'self' and 'identity'. Jean-Paul Sartre's notion of identity as a site in which the self struggles for authenticity is taken as a useful model for artists engaged in identity politics. An analysis of Mulvey's drawings and paintings examines their attempt to deal with men as 'providers' and 'warriors'. Research into the contents of men's social conditioning is examined as is the use of counselling to alleviate the negative effects of that conditioning. The changing nature of exhibitions about men is outlined, however, the development of post-structural theory is seen – in the main – as a hindrance to art that deals with identity politics. The chapter ends with a call for issue-based artists to understand more about how images are understood and made use of by spectators.

Watching the behaviour of others and acting out roles are vital parts of life. Can visual forms such as painting, photography and video help us to think about the identities we inhabit and roles we act out in everyday life? More specifically, can images help men think about the way they are expected to lead their lives and enable them to envisage possible futures?

A sense of self: the floating man
Firstly, in trying to answer these questions a great deal hinges on what we mean by the terms 'self' and 'identity', the understanding of these concepts is anything but easy. There is a range of hypotheses but fundamental questions about our make-up as individuals remain unresolved. Are we endowed with the roles we carry out or can we choose the parts we play? Is there a

central core to our being or are we an accretion of reactions to the way others have treated us?

The human being's 'sense of self' has been a perennial focus of attention in religion and philosophy across cultures. The mediaeval Islamic philosopher, Avicenna, posed the conundrum of 'the floating man'. A man who wakes up suspended in air, blindfolded, ears plugged, touching nothing and with all his limbs, fingers and toes spread out – in other words feeling and sensing nothing – would still be aware of himself.[1] Avicenna held fast to the idea that, deprived of all sense experience, we would have an awareness of 'self' from within us. We came into existence with this sense. Some centuries later Descartes whittled this sense of 'self' down to a single mental process. When all other propositions were deemed to be questionable, there was only one thing we could be certain of and that was our own thoughts or, to put it another way, our ability to be uncertain.[2]

Avicenna and Descartes maintain that the sense of self emerges from within us. Contemporary thinkers, by contrast, place an emphasis on self-awareness emerging as a result of encounters with the world outside. For the psychoanalyst, Lacan, our sense of self is formed externally. According to this account we first become conscious of 'self' by seeing ourselves in the mirror, and because the sense of self is gained by means of an image outside us and separate from us in the mirror, it is always unresolved, unstable and a fiction.[3]

The child psychiatrist, Winnicott, developing, among others, Lacan's ideas, describes the child's growing sense of self as an awareness that is created within the lap of the mother. As a site for play, the lap represents a loving space in which, given the right circumstances, our ability to make two crucial distinctions emerges at one and the same time.[4] By means of play, we begin to be able to distinguish between ourselves and others, as well as making a vital distinction between fantasy and reality. By this process, we become a complete person with a healthy and stable sense of inner and outer worlds. For Lacan, gaining a notion of 'self' and 'other' is doom-laden, for Winnicott its acquisition is the psychological basis of a healthy life.

The existentialist philosopher, Jean-Paul Sartre, comes at the problem from another angle fusing outward and inward accounts of the development of self-awareness. Crucially he adds an heroic dimension, bestowing the self with the faculties of choice and control. He lays out his thoughts on the topic in his book, *St Genet: Actor and Martyr*.[5] Sartre proclaims Jean Genet to be the prototype of the 'existentialist man' whose distinctions between good and evil are the result of personal choices and decisions. In doing so, Sartre gives his account of how our sense of who we are is shaped as children and adults by people's reactions to us. It is what we do with the roles and identities that we are given, which matters to Sartre. We 'know' ourselves from the outside, he opines and gives a poignant account of how he became aware of himself as a little boy. He remembers his curls being cut for the first time as a toddler: it was only by his mother's reaction to his newly uncovered face that he realized that he was 'ugly'. Sartre does not stop there; he does not want the individual to remain a passive victim of prejudice. It is how we react to the way the world reacts to us that matters. This choice over our action is at the centre of his existentialism. Identity is the way in which the self engages with society. For Sartre, this engagement is not a neutral site but an arena in which we confound the identities thrust upon us in a struggle to create our 'authentic' selves. The black civil rights movement in the 1960s shared this existential insight and seized identity or 'image' as a battlefield along with the struggle for political power and legal emancipation: so did feminists and gay rights activists in their turn. Such activists saw socially constructed identities as limiting and there to be contested.

Picturing men: providers and warriors

In the mid-1990s, I began to explore masculinity or male identity along with a number of other artists in and around London. Building on the feminist agenda and two or three decades of identity politics, it seemed a good point for men to start thinking about how their identity as boys had been shaped by models of manhood and expectations as teenagers about how we should spend our lives. The visual arts seemed to have a key role in dealing with awareness, identity and image since spectating others and exhibiting ourselves play such a big part in forming our identity.

My Brilliant Career, a set of drawings, focuses on a key aspect of the social conditioning for men in our role as 'providers'. Using fantasy and humour, I wanted to provoke a debate about the pluses and minuses of the privileged access men have to professional life. The series charts the career from the playground to retirement.

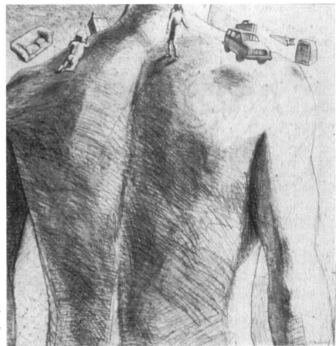

Fig. 19: *Responsibilities,* Mulvey, conte crayon on paper, 90 x 90cm, 1994.

Fig. 20: *Letting Go Over Acton: Wednesday Evening*, Mulvey, oil on canvas, 90 x 105cm, 1994.

Playground depicts the complex interweaving of life during 'breaktime' in a boy's school: the games, the fights, moments of intimacy and moments of isolation. A lot goes on in those frenzied gaps between lessons. Other drawings such as *Promotion* depicted moments with colleagues. *Responsibilities* and *Home/Work* looked at how men juggle work and family life. *Home/Work* looks at the double-career household. Finally, *Retirement: a sort of reward for something* looks at that dreaded moment for many men when the career ends.

Looking back now, this moment of reflection reflected in the creation of such work and gained its momentum from previous liberation movements, but adopting this 'liberation' legacy had its paradoxes. How could you speak of a 'liberation' movement for a group, namely men, who already had privileged access to resources in societies across the world? Were men oppressed and, if so, in what ways? Some of these contradictions needed to be analyzed, as will be seen in the section entitled 'Theoretical positions' below.

I came to see that *My Brilliant Career*, based as it was on watching my father and my uncles and my own career in art school management in the 1980s and 1990s, depicts the way things are for professional men. A question comes to mind. How did the freedom of boyhood change into the narrowness of adult life? I now wanted to create images that looked at how things could be different.

The *Letting Go* paintings and the *Free Fall*, a series of painted ovals, made for an exhibition at the Casa Elizalde in Barcelona, gave me the opportunity to explore pictorially how options might open up for men. The image of the falling or floating businessman and of things in flux tries to envisage the existential freedom that Sartre speaks of when all is to be decided and nothing is fixed. What would such a state of affairs feel like? The images try to encapsulate the mixture of exhilaration and fear that might ensue from such a realization: something like jumping out of an airplane with a parachute. The notion of a suspension of the rules of gravity in the home and in the office seemed to offer the possibility of things being up for grabs.

The *Office Hours* series mixes depictions of moments of quiet routine and absurd disruptions. *Monday Morning* and *Champ's Last Memo* are examples of such juxtapositions. Absurdity, disruption and incongruity are more ways of imagining futures opening up. In *Office Hours*, a formal incongruity accompanies the disruption of content: a monumental realist painting technique is used to represent the trivia of office life. Pictorial quotes from Renaissance and Baroque masterpieces are spliced into scenes of bureaucratic routine. The idea of religious visitations depicted in the lives of the saints offers a relief from routine. The pictures in *Office Hours* grow from daydreams to theatrical set-ups, which are shot on camera in a photographic studio. In the case of *Office Hours: Coffee break* – the set up is photographed on location with actors in a real office and then painted. The transition goes through a number of stages – from theatrical tableaux to photograph to drawing to oil painting. The length of the process is

Fig. 21: *Free Fall: briefcase*, Mulvey, oil on canvas 154 x 90cm, 2000.

important. Oil painting offers the possibility of depicting reality and fantasy with the same degree of palpability and this drawn out process gives time for the illusion to emerge and to be refined in terms of lighting, colour and focus.

Fig. 22: *Office Hours: Champ's Last Memo.* Mulvey, oil on canvas, 31 x 31cm, 2003.

Fig. 23: *Office Hours: Coffee Break.* Mulvey, oil on canvas, 35 x 35cm, 2005.

A pictorial model here is the sparse but eloquent scenes in Goya's *Caprichos*.[6] The psychologically taut compositions of Balthus and Rego are more contemporary models for what I was looking for. I wanted to picture a truth beyond and deeper than appearance: a kind of 'psychological realism'.[7]

These musings about loosening the ties of home and office life have given way more recently to a darker and sadder topic in my work. From the radical agendas for men that came out of the later 1980s and 1990s in publications like *Male Order: unwrapping masculinity*,[8] and magazines such as *Achilles Heel*, two overwhelming factors were identified as shaping men's lives which cut across class and nationality. These are the roles of 'provider' and 'warrior'. Much is made in criticizing men of their competitiveness, their aggression and their isolation. Little attention is given to how men, all men, are primed from childhood to be prepared in some form or other to kill other men and be killed, and to maim other men and be maimed. It lurks at the back of all men's minds. The focus on fighting in entertainment targeted at boys is still with us today and the readiness of some nations to send young men into battle is a startling reminder of how this aspect of many men's lives remains in place.

In a set of four paintings, entitled *Aftermath*, I look at this issue. These images are aimed at creating a pause in the media rush to move attention away from examining the consequences of military campaigns for the warriors themselves, their families and for society as a whole. The titles of the work in the set are *Counting the Cost: Iraq 2003*, *The Angel of History*, *Homecoming* and *Peace*.

The issue of war is rarely, if ever, connected with the fundamental role that militarization plays in shaping boys' identities as men. Notable exceptions are Mary Kelly's installation, *Gloria Patriae* and Paul Smith's digitally manipulated photograph series, *Artists Rifles*. Kelly looks at how the individual becomes invisible and lost in the uniform and insignia of rank and battalion. In *Artists Rifles* Smith looks at how his youthful sense of adventure was co-opted and manipulated

Fig. 24: *Artists Rifles*, Paul Smith, digitally manipulated photographs, 1993.

Fig. 25: *Make My Night*, Paul Smith, digitally manipulated photographs, 1998.

by the army. 'Joining up' for him as a working class teenager was a way of 'being a man'.[9] In *Make My Night* he looks at a drunken night out celebrating with his friends in his squad.

In a haunting and amusing way, Smith's digitally-manipulated photo-series deals with the dilemma of trying to be oneself and 'one of the lads' at one and the same time. In Sartre's terms, the hero in these photos struggles against losing his sense of self and having it replaced by a military identity – distinctive but anonymous. Being 'one of the pack' is made attractive by the loyalty and the camaraderie it offers. In these photographs, the battle is not with the enemy, which Smith tells us was always identified as the Russians when he was posted in Germany in the 1980s. The struggle is within the hero of the photographs himself. The battle is to make sure the teenager's courage and craving for a real meaning to his life is not taken from him and substituted by an inauthentic military persona.

Theoretical positions

In any issue-based art, the artist has to prepare the ground by choosing a theoretical position. The art is part of a greater purpose and not an end in itself. In dealing with issues of male identity in the 1990s, artists availed themselves of information from a variety of sources: women studies, the emerging gender studies, sociology, history, psychoanalysis, genetics and counselling. The development of critical practice courses in art schools undermined the old anti-intellectual tradition of art schools and saw the creation of generations of graduates who were at ease with image-making and theoretical analysis alike. Seminal examples of such courses are the Critical Theory course on the BA (Hon) Degree in Photography at the Polytechnic of Central London started by Victor Burgin in the 1970s and the BA (Hon) degree in Fine Art and Critical Theory at Central St Martins, established by Roy Trollope and Simon Pugh in the 1980s. However, the theoretical approaches listed above do not dovetail neatly and are frequently at odds with each other in explaining the nature of men and their behaviour. Decisions have to be made. The theory that artists choose to base their work on will depend on the political aims of their art. The historical, sociological and counselling sources that I drew together needed to have conceptual coherence to be of any use as a basis for creating images and curating exhibitions.

I was drawn to theories that offered the possibility of individual autonomy in Sartre's heroic sense. Certain strands within gender studies provided an analysis of the contents of male conditioning. In these accounts, male identity is socially and historically constructed, not genetically 'hard-wired'. Secondly, in line with the demands of Sartre's existential project outlined above, I was drawn to counselling theory and practice because it offered ways of freeing the individual from the constraints of social conditioning.

Victor Jelienewsky Seidler, Professor of Social Theory at Goldsmiths College, London University provided the most thorough analysis of the historical formation of European masculinity drawing on religious, philosophical and sociological accounts of the nature of men and women. In his paper, 'Image, Experience and Masculinities' he defines the dominant model of masculinity in western society tracing its origins in the religious and philosophical ends.[10] He describes a sense of manliness that is full of uncertainties and contradictions defined only in terms of what it is not – a sense of self only as distinct from others. In dealing with the multiplicity of masculinities, he describes a dominant form which defines itself against marginalized 'others', showing how men are conditioned to treat each other today is a construction that has developed over millennia.

A synopsis of these two papers gives Seidler's account of formulation of masculinity. He firstly focuses on dominant notions of male identity defined in terms of difference from women, children and nature. He then goes on in a later paper to look at the subject of 'man-to-man' relations in terms of a wide range of identities; class, race, religion, sexuality, geographical displacement and able-bodied-ness.[11] Seidler sees the dominant white Christian heterosexual masculinity alone at the centre of a new modern world as part of the imperial enterprise. As with women and children, these male 'others' are marginalized and are seen as closer to nature needing to be organized and spoken for.

Seidler traces a historical sequence of differences in the European tradition, which distinguishes those males within patriarchy from those outside it. According to the anti-Semitism of mediaeval Europe, the gentile, the Christian gentleman, saw the Jewish man as 'other', carnal Israel, blindly sensual and lacking in self-control. This early European model prefigures the enlightenment definition of man as superior to women and the white man to men of colour. As part of the colonial enterprise, these 'others' were to be exploited: to be 'made useful'.[12] Seidler refers to the work of bell hooks and her analysis of the complex relationship between the white man and women and the black man and women and the effects of the black man's exclusion from patriarchy.

To difference as inferior and exploitable, is added the notion of difference as threat. Fear of gay men becomes important because they bring to the surface inner uncertainties for the dominant heterosexual man. Seidler looks at accounts of masculinity at the turn of the century in which 'otherness' is represented as sickness. He sees such re-workings of European notions of masculinity as central to the developing ideologies of fascism and Nazism. Difference is considered to be a threat to order, civilization and genetic purity. Pathologized 'others' – Jews, gays, gypsies and the disabled – are seen as contagious and are, therefore, not just to be broken and exploited as part of an earlier imperial enterprise but destroyed.

References to difference, says Seidler, sit all too easily on the page unless we recognize how threatening images of difference are to the dominant culture and the whole project of modernity, which characterizes contemporary western history. He connects a detailed historical analysis of masculinity to the violent reality lived out by so many men, to the terror, rage and humiliation that are part of these identities. This historical analysis is part of a larger process of change and, for Seidler, connecting this analysis to everyday life is a crucial stage in this process. Being made aware of how boys and young men are brutalized as individuals is a vital part of disempowering the conditioning and confounding the stereotype.

This way of thinking about masculinity in the 1990s expressed in Seidler's work and the pages of *Achilles Heel* magazine would have been impossible without the insights provided by feminism and the black and gay liberation movements of the preceding decades. However, an intellectual grasp provided by these analyses does not automatically lead to the desired change in behaviour. Knowing that domestic violence is wrong does not lead to its elimination. The rapid grasp of these insights heralded by the radical men's literature of the 1980s and 1990s needs to be accompanied by a process in which individuals could 'undo' the conditioning to enable them to resist the pull to behave in certain ways when under pressure.

Re-evaluation counselling theory and practice offered an agenda for men that complemented the liberation agenda for women and brought the competing identities together in a coherent matrix. An integral part of such a programme was an understanding of the brutal process by which the conditioning becomes instilled in men, and a counselling practice that aimed at relieving the emotional hurts that keep the conditioning in place.[13] By being allowed to tell one's story in a non-judgemental setting and through the emotional catharsis that results – in terms of anger, tears and laughter – an individual can reclaim their inherent flexible intelligence. By means of such a process, Sartre's model, mentioned earlier, of the existential hero – whose distinctions between good and evil are the result of personal choices and decisions – becomes feasible.

Many useful projects were established beyond the art world using such theory and practice. Therapists and trainers employed in public and private institutions to address sexism in the work place used these methods to provide more effective teamwork. The insights gained from understanding the nature of male identity inform family mediation and contribute to the therapy used to help the perpetrators and victims of domestic violence. Today they underpin government initiatives set up to address problems in professions with 'macho' cultures, such as, the police force and the fire service.

However, in the art world things were different. Historically speaking the new understanding of masculinity, and its conditioning in the 1990s, was accompanied by a shift away from identity politics in galleries and funding bodies towards a more formalist and conceptual agenda. This was underpinned by an increasing adoption of post-structuralist theory by art institutions. The ethos of re-evaluation counselling with its postulations about the individual's inherent goodness and the ability to recover from the effects of social conditioning were antithetical to this theory.

Post-structuralism is characterized by a number of key positions: namely the problematization of the concept of the 'autonomous individual',[14] an emphasis on culturally determined accounts of behaviour and a resulting marginalization of ethics. All these stances distance it from the critical practice of the preceding decades. Thus, the heroism of Sartre's 'existentialist man' is rendered impossible and the promise of re-evaluation counselling to connect the empowerment of individuals with social justice is rendered naïve.

In many ways, post-structuralism provided an inappropriate theory for issue-based art, which aimed at enabling people to make choices about their lives. Theory as a basis for action had become 'over-theorized', easing the art world's shift from politics to aesthetics and conceptualism at the end of the twentieth century. The shift may be temporary. For some, post-structuralism still holds the possibility of oppositional politics. Jeffrey Weeks feels that the use of discourse theory does not lead inevitably to abandoning the idea of individual autonomy. Quite the opposite. In fact, it enables us to relocate the site of political action to identity itself. As he put it in discussing how the gay community should address the rampant homophobia caused by the Aids epidemic in the 1990s: 'Identity may be a historical fiction, a controlling myth. But it is at the same time a necessary means of weaving a way through the hazard-strewn world and a complex web of social relations.'[15]

Similarly, Gayatri Spivak offers a way forward for issue-based art and notions of the 'self in progress', by means of her concept of 'strategic essentialism'[16] – a means of using identity tactically.[17] More recently, Moya Lloyd in Beyond Identity Politics argues that the turn to the 'subject in progress' of post-structuralism does not entail the demise of feminist politics as many feminists have argued.[18] She rethinks ideas about subjectivity to open up spaces for political contestation.

As the women's movement of the 1970s allowed men to think about their lives in new ways, so now a contemporary re-engagement with feminism offers the possibility of continuing the development for men. The opening of the Elizabeth A. Sackler Centre for Feminist Art[19] and the Los Angeles Museum of Contemporary Art's exhibition, entitled 'WACK! Art and the Feminist Revolution', are examples of the plethora of feminist-related arts activities in the United States in 2007. This activity may herald a genuine revival of an interest in identity politics or just another faddish discussion topic for symposia and conferences. Amelia Jones' interview for frieze with the curator of the 'WACK!' show, Connie Butler, explores the complex legacy of feminism and looks at a re-engagement with gender issues in new ways for a younger generation of women artists.[20]

From guilt to empathy

Unknown to me at the time, my engagement with masculinity in the 1990s was part of a broader artistic movement in Australia and the United States. A history of exhibitions about masculinity in that decade reflects shifts in the broader debate on the topic. The first shows in 1991 in California, on campuses and in radical art centres in the San Francisco Bay area entitled 'No more heroes', 'Re-imaging Masculinity', and 'Articulating Disparity: renegotiating masculinity' set the ball rolling and broadly speaking came out of feminism.[21] Being a man was presented as something to feel guilty about. Male experience was seen as homogenous with a focus on heterosexual male stereotypes such as the boy scout, the soldier and the businessman.

Subsequent shows gave the debate greater depth by raising the issue of diversity. The Whitney Museum's 'Black Male' focused on gender and race and shows such as Michael Yamamoto's 'Meet Me in the Green Room' explored gender and sexuality and so a wider range of male experience began to be pictured. 'The Male Masquerade Show' at the List centre at MIT in 1995 reflected this growing sense of diversity and inclusion. However, there was still an emphasis on the horror story of the heterosexual bogeymen: installations of a teenage boy's bedroom with his war toys, sculptures of the chilling paraphernalia of military academies, a video of a phallocentric satyr and photographs of an immaculate corporate male and his sons. The only way to deal with the dominant forms of masculinity offered here is to stereotype them in revenge.

Notable exceptions in this exhibition were works by Michael Yue Tong and Keith Piper. Their images deal with the pressure and brutality involved in 'being a man' from the point of view of a feeling subject. Their pictures give a rare view from inside the stereotype of what it is like being caught up in the brutal processes of male conditioning. Their work enables others to empathize with those undergoing the processes by which boys and young men become separated from each other, and defensive, arrogant adults. Piper's video Go West Young Man[22] focuses on a struggle between father and son: set against a background image of bodies stacked in slave ships, the father tells the son about the terrible things that await him when he grows up and that he must prepare for.

Agendas and models for men

A post-structural gloom pervades the majority of the articles in the catalogue that accompanied 'The Male Masquerade Show' with two notable exceptions. Pieces by bell hooks and Simon Watney stand out as lone witnesses to the possibility of recovery and change for men. Watney has no time for doom-laden theorizing. Instead, he challenges artists to create more realistic images of HIV/AIDS so that those untouched by the epidemic can share the experience of those who are.

In 1995 art still had a role to play for Watney in undermining the vicious homophobia that was raised by the 'gay plague'.[23] He calls not only for images of illness and isolation but also for images of the rich fulfilment of gay men's lives. In a talk he gave in 1996 at an exhibition entitled 'Men and Masculinities' in London at Watermans Arts Centre, Watney held up the work of Felix Gonzalez-Torres as an example of one who pictured the tenderness and commitment between men who were coping with life-threatening illness and loss.[24] Art and exhibitions are vehicles by which marginalized men could share something important about their lives with society as a whole.

In her essay, 'Reconstructing Black Masculinity', bell hooks offers a model of how the analysis of masculinity can be linked to progress.[25] The essay focuses on black masculinity and the behaviour of black men in the United States but it is relevant to all men. hook's rejection of deterministic models of human behaviour is explicit in her challenge to black male celebrities to reject the misogyny and sexism of the black stereotypes of the 'playboy' and the 'drifter' so beloved of the white entertainment business. For hooks these caricatures of male behaviour are a burden to the black community and re-inscribe the phallocentrism of the dominant white culture, which, she maintains, a growing number of white men, in the wake of feminism, are attempting to throw off.

hook goes further and offers an alternative model from black culture for men to build on. The essay is dedicated to her brother, who never learned to be tough or hide his feelings, and a beloved and partially remembered and undocumented type of man from her childhood in the black segregated community in the rural south: the hobo. Involved in no permanent labour, these figures had time for contemplation and reverie and time to develop responsible and loving relationships with women and children. In doing so, they subverted norms, repudiated patriarchy, and its concomitant sexism and developed new ways of thinking about masculinity.

For hooks there is in the lives of these men a basis on which to develop a notion of masculinity that has existential authenticity beyond homophobia, sexism and 'adultism' in which men are able to remain connected to themselves, other men, women and children.

Re-thinking men's lives: a long-term project

There is a major problem. The vicissitudes of the art world – driven by commercial pressures and topical agendas – do not favour a sustained project that deals with the complexities of a topic such as men and male identity. The development of art research in universities in the United Kingdom offers a more conducive setting. However, because it draws its benchmarks of excellence from the art institutions and commercial galleries, art research in academic institutions runs the risk of being compromized by the very same vicissitudes.

It is not surprising that one of the most profound and radical developments in modern art was accomplished by an artist, namely Cézanne, working in deliberate isolation. His search to find a new way of representing space and form in painting was accomplished over a period of thirty years supported by personal wealth and a correspondence network of valued peers but, crucially, a long way from the artistic hubbub of the French capital. Is it possible to have sustained research campaigns in the art world similar to those that characterize other disciplines such as sociology, economics and science?

The exhibitions about men in the 1990s described in this chapter were all shown in art galleries. An important development would be to locate exhibitions about men in relevant spaces outside the gallery, such as war museums and sports halls where the issue of gender already has a high profile. The Museum at the Scott Polar Research Institute in Cambridge, for example, is a place in which powerful elements of manliness such as adventure, endurance and empire, are brought together and enshrined. Memorabilia such as the little pencilled note from the dying Scott scribbled to his son back in England bear further reflection. Here is an opportunity for a fresh look at 'heroism' and how its social construction drives and shapes human endeavour. In Scott's case lying in his tent in the wastes of Antarctica, being heroic drove his behaviour up to the very moment of extinction. Images would be an effective way of reflecting on these issues and offering ways of re-imagining heroism.

The mechanics of spectating

Earlier in this chapter, I wrote that issue-based art such as we are dealing with here, is part of a greater purpose and not an end in itself. This thought should shape the images and the curation, but it also needs to include the effects we want to achieve in the viewer's response. The 'art for art's sake' tradition of western art not only places aesthetic considerations at the centre of practice to the exclusion of all else, but it is also accompanied by a reluctance to be concerned with the response of the viewer. According to this philosophy, art should not have a message nor should the artist preach. If you want to have art with messages, goes the much-quoted cry of the abstract expressionists, use the Bell Telephone Company.

Issue-based art by its nature has to be concerned with the effect of the work on the viewer as an integral part of its practice. Too often artists and curators promote an exhibition as 'enabling the audience to focus on' this or that issue, but very rarely do they find out whether any such focusing takes place. By and large, the professionals of the art world talk to each other at openings and may do little more than read the comments book to elicit feedback.

My involvement with the Cambridge 'Open Studio' programme over the past eight years has given me a chance to watch how people respond to pictures. At the beginning, I was keen to steer audience attention in a particular direction by supplying texts to accompany the exhibition. Over the years as I witnessed the discussions among the public about the work on show I have become more and more aware of the creative way people react to pictures. I have become conscious of the process by which viewers enter the imaginative space of the painting in order to fulfil needs of their own.

We need to re-think the way people enjoy and make use of images. I have noticed with the Open Studios that pictures seem to be vehicles that viewers take to go on narrative journeys of their own unhindered by 'correct' readings or predetermined responses. A landscape or still life will offer harmony and balance and by doing so will contrast with inner turmoil the viewer may feel inside. Thus, the viewer is moved by the painting due to the variety of possible meanings. Images provide the mind with the raw material for infinite paths of flight.

According to psychoanalytic theory, the mind is always seeking to resolve its distress in whatever ways it has to hand. The child psychologist, Donald Winnicott, watching children playing, noticed that the play the child became engaged in was not for pleasure alone but had therapeutic intent.[26] Accordingly, the seemingly random daydreams prompted by a picture are driven by some mental purpose. There is, therefore, a relationship between counselling and looking at art. The counsellor asks questions aimed at helping the client to look at painful memories. Alternatively, suggestions may be made that allow the client's attention to soar to new, unaccustomed heights.

The picture could be seen as a visual manifestation of this process: questioning, giving permission and perhaps restoring the viewer's peace of mind. With better understanding this process of spectating could be harnessed as part of a strategy aimed not merely at the re-evaluation of the viewer's individual life but aimed at enabling individuals to reconsider and transcend the social groups they find themselves placed in or 'identities' they have thrust upon them.

I have since dispensed with gallery notes in the Open Studios, reducing the written content to a title deployed as a counterpoint to the image, hinting at possible readings of the image. Gallery workshops are a good opportunity for the artist to listen and find out how the work and the audience engage with each other. These encounters are not opportunities for instruction and explanation but a chance for the artists to gather feedback and gauge how their practice might be adjusted to achieve desired results. Business studies models developed to assess whether training events lead to long-term changes in participants' behaviour may offer promising expertise here.

In creating images, which enable people to understand the ways men are conditioned and help viewers to imagine future possibilities a number of key issues need to be considered. The artist has to judge the ideas that form the basis of the image, the images themselves and the how and where they are displayed. The 1980s added critical theory to the artist's armoury; the 1990s, marketing skills. In the twenty-first century understanding, the mechanics of spectating and being able to measure audience response should be a vital part of the issue-based artist's practice.

Notes

1. Wisnowsky, R. (2005), *Avicenna's metaphysics in context*, London: Duckworth and Co.
2. Grayling, A,C. (2006), *Descartes: the life and times of a genius*, 1st Edition, New York: Walker Company.
3. Lacan, J., Millar, J-A., Sheridan, A. (2004), *The Four Fundamental Concepts of Psycho-analysis*, London: Karnac Books.
4. Winnicott, D. W. (2005), *Playing and Reality*, London: Routledge.
5. Sartre, J-P. (1963), *St Genet: Actor and Martyr*, (trans.) Frechtman, B., New York: George Braziller.
6. Goya's etching series entitled *Caprichos* provide the viewer with a series of small tableau in which significant scenes are acted out by a small group of players. The pictorial format is pared down to a few protagonists set against a vestigial landscape: a tree, distant hills and sky. The viewer is forced to focus on the scene which could be a fantastic metaphor, such as donkeys riding men (Capricho no.42 *Tu que no puedes*), or elsewhere a realist glimpse of urban life in eighteenth century Madrid (Capricho no.27 *Quien mas rendido?*). This dark visual distillation contrasts with the comedy and busy details of English and Dutch eighteenth century prints.
7. The term 'psychological realism' is coined here to identify an element in contemporary narrative painting which tries to depict the reality of the way a person feels about the situation they find themselves in rather than the appearance of the scene. I prefer this term to 'surrealism' or 'magic realism' as there is an emphasis on the irrational in the first and an arbitrary element implied by the use of 'magic' in the second. Our feelings are real and not random or mystical. The way a scene is re-interpreted by the artist in 'psychological realism' is driven by a need to expose an underlying psychological fact. Examples of this type of picture are Balthus' portrait *The Blanchard Children* (1937) and Paula Rego's *The Family* (1988). Many more examples can be found in the work of the North American painters, for example, Edward Hopper and Eric Fischl.
8. Rutherford, J., Chapman, R., (eds.) (1988), *Male Order: Unwrapping Masculinity*, 1st Edition, London: Lawrence and Wishart.

9. This reference is a quote from an unpublished research seminar paper Paul Smith gave on his work at Anglia Ruskin University as part of the 'Identity, Representation and the Body' Research Group Presentation, 17 January 2008.

10. Seidler, V.J. (1996), 'Image Experience and Masculinities' in Mulvey, J.F., Joiner, B.S. (1996), *Men and Masculinities*, London: University of Westminster, pp. 3–9.

11. Seidler, V.J. (1999), 'Images, Masculinities and Difference' in Mulvey J.F., Joiner B.S. (1999), *Machos y munecas: images of masculinity*, London: University of Westminster, pp. 20–9.

12. ibid.

13. Jackins, H., et al. (1999), *The Human Male: A Men's Liberation Draft Policy*, 1st Edition, Seattle: Rational Island Publishers.

14. A number of post-structuralist writers, such as Foucault and Derrida, placed an increasing attention in their writing on the way an individual's behaviour was driven by their social conditioning. Less emphasis was placed on the subject's ability to contest this conditioning. These post-structural models of humanity exemplified by Foucault's late text, 'Technologies of Self' give little or no space to the idea of an autonomous stable subject on which identity politics and the hope of improving society depend.

15. Weeks, J. (1991), *Against Nature: Essay on History, Sexuality and Identity*, 1st Edition, London: Rivers Oram Press, p. 85.

16. There is, however, a way in which identity politics and post-structural theory can be reconciled. In her book, *Beyond Identity Politics*, Moya Lloyd looks at the problem created when political movements are based on identity. These movements have relied on the idea of a stable, sovereign subject for their political dynamism. As we have seen, the post-structural idea of the subject-in-progress, formed culturally, saturated and determined by power-relations, raises a problem for activist movements. Who or what is the 'we' the movement is fighting for? Instead of seeing the post-structural 'unstable' subject as a problem for activists, Lloyd sees it as offering the possibility of more effective forms of 'essentialism' elaborated in her review of the work of the Subaltern Studies Group. According to Spivak, politics creates the sites in which struggles have to take place. There is nothing essential or permanent about black, gay or female identities but they are, for the time being, the culturally formed arenas within which oppression operates and battles have to be won. Spivak argues for an 'operational' or 'strategic' essentialism which is neither completely essentialist nor anti-essentialist but which synthesizes the post-structural understanding of self and the activists' demand for political solidarity. Spivak, Gayatri Chakravotry (1988), 'Subaltern Studies deconstructing historiography' in Spivak, Gayatri Chakravotry, *In other Worlds: Essays in Cultural Politics*, New York: Routledge, pp. 197–221.

17. Spivak, G. C. (2000), 'Feminism and Critical Theory' in Lodge, D.,Wood, N. (eds.), *Modern Criticism and Theory: A Reader*, 2nd Edition, UK and New York: Longman, pp. 475–93.

18. Lloyd, M. (2005), *Beyond Identity Politics: Feminism, Power and Politics*, 1st Edition, London: Sage.

19. Elizabeth A. Sackler Gallery; Centre for Feminist Art at the Brooklyn Museum, New York. The centre, opened in 2007, is an exhibition space and educational facility dedicated to feminist art: its past, its present and its future.

20. Jones, A. (2007), 'History Makers', in Higgle, J. (ed.), *freize*, Issue 105, March 2007, pp. 134–9.

21. 'No more heroes: unveiling masculinity' 1991 at the SF Gallery San Francisco California; 'Reimaging Masculinity' September 1991 at the WORKS Gallery, San Francisco, California; 'Articulating

Disparities: renegotiating masculinity' at the Gallery 1 San Jose State University, San Jose, California, 10 September–10 October 1991. These three San Francisco Bay area shows were organized by Barbara Degenevieve. Her account is written up in her article 'Unveiling Masculinity at the SF Gallery', *Art Issues*, January 1992.

22. Keith Piper's animation *Go West Young Man* was made in 1996 and lasts 3 minutes and 42 seconds, and was shown in at the Ikon Gallery in Birmingham in 1998, in a solo exhibition of the artist's work entitled, 'Relocating the Remains'.

23. Watney, S. (1995), 'Lifelike: Imaging the bodies of people with Aids' in Perchuck, A., Posner, H., *The Masculine Masquerade*, Massachusetts: MIT, pp. 63–69.

24. Watney, S. (1996), *Men, Sadness and Redemption,* a paper given at 'Men and Masculinities' conference held at the Waterman's Centre, London, 11 October 1996. These unpublished papers are held in the Male Identity Group Archive at Anglia Ruskin University.

25. Hooks, B. (1995), 'Reconstructing Black Masculinity' in Perchuck, A., Posner, H. *The Masculine Masquerade*, Massachusetts: MIT, pp. 69–89.

26. Winnicott, D.W. (2005), *Playing and Reality*, London: Routledge.

11

Haptic Visuality: The Dissective View in Performance

Gianna Bouchard

This chapter examines the staging and representation of the anatomized body in contemporary performance. Exploring the dynamics of touch in systems of representation, this chapter asserts that the anatomized and opened body de-stabilizes and even ruptures the representational strategies within which it is situated. It argues that these ruptures occur around the excessive nature of the opened body and that, in certain instances, the frame of representation cannot contain or sustain these sights without altering them. Through focusing on a work by Caravaggio and a performance piece by Annie Sprinkle, the chapter considers the possibility of vision becoming like touch in certain instances of representation, where a haptic encounter seems to be produced for the spectator, and asks what is at stake when these moments occur.

Michelangelo Caravaggio's painting of 1603, titled *The Incredulity of Saint Thomas*,[1] depicts one scene from the New Testament biblical narrative concerned with the resurrection of Christ, described in detail in the Gospel of John. Following his crucifixion, Christ appears to the disciples and reveals the wounds of the crucifixion as proof of his identity, death and resurrection. For reasons not articulated in the narrative, Thomas, another disciple, was not amongst them for this visitation. Unable to accept on faith what his fellow apostles describe, Thomas demands proof of his own before acknowledging the truth of the resurrection: 'Except I shall see in his hands the print of the nails, and put my finger into the place of the nails, and put my hand into his side, I will not believe.'[2] He desires to touch and explore Christ's wounds and only by thus invading the body interior, by mimicking the trajectories of the penetrating objects through firstly vision and then tactility, will Thomas concede the miracle of the resurrection. For Thomas at least, seeing is not fully believing.

Fig. 26: Michelangelo Caravaggio, *The Incredulity of Saint Thomas*, 1603.

Some eight days later, Christ again appears to the disciples and Thomas, this time amongst their number, is invited by Christ to dispel his scepticism: 'Put in thy finger hither, and see my hands. And bring hither thy hand, and put it into my side: and be not faithless but believing.'[3] Here, there is a strange aporia in the text, for it is not clear whether or not Thomas does touch any of the wounds or whether the sight of the dead Christ embodied is simply enough to dispel his doubt. He moves instantaneously from seeking tactile empirical evidence to articulating a rhetoric of belief: 'My Lord and my God' is his only reply, according to the narrative.[4] In religious iconography of the scene, however, the aporia in the text is often negated in favour of a Thomas who is compelled to make contact with the wound. Caravaggio likewise makes no bones about the aporia – Thomas impinges upon the marks of the crucifixion by plunging his finger into the spear wound on Christ's torso, guided there by the touch of the resurrected man himself and embedded in the flesh.

Thomas invades this particular wound, located within the painted image, for the purpose of interrogation: it will be a conversion of thought and belief from one path to another through testing the evidence of the body before him. Proof of the resurrection is here, supposedly, verified by sight of the wound and an intimate tactile penetration of its boundaries. Taking my lead from Thomas in Caravaggio's painting, who occupies a central viewing position in relation to Christ's body, I am going to interrogate a radically different spectatorial response from that of a passive on-looker and discuss what happens when we are invited to consider the body in close proximity.

Although the image is not explicitly one of medicalized anatomical dissection, it parallels many of the same concerns inherent in the dissective scene and opens onto some provocative questions. I am going to consider touch as an integral part of the dynamics of corporeal intervention through the incision or opening within representational structures – Thomas's literal pointing into the wound. The tactility of dissection will be explored through the slide between vision and touch that this image seems to offer. I will then seek to identify a haptic encounter in performance and ask what is at stake when these instances occur. To speak of haptics in relation to theatre and performance may seem fruitless, as a dynamic that theatre cannot replicate. I want to argue, however, that there are instances when performance can and does, approximate this experience.

In order to undertake an interrogation similar in nature to that of Thomas's in terms of beginning with a surface that can then be critically incised and lifted for deeper insights, the painted plane needs to be considered as only a first layer or membrane, covering that which exists under it. I am suggesting that the surface is viewed, therefore, as a kind of 'skin' – the delineation of which will enable the depth analysis to be effectual and sustainable. The metaphor is not an uncommon one amongst those considering art and the sensate. Richard Shiff asks how 'the visual arts of painting and sculpture actually operate' and answers that they 'are media of surface appearance. Yet they also extend beyond the visual effects of the surface, as if to lead through the skin to the flesh.'[5] Artists themselves have often been preoccupied with this notion, deliberately manipulating the canvas to imitate flesh and woundings more closely. Anish Kapoor, for instance, created an incision through the material surface of the artwork in *The Healing of Saint Thomas*, 1989, that evokes the wound of Christ found in Caravaggio's painting. The viewer is only aware of this literal cut in the surface when they position themselves anamorphically to the work, where the depth of the incision can be perceived in a way that is denied by a normative viewing point.

Didier Anzieu undertook a rigorous analysis of the skin, from a psychoanalytical perspective, that pared the skin's functions down to the following three principal capacities:

> The primary function of the skin is as the sac which contains and retains...Its second function is as the interface which marks the boundary with the outside and keeps that outside out; it is the barrier which protects against penetration...Finally, the third function... is as a site and a primary means of communication with others, of establishing signifying relations; it is, moreover, an 'inscribing surface' for the marks left by those others.[6]

These insights appear transferable to a contemplation of the surface of the Caravaggio painting. Where this two-dimensional plane contains and protects the pictorial detail, it provides a clear boundary between representation and reality, whilst being inscribed with a picture that communicates with the spectator. The surface acts as a point of interface and communication between viewers and viewed.

The 'skin' of the image consists of the materiality of paint, the oils in this case, selected by the artist and applied in such a way as to invoke pictorial details of a specific scene, and the canvas upon which the paint adheres. The realism of the image, however, serves to draw attention away from the physicality of paint and the brushstrokes employed in its creation. This becomes more apparent when looking at reproductions of the image, whose glossy surfaces smooth all the texture and materiality of the picture. Both the mechanisms and 'work' of painting at the surface of the canvas are somehow obfuscated by the form and content, so that the viewer is not fully aware of its painterly constructions, or if they are, it is only peripherally. It is as though a perceptual switch has to occur in the viewer in order to address its materiality and form. What is at the centre of viewing, the focus, pushes its alternate to the periphery. In other words, if viewing is focused on the pictorial details, perception is only vaguely aware of the paint and its operations, whilst if one concentrates on the paint and its physicality, one loses focus on the content.

James Elkins, art theorist and critic, discusses viewing positions for the spectator of the artwork and associates those positions with our perceptions of relations between bodies and scale. For instance, he describes a 'normative distance' from a painting as 'conversational', meaning that it roughly equates to the distance one would stand 'from a person to whom I am talking'.[7] For those pictures complying with the perspective schema, such as Caravaggio's, Elkins suggests that his positional 'choices are quite clear: either I walk close up to one of his paintings and try to see how it was done, or I can stand back near the place specified by the perspectival or structural cues in the picture.'[8] He points out that perspectival viewing positions are 'usually within touching distance of the painting because they correspond with the distances from which the painting was made', drawing it back to his idea of a relation between bodies and paintings that echo interpersonal relations with each other.[9]

As part of his work on relations between body and picture, Elkins draws up a schematic list of viewing positions for the spectator of the image, ranging from his definition of the 'myopic', which is deliberately too close to the surface, to its exact opposite; the 'hyperopic', which sites the viewer too far away from the painting to gain much insight.[10] He describes these extreme positions as 'improper' and identifies them as ways of 'spying on the painting, seeing it from places it does not sanction.'[11] This usurpation of normative viewing positions allows the spectator to begin to unravel the illusions at work in the picture, to see below or beyond the surface communication.

Elkins more fully explicates the 'myopic' viewing positions as determinedly 'pathological or medical' and, as such, 'beyond the bounds of common human intercourse'.[12] The pathological viewing position refuses the normative in favour of a fragmented, partial and, to a certain extent, decontextualized sight of picture/object/body. The spectator can choose to occupy such a position in relation to the painting by moving towards the surface and eventually being in extreme proximity to its physical form. In a similar kinaesthetic movement, Thomas himself, within the representation, stoops towards such a myopic or pathological relation to the flesh and, more accurately, the wound. We could infer that he seeks a 'better' view but perhaps it is an essentially different viewpoint that he now occupies, that is not necessarily advantageous but problematic in its proximity. His myopic position doubles the viewer's approach to the painting as both figures desire the details to come into focus but perhaps there is a fundamental shift in perception at this point for Thomas and spectator.

Close proximity to the object of study, allied with intense looking found a new emphasis during the early modern period as the scientific methodology of empiricism took root, focusing on observation and sensate knowledge as 'truthful' providers of requisite knowledge. The importance of keen observation around the pathologized body had been signalled by Hippocrates as the most fundamental diagnostic tool for the medic, taking in both the body's immediate environment and its physical appearance, symptoms and excretions. With the birth of dissection as a public and sanctioned event from the fourteenth century onwards, the sense of sight as a revealer of truths and knowledge took on an even more significant role. Reflecting upon the influence of science on art and constructions of the self during this period, Jonathan Sawday suggests that these revived concerns did not escape the notice of the artist:

> in this image...Caravaggio also seemed to be responding to a new emphasis, in the realm of science or natural philosophy, on the vital importance of personal experience of the phenomena which were under investigation. In the field of medicine and anatomy, such a stress on direct, visual, sensory experience at the expense of the textual...involved the cultivation of 'autopsia' – literally, seeing for oneself.[13]

Not only then does Caravaggio produce an image reflective of 'surgical detail' in its attention to anatomy, but Thomas occupies the new place of looking being investigated by artist and physician. As representation and display is progressively given more status within the medical faculty as a means of underpinning and demonstrating textual accounts of the body, so the exact 'how' of looking comes under scrutiny.

It is my contention, however, that such pathologized bodies and viewing perspectives demand more from their viewers than vision alone can provide. Surely, also, there is a fascination with the myopic viewing position – we desire the collapse of scopic and tactile distance. As the interior is revealed, so the adage 'seeing is believing' seems to fade into insignificance, epitomized by Thomas who is not content to simply look on the resurrected Christ within the pictorial frame. Thomas claims in the narrative that his doubt can only be negated through direct tactile contact with the wounds of the crucifixion found on Christ's feet, hands and chest. In the painting, he pursues this desire to the point where he inserts his finger into the trauma caused by the soldier's spear. Thus, the wound requires more than visual affirmation to instil belief within its representation – the tactile is incorporated as final arbiter. Touch is the significant sense here, implying that doubt must be worked through by establishing an epistemology of the sensate to reach understanding.

In the image, it is vital to note, however, that Thomas is the figure who touches and is touched, not the viewer, who can only see the touch, in the same way as the dissector has the authority to touch and dismember whilst spectators can only watch these actions and sensations. Somehow, sight of the interrogative touch of Thomas must suffice to create or sustain belief in the resurrection for the spectator, or does it? I want to explore the possibility that, far from being mutually exclusive senses, vision and touch may slide into each other at certain moments, so that vision itself becomes, in a sense, tactile.

The idea of the haptic and its relation to representation can be traced historically to the work of Alois Riegl, a prominent art historian in the nineteenth century (1858–1905) who specialized in researching the art of classical civilizations and the early modern period. He developed the notion of two different modes of vision available to the spectator: 'the near or haptic, is analogous to the sense of touch in the way that it must synthesize mentally a number of discontinuous sensory inputs. The distant or optic view, on the contrary, takes in a synoptic survey of objects in space.'[14]

Unlike Elkins, Riegl did not set these differentiations into a hierarchical order of success, with the haptic identified as problematic, but he rather argued for a 'schematic history and typology of style based on a progression from the near to distant view, that is, from Egyptian art to impressionism.'[15] This avoidance of privileging the distant, normative view established by perspective has continued to be reflected in work on haptics, where critics have employed its tactics to negate the mastery of the viewer implicit in traditional understandings of optical relationships. Hence, Laura Marks's interest in its potential as a tool, in more marginalized film work, for undermining dominant ideologies and representational strategies. She claims the haptic as a device for subverting visual dominance in favour of a relation 'between viewer and image' that is predicated on 'mutuality' in a manner that resonates with phenomenological explanations of perception and embodied engagement with the world.[16] But what is haptic visuality and how does it operate?[17]

For Marks, haptic visuality means, 'the eyes themselves function like organs of touch' because of their proximity to the object.[18] In entering into a more proximate dynamic with the image, the viewer negates the illusions of representational strategies, which leaves vision to traverse the surface planes of the image, to perceive texture and materiality rather than depth or form.[19] Intrinsically connected to this visuality is its relationship with the body of the viewer that engages both 'touch and kinaesthetics' more than is usual in traditional optical dynamics.[20] So, the analysis laid out previously, concerned with perceptual shifts and kinaesthetic motion, here becomes identifiable with aspects of haptic visuality.

As distance between image and viewer collapses, so do distinctions between subject and object that usually define relations between art and spectator. Instead, there emerges a reciprocal engagement in which the viewer 'relinquishes her own sense of separateness from the image' to succumb to its perceptual intricacies and detail.[21] In close proximity to the artwork it becomes difficult to identify any interstices between viewer and surface as the communicative interfaces of both skin and canvas open themselves to a melded interchange. For the viewer, this sensation of indistinguishable elements stems from a proximity that negates the possibility of defining edges or boundaries to the object as the eyes are seemingly surrounded by infinite surface. Content and illusionary definition are too near to the eyes to be normatively perceived or comprehended, rather the eyes flick across the surface rapidly, taking in its materiality and 'feel', operating in an analogous mode to touch.

Haptic visuality can also be encouraged by the artwork itself in Marks's analysis, stimulating this visual intimacy over surfaces by creating 'an image of such detail, sometimes through miniaturism, that it evades a distanced view, instead pulling the viewer in close.'[22] She goes on to examine various filmic instances of such incitement to the haptic, where a film focuses on extreme close-ups of its objects that over-ride visual comprehension, leaving the eyes to engage with texture and substance rather than narrative form and content. This is precisely the point where Marks believes that haptic images open alternate potentialities within filmic discourse, slipping away from more dominant modes of viewing and subjectivity into this reciprocal space, where meaning is more indeterminate and shifting.

Although Marks has produced an analysis concerned with filmic haptics, her sources are derived from visual art theory and such analyses are useful in opening questions around the Caravaggio image. By filling in the aporia in the Biblical narrative with Thomas's finger (in the Biblical text it is ambiguous as to whether Thomas does actually touch Christ), Caravaggio explicitly introduces tactility within surrounding structures of vision. At the very heart of vision and its operations, Caravaggio intercedes powerfully and unreservedly with touch, penetrating these edifices and pointing towards their inadequacies as potential guarantors of meaning or stability within representation. Paradoxically then, the central focus in this visual representation is touch – the immediate tactile contact between two bodies that the spectator can seemingly only watch from a distance. This touch that is another's, has to be seen and comprehended visually so that belief in this moment is allegedly reinforced.

With vision usurped so poignantly at the very centre of the image and its structures, a slippage into the haptic is offered as a potential mode of sensuous and perceptual exchange, both between Thomas and Christ and between image and viewer. Clearly, Thomas adopts a haptic stance in relation to the wound, taking a 'near' view to the surface of the body where the details of the physical trauma as an intervention into the flesh will dominate his vision. Desire for haptic visuality draws him close to the wound site, for it is not Christ as a whole entity or complete form that interests him, but just the site/sight of the incision. At this proximity he has, to some extent, lost his awareness of this wholeness in favour of the partial view that concerns itself with surface and materiality. Any structures of illusion created by Christ's physical embodiment is passed through in the approach from distance to closeness to situate the gaze on the minutiae of the wound as the provider of proof and resolution of scepticism. I want to argue that the touch of Thomas and the instance of haptic visuality enables the spectator to likewise experience this moment haptically and thus belief is strengthened in this enabled space of mutual perceptual intertwining. Seeing the touch becomes more significant when vision becomes tactile but I am not sure that it strengthens the supposed theological narrative of the painting.

The image is not perhaps Marks's ideal paradigm of a haptic work in that it offers more to view than pure surface through extreme close-up, but there are structures and forms operating here that are resonant with haptic images. For instance, the whole painting is compositionally focused on the physicality of surfaces, from the detailed depictions of draped and falling fabric to the various exposed areas of flesh, which pivot between the excessively undulating brow of Thomas to the smooth firmness of Christ's chest. This concentration on materiality provokes in the spectator an awareness of tactile experience that is then exacerbated by the insertion of the finger through the surface. Suddenly the viewer is plunged deeper than the surface into the wound that opens itself beneath or beyond. Thomas foregoes an interrogation even of the wound's façade, which could be overwhelming in its pathological substance, and seeks instead internal contact. Interestingly, Caravaggio has circumvented this potential for looking on the physical trauma of 'stabbing' by rendering sterile and perfect the site of the intervention. The wound edges are clean, enveloping Thomas's finger within its gently folded opening. This again seems to emphasize the tactility of the touch that enters within the body by making its penetration explicitly visible. Once more, the image instigates a slide in perception between touch and sight.

Haptic understandings of representation, as already noted, depend upon a proximal relation between viewer and viewed that Elkins has described as pathological because of its direct problematization of normative viewpoints. Although Elkins does articulate his schema based upon kinaesthetic action in relation to paintings, the viewer's walking to and from the canvas, haptic visuality is not always predicated on actual proximity. Positions for haptic responses are focused too closely on the surface to be able to interpret form or composition as delineated by geometric constructions of perspectival space. Although Caravaggio has utilized such formulaic compositional rules in this painting he has also seemingly established a dialectical tension between the two positions that encourages the viewer to explore both. There are obvious factors at work here that draw the viewer in closer to the surface whilst also offering the illusion of depth and vanishing point. Something about the physical stance of the depicted figures – their intense focus on the touch that manifests itself in imaged embodied reactions to its occurrence – encourages a similarly embodied and kinaesthetic counterpoise in the viewer.

Part of the spectator's desire for a mutuality of physical engagement with the body of Christ is that 'the issue of rivalry is not only physical but also *visual*', according to Bal.[23] She argues that 'difficult visual access is stimulating: it enhances desire, and visual attention.'[24] Not only then is the view being obfuscated but the displayed body is being penetrated in a homoerotic gesture of necrophilic love. The viewer is positioned to occupy the remaining space within its frame, to close the circle of looking and desire around the wound, as well as to encourage the viewer to want to touch. Of course, this action is impossible but optical visuality can now be exchanged for the haptic, allowing the viewer to sense the touch through vision at least.

These various openings onto haptic perception through the image permit the viewer to access the touch sensuously as an embodied awareness. There seems to be an implicit acknowledgement from Caravaggio that just as Thomas is not content with visual proof alone, there is the possibility that it does not suffice for the viewer either. By creating haptic opportunities, the viewer is able to perceive the touch visually by engaging with its detail and materiality, by studying the uncomfortable stretching of the wound that enables the penetration. By drawing close to the surface, the eyes are permitted to rove over these fleshy folds and openings that negate narrative in favour of perceptual awareness of tactile experience and feeling. This affect, then, replicates doubt, by undermining the story and providing a fundamentally different experience. Moving into a mutual intertwining with the image, where sight is overwhelmed by the physical presence surrounding it, the touch of Thomas becomes a moment of reciprocal touching. The touch is reinforced by the potential for a mutuality of touching through haptic visuality, thus we can not only see the touch, but sensuously perceive the touch through vision.

In her study Marks makes the following important statement:

> haptic visuality inspires an acute awareness that the thing seen evades vision and must be approached through other senses...Haptic visuality implies a fundamental mourning of the absent object or the absent body...it acknowledges that it cannot know the other.[25]

As a result of proximity to the surface and materiality of the object or image, haptic visuality offers the viewer only indirect access to knowledge, so that understanding is not provided 'about' the object but 'nearby' or next to it, in a metaphorical shift of perspective.[26] Unable to deliver concrete knowledge around content, haptics produces other readings and interpretations that are not concerned with total analytical control. It opens instead a 'power of approaching its object with only the desire to caress it, not to lay it bare.'[27] Haptics relinquishes the desire for control and mastery over the object of vision, so that a reciprocal exchange can occur that denies the binary opposition of subject and object.

It seems that these claims by Marks are borne out in the image of doubting Thomas, which captures a moment of haptic engagement with the resurrected body. From the first time he is told of Christ's return from death, Thomas denies the power of vision to prove the legitimacy of its occurrence, demanding tactile contact as his material of proof. He will only concede the miracle if he can both see and touch the body in question, thereby acknowledging Marks's contention that somehow the thing seen carries the potential of eschewing vision.

In thinking about theatre and performance practice, my sense is that, similarly to Marks and her interrogation of film, the haptic and haptic visuality operate as structuring principles within performance practice and that when they do appear as sensory opportunities they simultaneously open out new perceptions in the viewer and elicit particular problematics around the body on the stage. It is my contention that moments of haptic visuality within performance have an equally powerful potential to subvert conventional representational and visual strategies that

Marks finds in filmic instances and that have been explored in relation to the Caravaggio image.

The particular performance that I want to consider in terms of haptics is a section of Annie Sprinkle's show *Post Porn Modernist* (1989) called 'A Public Cervix Announcement'. Sprinkle is an American performance artist, whose career as both a prostitute and a porn star informs her practice through the development of autobiographical pieces that focus on her life and experiences. Her body troubles the theatrical frame and worries at conservative distinctions between art and pornography. In staging her body, she challenges dominant regimes of vision and representation with excess and revelatory sight of her female body.

She adopts a medico-scientific frame for this part of the performance, which begins with Sprinkle lecturing to the audience on the location and function of each part of the female genitalia, which she illustrates with the use of a sketch of the female anatomy. Image and text intermingle within this introductory mini-lecture in a manner that Sprinkle hopes will begin to demystify the female body by establishing objective and scientific 'truths' about its nature. Just as anatomists claim the value of actually seeing these realities revealed in the dissected body, so Sprinkle encourages a similarly immediate and proximal engagement with her genitalia that emphasizes vision as a perceptual and epistemological tool for the spectator. Here I want to suggest also the possibility that she not only invites a visual encounter but her performance opens onto elements of haptic visuality that provoke mixed interpretations and reactions to this piece.

Following the lecture on the female genitalia, Sprinkle would labour 'in the awkward project of inserting' a speculum into her vagina whilst announcing that audience members could come to the stage and look at her cervix, previously identified diagrammatically and now to be on show physically.[28] Spectators formed a queue in the auditorium, monitored by ushers, each taking it in turn to see her cervix: 'There Annie sat, legs spread, inviting the audience to peek inside her with the aid of a flashlight.'[29]

Sprinkle's use of a speculum in 'A Public Cervix Announcement' is of particular interest here as an instrument specifically associated with the medical establishment. Designed to enhance visibility within the body through its insertion into any of the orifices, it has become synonymous with surveilling the interior of the female reproductive organs. For feminists such technologies:

> reinscribe dominant narratives of gender identity on the material body by providing the means for exercising power relations on the flesh of the female body. They do so in two ways: first by intervening in the physiological functioning of the female body, and secondly by providing the technological infrastructure for the institutionalization of surveillance practices.[30]

The speculum is perceived then as an instrument of control over the female body, a body which requires domination by the masculine medical gaze in order to calm its excesses and unruly nature. Sprinkle subverts these gender-power relations through inserting the speculum herself outside of the institutions of medical science. By controlling the technology of surveillance she recuperates agency over her own body, deciding when and how this instrument will be utilized in relation to her own subjectivity. Caravaggio seems to have provided Christ with a similar degree of control over access to his body in the painting by directing and guiding Thomas's hand into his wound. Both Christ and Sprinkle seem to be invested in assuming agency over their own subjectivity by manipulating access to and offering views of their interiors.

Once the speculum is in place audience members can choose to come to the stage to take a closer look through it to Sprinkle's cervix. Just as Christ invites Thomas to see and touch his wounds, Sprinkle encourages her spectators to occupy a myopic viewing position in relation to the performance and her body. She collapses the conventional spatial boundaries of the theatre by offering such an extreme proximal viewing position that simultaneously puts the spectator in the privileged position of the physician in relation to the corporeal interior. Thus Sprinkle establishes multiple desires in the spectator that apparently few can resist – desire to be close to the performance, desire to see and desire to see inside the corporeal.

Approaching the stage during a performance is fraught with contradictory sensations, even though this movement has been explicitly authorized by the performer. As an invite to transgress conventional behaviours and spaces that usually separate the binary opposites of stage/ auditorium, performer/audience, so the blurring induces a certain amount of anxiety, described by Rebecca Schneider: 'Standing in line…I felt a mounting sense of confusion about my choice. How was I to focus my particular gaze? Who was I when I looked?'[31] As the spectator nears the performance area there is a perceptual shift that recognizes the potential slippage between viewer and performer now released. Apprehension is aroused by the sense of an approaching unidentifiable moment when spectator will become performer, performing their looking for those still spectating. This transformative dynamic, involving kinaesthetic engagement and proximal viewing, moves the spectator from an encounter with depth and illusion to one that confronts the materiality of the performance and the physical manifestation of the performer's body. Here the spectator becomes self-aware and fully cognisant of the work of performance that has the capacity to make them fully complicit in its actions.

Flashlight in hand, the spectator draws close to Annie in order to look through the speculum, exchanging part for whole as the anatomist does and thereby opening the possibility of a haptic visual encounter during the performance. The visual field is effectively reduced to the material and physical aspects of Annie's genitalia and vaginal cavity. From this pathological viewing position comes the autoptic moment of performance – the empiricist experience of seeing for oneself that operates over and above any textual or representational knowledge. Annie, as the good teacher and physician, has shown images of the cervix and now enters the realm of empirical science with the spectator. The supposition of a haptic autopsia is borne out by Schneider's brief description of 'the round pink cervix peeking back at me.'[32] In Kristeva's terms, what is seen is 'incapable of signifying' anything: the cervix is simply what it is, a fleshy organ hidden within the female body.[33] In these rather banal words, however, lies tantalizing evidence of a haptic visual engagement that describes surface and texture rather than meaning or content in this moment of proximal sight. In Schneider's terms it explicitly confounds her ability to cognitively process the moment in terms of constructing meaning and she becomes more aware of confusion and apprehension as effects of the haptic visual encounter.

Seemingly unable to consider the experience through anything other than visual theories but aware also that she is unable to make much sense about what she saw in that speculative revelation, she falls back on visuality and identifies within the moment of looking a sense of reciprocity that she explains as a 'theoretical third eye...meeting the spectator's – my – gaze. I imagined that gaze as a kind of counter-gaze...'[34] Echoing Marks's contention that haptic visuality is a 'mutually constitutive exchange', it seems that Schneider's experience did incorporate a slippage between vision and touch, whereby relations between subject and object become mutual rather than predicated on domination. However, she is unable to relinquish her position fully and undertake an analysis that caresses the object, rather than laying it bare, in Marks's words.[35]

What was available to sight through the speculum? Few accounts of the performance pursue any interest in this question, preferring instead to take the long view from an analytical perspective that critiques the overall meaning and impact of the show. In this proximal interrogation, it seems appropriate to consider or speculate on the image through the speculum. Apart from Schneider, whose response we have already noted, only Carr makes reference to the sight: 'to look inside someone's body is to see too much.'[36] In a strange paradox, the revelation of corporeal interiority, or indeed the wound, marks an inability to see anything except an excess that obfuscates meaning. Sprinkle acknowledges this excess that over-signifies when she remarks: 'Fuck you guys – you wanna see pussy, I'll show you pussy!'[37] It is as if this extreme voyeurism will not satisfy desire but overload it with sight, destroying the pornographic effect and overlaying it with surplus.

If the speculum did invoke a moment of haptic visuality for Schneider in the cervix's 'tactile and viscous pinkness'[38] we can return to Marks's argument that such an engagement 'inspires an acute awareness that the thing seen evades vision'.[39] Enigmatically, occlusion occurs even though the performance apparently works to heighten any experience of the visual field. Sprinkle performs under bright stage lighting and occupies a space at the edge of the stage, as close as possible to the audience. Sight is then supposedly helped by the insertion of the speculum, a technological device to enhance viewing and the use of the torch with which to illuminate the now open vagina. Finally, the spectator is admitted to within inches of its objective, in Carr's account on hands and knees, only to be confronted with a plethora of vision from which little sense can be derived.

I want to argue then that in both cases, where proximal visuality is offered as the apparent guarantee of truth and revelation in relation to the opened and penetrated body, a slippage between vision and touch becomes apparent that throws the system of representation into question. Hapticality figures in both moments and confounds the view, dissolving the possibility of any final resolution within these two frames. Caravaggio's evocation of the instance of the touch puts into play a haptic effect, which questions and opens the representational system and theological content of the painting. Far from dispelling doubt in Christ's resurrection, founded in his capacity to transcend the flesh, this effect may evoke for the spectator the doubtful scene of touch itself: that it is no guarantee of the truth, of faith or of the meaning of the interiority of the body. Similarly, when Sprinkle, like Christ, invites her spectators to test the meaning of their object of vision through the opening of the interior of the body to sight, visual representation becomes insufficient and sight approximates the conditions of touch. Far from verification of sight or of representation, the instance of the opening brings the spectator's vision into the confounding affect of touch, whose force infinitely resists the finalities of any representation. In these moments, the body is paradoxically empty and excessive in its materiality and fleshiness.

Notes

1. Caravaggio, Michelangelo (1603), *The Incredulity of Saint Thomas*, Preussische Schlösser und Gärten, Berlin-Brandenburg, Potsdam, 107 x 146, oil on canvas.
2. King James Bible, John, paragraph 20, verse 25.
3. Ibid., paragraph 20, verse 27.
4. Ibid., paragraph 20, verse 28.
5. Shiff, R. (1996), 'On Passing Through Skin: Technology of Art and Sensation' in Tomas, D., (ed.), 'Touch in Contemporary Art' in *Public 13*, Canada:Public Access, p.25.
6. Anzieu, D. (1989), *The Skin Ego: A Psychoanalytical Approach to Self*, (trans.) Turner, C., New Haven & London: Yale University Press, p.40.
7. Elkins, J. (1999), *Pictures of the Body: Pain and Metamorphosis*, Stanford: Stanford University Press, p. 16.
8. ibid., p. 17.
9. ibid.
10. ibid., p. 16.
11. ibid., p. 17.
12. ibid.
13. Sawday, J. (1997), 'Self and Selfhood in the Seventeenth Century', in R. Porter (ed.), *Rewriting the Self: Histories from the Renaissance to the Present*, London & New York: Routledge, p. 35.
14. Riegl cited in Iverson, M. (1993), *Alois Riegl: Art History and Theory*, Massachusetts: MIT Press, p. 9.
15. ibid., p. 76.
16. Marks, L.U. (2000), *The Skin of the Film: Intercultural Cinema, Embodiment and the Senses*, Durham: Duke University Press, p. 185.
17. Marks is careful to distinguish between 'haptic images' which the film or video offers and 'haptic visuality' which 'emphasizes the viewer's inclination to perceive them', ibid., p. 162.
18. ibid., p. 162.
19. ibid.
20. ibid., p. 163.
21. ibid., p. 183.

22. ibid., p. 163.
23. Bal, M. (1996), *Double Exposures: The Subject of Cultural Analysis*, New York & London: Routledge, p. 126.
24. ibid.
25. Marks, L.U. (2000), *The Skin of the Film: Intercultural Cinema, Embodiment and the Senses*, p. 191.
26. ibid.
27. ibid.
28. Schneider, R. (1997), *The Explicit Body in Performance*, London & New York: Routledge, p. 53.
29. Carr, C., (ed.) (1993), *On Edge: Performance at the End of the Twentieth Century*, Middletown: Wesleyan University Press, pp. 175–6.
30. Balsamo, A. (1997), *Technologies of the Gendered Body*, Durham & London: Duke University Press, p. 160.
31. Schneider, R. (1997), *The Explicit Body in Performance, at the End of the Twentieth Century*, p. 55.
32. ibid.
33. Kristeva, J. (1982), *Powers of Horror: An Essay on Abjection*, (trans.), Roudiez, L.S., New York: Columbia University Press, p. 3.
34. Schneider, R., *The Explicit Body in Performance at the End of the Twentieth Century*, p. 55.
35. Marks, L. U. (2000), *The Skin of the Film: Intercultural Cinema, Embodiment and the Senses*, p. 183.
36. Carr, C., (ed.) (1993), *On Edge: Performance at the End of the Twentieth Century*, Middletown: Wesleyan University Press, p. 176.
37. Juno, A., Vale, V. (1991), *Angry Women*, San Francisco: Re/Search Publications, p. 34.
38. Schneider, R. (1997), *The Explicit Body in Performance at the End of the Twentieth Century*, p. 56.
39. Marks, L.U. (2000), *The Skin of the Film: Intercultural Cinema, Embodiment and the Senses*, p. 191.

12

TOUCHED BY HUMAN HANDS: CITY AND PERFORMANCE

Roma Patel

The boundaries between the play and life are intentionally erased. Life is on stage.[1]

On the morning of Thursday 4 May 2006 a large wooden rocket landed in Waterloo Place in central London, breaking the tarmac. No one knew what was happening. Then on Friday a sultan of the Indies arrived, on his forty-foot-high time-travelling elephant. The wooden rocket then opened and a twenty-foot-tall girl giant disembarked, and was greeted by the elephant. The drama[2] unfolded for thousands of captivated audience members who joined the giants on their journey through the streets of London. By Sunday evening it had all come to an end: the girl returned to her rocket; the elephant left for Antwerp. The weekend's goings on were seen by a million people, the largest and most successful public theatre performances ever to be staged in the city of London.

The Royal de Luxe's performance, that spring, challenges one's perception of public space through the re-appropriation and disruption of the city's streets. It compels us to re-contextualize their use. Such street performances are a rare sight in England. In this chapter I shall attempt to describe how theatre interventions such as these can become a catalyst for 'interrupting' and re-animating the spectator-space interaction, for recapturing their attention and in so doing can reinvent their memories of public space. It will be illustrated through two personal experiences; one of developing site-specific performances with Corcadorca Theatre Company; the other as one of the spectators witnessing 'The Sultan of the Indies on His Time-Travelling Elephant'.[3]

Fig. 27: 'A million people came to central London to enjoy a staggering spectacle that has changed the way we think about street theatre...The Sultan's Elephant was a marvel.'[4]

Negotiating with the city

Street theatre is one of the oldest performance art forms, common in the market towns of mediaeval England. Its early success lay in drawing together large numbers of people to experience elements of spectacle, theatre, music, celebration and comedy. Mantzius' research into eyewitness reports of early sixteenth century mysteries reveals how the support of the city authorities made this event significant.

> To a mediaeval town the performance of a mystery was an event of immense interest... the magistrates ordered all the shops to be closed, and forbade all noisy work. The streets were empty, the houses locked up, and none but solitary armed watch-men, specially engaged for the occasion, were seen about the residences. All were gathered in the public square.[5]

The decline of the mysteries was the result of a conflict within the church that led to prohibition of religious plays in Europe,[6] together with an increased interest in classical studies that affected staging and playwriting. Street performances moved to inn yards and open-air amphitheatres, then to purpose-built indoor spaces; the playhouses.

By the Victorian age, theatre audiences were mostly made up of the educated classes and these spaces became a sign of high culture. The revolutionary moments of the twentieth century spawned experimental theatre companies such as CAST and The People Show in the 1960s. Whilst Welfare State and I.O.U. ushered a new age in British theatre where, once again, theatre could be seen on streets, in parks or in disused buildings. Nevertheless, theatre in public spaces still remains a relatively rare phenomenon in Britain. The reasons for this must be wide ranging and complex but may lie in the British theatre hierarchy, as Helen Marriage, lead producer of The Sultan's Elephant in London, of Artichoke Productions, points out:

> We have carnival, but we tolerate carnival. We don't celebrate it. We don't really invest in it in the way it should be invested in, because it's free, because it doesn't fit with a British sense of hierarchical values. And, for me, this is a huge tragedy, because this is the way in which one touches the most people – it's not just about 120 people sitting in a black-box studio. The real power of this work is about being out there on the streets and experiencing your world.[7]

This situation is different on the continent, where the tradition of open-air spectacle has been retained. Even in northern European countries like the Netherlands, during summertime, and annually, theatre festivals take place in shipyards and fields, on beaches, by canals, on city streets and in squares where a host of national companies such as The Lunatics and Dogtroep perform alongside their European counterparts. De Parade for example, is a touring theatre caravan where you will find a diverse market- place of performance, colourful tents luring visitors to the delights of dance theatre, musical performance, cabaret and comedy. Children's activities are set along side-tables where adults enjoy culinary pleasures in the backdrop of a summer evening.

Performing theatre in public spaces is often a reaction to the commodification of theatre and the desire for inclusivity. Therefore, ticket prices are often low or free. However, these events are difficult to organize and negotiate, because they are, at one level, inconvenient and challenge how public spaces are used. They are usually expensive to run and companies often rely on the dedication of the people involved and the full cooperation of city authorities. Courcoult, the artistic Director of Royal de Luxe said in an interview:

> I am proud that the shows we produce are financed by taxes. It seems fitting and beautiful that some tax money is dedicated to popular culture. By putting on the show in the public arena and free of charge I can reach people as they are whereas in traditional theatres you only meet those who have dared cross the threshold. I want to contact everyone, adults and children, whatever their sociocultural milieu. This is a mythical story and it concerns everyone.[8]

Every summer since the late 1990s, Corcadorca Theatre Company[9] has made the city of Cork their performing space. The poetic texts of Shakespeare and Büchner have been heard echoing in the halls of disused buildings, through city streets, crowded parks, watersides and industrial sites. These performances enthral the public and have been critically acclaimed but they are usually accompanied by months of negotiating and compromise with the city authorities, although now that the company has established its place within the fabric of the city these relationships have become somewhat easier.

Even more starkly, it took Artichoke Productions' event organizers Helen Marriage and Nicky Webb no less than five years of fundraising, organizing and approval applications before the puppet elephant was allowed to roam the streets of London, rather than be confined to one route between Hyde Park and Trafalgar square. It was no mean feat as Webb recounted at the event 'How many elephants does it take...?' held at the South Bank Centre after the spectacle:

It's taken us five years to get this show together and 90 per cent of that time has been spent persuading people that we should be allowed to do it.

This show is a living thing and they need to do what people who visit London do: they need to walk about and shuttling back and forth isn't the answer.

Fig. 28: *The Tempest* On the Pond, Fitzgerald Park, Cork, Ireland, 2006, Corcadorca Theatre Company.

There are three things needed to make something like this happen: faith, hope and love. For me, the most important of these is – and here I'll probably cry, as I have for most of the weekend! – love.[10]

The recent popularity of PunchDrunk's promenade production that re-appropriated buildings in London may signal a change in the staging of performances in the city. Whether this is merely the latest vogue or reflects a permanent shift in audience preference towards an experience, over sitting in dark theatres remains to be seen, but at £40 a ticket for Punchdrunk's *The Masque of the Red Death* (2007) was certainly not inclusive. Consequently, as more audiences and critics seek out established UK site-specific companies such as Grid Iron, Shunt, Kneehigh and the Factory, it may mean more productions will be commissioned and the various city agencies and authorities will have to go beyond their bureaucratic difficulties and recognize the social value of performing theatre in our cities' public spaces.

Humanizing the city

The increased prevalence of conditions such as agoraphobia and claustrophobia has convinced many psychologists of a link with the alienating environment of the modern city. Walter Benjamin's proposition that the city streets have now become 'invisible' to its citizens and are now mere backdrops to their lives, 'felt' rather than 'seen',[11] needs to be addressed by our city planners and ministries of culture. The public art displayed in our urban spaces frequently appears to have become a token, disappearing into the fabric of the city, taking a subordinate position. Often it is impersonal and commissioned as signatures of famous artists and bears no relationship to the 'public'. The underlying issue is about commissioning 'public' art and performances that can humanize and animate our city – where the flow of people replaces the flow of traffic; where people stop, spend time and gaze.

In 'The City and the Soul', psychologist James Hillman, describes graffiti as a compensation-symptom of the soullessness of the city, where the human hand needs to 'leave its touch'.

These marks made in public places, called the defacing of monuments, actually put a face on an impersonal wall or oversized statue. The human hand seems to want to touch and leave its touch, even if by only obscene smears and ugly scrawls. So, let us make sure that the hand has its place, in the city, not only by means of shops for artisans and displaying crafts, but also animated and bringing culture to the walls and stones and spaces left bleakly untouched by human hand. Surely, a city is a masterpiece of engineering form and architectural inspiration that would not be despoiled by the presence of images that reflect the 'soul' through the hand.[12]

I was sceptical when I first heard about Royal De Luxe's show; I assumed it would just be a spectacle parading through the streets. Nevertheless, I joined hundreds of spectators for my first sight of these machines of spectacle in Trafalgar Square and within a short time I was rethinking my position. These machines are the ideal scale for a city like London. One of the major issues with large-scale street theatre is how to preserve the drama at a human scale. So

Fig. 29: On the steps of Trafalgar Square, the visitors rest.

how did an over-scale motorized time-travelling elephant and wooden girl giantess requiring a team of 112 performers and technicians 'leave its touch' on so many spectators? It had to do with a combination of a high level of craftsmanship in making the objects lifelike, creating intimate moments, and attractive and imaginative storytelling. The girl did all the things that a real little girl will do; she changed into her bed-clothes at night, had showers, licked lollipops, rode a bus and cheekily peed on the street.

Delarozière, the scenographer/engineer for Royal De Luxe, exhibited an extraordinary attention to detail: every step of the elephant was accompanied by stomp-simulating spurts of dust; from time to time the elephant would trumpet and flap its brown leather ears. Onlookers were given surprise soakings from its trunk, fed from an on-board 380-gallon reservoir. The latter became a natural way to disperse the crowds as the elephant travelled around the streets.

The little girl giantess sat in St James Park for hours with her keepers and with no metal barriers around her, passers-by would come close enough to experience intimate moments and even sat on her arms. Likewise, the elephant sometimes rested on the street and on its back, from the howdah, the sultan, his servants and courtesans, periodically put on a show for the crowds.

Angharad Wynne-Jones, Director of London International Festival of Theatre, talks about the shared experience of the weekend and describes the elephant and the little girl as impossible objects:

Fig. 30: The onlookers are given a surprise soaking from the elephant's trunk to disperse them.

I think the elephant and the little girl are impossible objects, yet they were moved to and through this city by the collective will, the extraordinary imagination and the sheer logistical virtuosity of a group of people brought together because of these mechanical puppets. But it is really in the response of the public that the event lives, and will continue to change and charge our perceptions of our city and of each other.[13]

Fig. 31: 'The Little Girl Giantess' travelling through the streets of London.

The shared experience of moving through a city layered by actions and stories involves the spectator, confronts him, obstructs him and commands his attention and response. This is where performance in public spaces works best. My journey through London streets in search of the elephant one Sunday morning, was altogether unusual, not simply because the streets were relieved of traffic for the weekend but because the story of The Sultan of the Indies on His Time-Travelling Elephant created living reverberations that were still alive on the streets of London even after the puppets had passed on.

Fig. 32: The curious passer-bys gather around the story trail of the sewn cars.

A constant stream of spectators revisited the story and trail of broken tarmac and sewn cars, as if on a pilgrimage. This exchange between making-known and making-believe is expressed in Marinis' and Dwyer's article 'Dramaturgy of the Spectator':

> One side of this 'theatrical relationship' – the relation of performance to spectator – comprises a manipulation of the audience by the performance...This manipulative aspect of the performance can be expressed in terms of Algirdas J. Greimas' theory: the performance or, better still, the theatrical relationship, is not so much a making-known (*faire-savoir*) – that is, an aseptic exchange of information/messages/ knowledge – as it is a making-believed (*faire-croire*) and a making-done (*faire-faire*).[14]

Street theatre of the Royal De Luxe variety has a significant role to play in our cities. The relationship between the spectator and the performance is based on freedom, which makes it a valuable art form. The spectator can arrive and leave at any point he or she wants to, or stay and participate in the celebration. The spectator can now find new meaning, and escape from the monotony of city living into the unexpected. New emotional memories are forged interrupting the monoculture.

The city as inspiration

Royal De Luxe's large-scale shows are the exception, only produced every few years. Performances made by site-specific theatre companies are more common. These take place in a variety of public spaces and disused buildings and tend to attract audiences that normally don't go to theatre. They are seen as unique, innovative, exciting and unpredictable events that blur the boundaries between the spectator and the drama. Wilkie's survey of site-specific performance in Britain, 2001, refers to Carolyn Deby, of the dance company, Sirens Crossing and their experience of the relationship of the audience to site-specific work.

> Deby also reminds us that the challenge in site-specific work is not only to attract a wider audience but to enable this audience to have a 'radically different relationship' to the

Fig. 33: ACT II Inside the Distillery. *The Merchant of Venice,* (2005), Corcadorca Theatre Company, Cork, Ireland.

performance. Potential new relationships might be explored through 'degrees of scale, intimacy, proximity...the possibility of the audience member moving through or past the performance...the lack of usual theatrical conventions...the challenge to focus the viewer's eye without the usual tricks...'[15]

Site-specificity implies that a performance is tied to the identity of the location, its size, shape, and history; consequently it cannot be relocated: 'to remove the work is to destroy the work'.[16] However, in recent years the meaning of 'site-specific' has become contentious as companies relocate work once specific to a certain site. In Wilkie's survey of site-specific companies in the United Kingdom, many of them felt that performances that moved location never quite manifested as they did in the original site and were sometimes re-contextualised for each site. However, this was often dependant on finances. Many of the practitioners suggested that the term site-specific may not be the most suitable description for their work and could be replaced. [17]

When I first visited a disused distillery, in search of a possible location for *The Merchant of Venice*, 2005, with director Pat Kiernan, we found two large empty warehouse spaces. In the second warehouse, we discovered a blue cage spanning 34 metres across and 16 metres high (Figure 33). Instantaneously we felt that it was the right location for Portia's house. This was our starting point. The site had inspired our first steps toward a performance.

The spectators only saw Portia behind the cage, until Bassanio selected the right casket and the doors were left open. The design of Portia's house was influenced by Georgian and Palladian architecture found in the villas of Cork and Venice. The set and the back wall were painted to look like white Venetian marble and were complemented with red upholstered, gilded wooden furniture.

In *One Place After Another* Kwon[18] discusses two opposing artistic responses to a site – integration and intervention. In integration the work merges into the fabric of the site whereas intervention emphasizes the work as 'response' to site. These are issues that a scenographer should consider when designing for non-traditional spaces and raises the age-old debate about the role of the scenographer in theatre. When responding to a site the scenographer must be aware when to leave the site as found and when to intervene.

The spectator and the city

Manipulating and mapping the spectator's theatrical journey in promenade performances requires the scenographer to structure the spectators' location throughout the performance. Particularly when working with a play the movements between acts are important to consider. Otherwise, losing the spectator's attention could lead to the experience fragmenting. In Corcadorca's adaptation of *The Merchant of Venice*, the journeys between acts were considered as part of the narrative experience. The drama travels through buildings containing immersive videoscapes, stops for scenes staged in disused factory cages, and then rushes into placard wielding crowds through the streets on to the city court-house for the climactic scenes. (Figure 34.)

> The more the performance allows audience members their own experience of the staged experience, the more it must also guide their attention so that, in all the complexity of present action, the spectator does not lose the sense of direction...To give life to the drama is not simply to plot the actions and tensions of the performance but also to structure the spectator's attention, ordering its rhythms and invoking its moments of tension without, however, imposing any one interpretation.[19]

The spectator can be considered as 'dramaturgical object' besieged for/by the actions of the performers, where their attention is considered and structured as expressed in Karen Fricker's review of the performance: 'The sense of audience implication in the action is taken up a notch

Fig. 34: The journey through the city streets of Cork, *The Merchant of Venice* (2005).

as extras bearing torches and placards with hateful racist slogans lead an uneasy journey over the River Lee to the city courthouse.'[20]

Performances in public spaces are in non-controlled environments, they are interventions that 'interrupt' the public space. For Corcadorca's adaptation of *The Tempest* we took up residence in Cork's largest park and set up a temporary workshop in the gardener's yard. The natural amphitheatre of the pond became our stage with audience space surrounding the action on three sides (Figure 36).

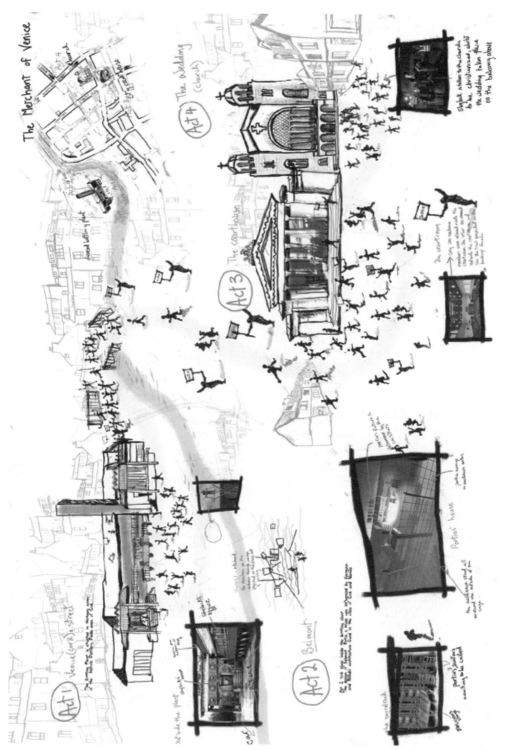

Fig. 35: The audience route in *The Merchant of Venice*, Act I. All of the street scenes are condensed and take place in the courtyard of the bottling plant. For Act II, Portia's mansion was set in a warehouse space inside the plant. We decided not to attempt to portray the continuous shift between the streets of Venice and Belmont that takes place in the original text. Act III took place simultaneously inside courtroom no. 1 and outside the courthouse. Act IV combined the christianization of Shylock and the wedding/ring scene and was set outside of the church.

Fig. 36: Transformation of the pond at Fitzgerald Park, Cork, *The Tempest*, Corcadorca Theatre Company.

Four weeks of the rehearsal took place in the park and the good weather meant that we were working in the public eye. As a result our theatre-making became transparent; we all became performers for the park visitors. Passers-by became privy to the artistic process, sometimes venturing on set.

Fig. 37: Scenes from *The Tempest*, Corcadorca Theatre Company.

Fig. 38: Crowds gather around the projections on the façade of the Courthouse for *The Merchant of Venice*.

For the last two acts of *The Merchant of Venice*, the roads were blocked for vehicular traffic whilst audiences filed inside the courthouse or stood and sat on the road with passers-by from the pubs nearby. Large-scale projections on the façade of the Courthouse drew the attention of onlookers who sometimes taunted the actors, adding to the drama and at times the 'city and production seem to merge'.[21]

Much of the public space in British cities is intertwined with commerce. We need to experience interventions that re-appropriate these spaces for a wider variety of social interaction and discourse. The performances discussed above surprise and disrupt the spectator's attention drawing her out of herself, encouraging her to find new ways to connect to the city, creating a sense of celebration that harks back to the mediaeval pageants, as spectators gather joyfully and harmoniously promenade through the city streets, sit under stars and walk through projected seascapes. This is how the city renews its soul. These celebrations, to my mind, are one first step towards humanizing our cities.

Notes

1. Bakhtin, M., *Rabelais and His World*, (trans.), Isowolsky, H. (1993), Indiana University Press, p. 256

2. Synopsis from the Sultan's Newspaper:

   'Once upon a time, there lived a sultan who was tormented in his dreams by visions of a little girl who was travelling through time. This is his story, incredible but true. The sultan could no longer sleep, his growing anguish diverting his attention from affairs of state. In order to cure his sickness, and believing that he would find the girl in the land of dreams, he commissioned an unknown engineer living in 1900 to construct a time-travelling elephant. A few months later, the sultan set off with his court in search of the little girl giant, which, in the course of his nightmares, had been transformed into a marionette 5 meters high. The trip was awful, but they found a series of clues as to her whereabouts. The little girl giant loved sewing – she liked to stitch cars to the tarmac...The elephant followed the trail left. And as in all love stories, strange things began to happen. Such was his happiness at getting closer to her, he began to expel hundreds of living birds which disappeared into the sky in a burst of joy.'

3. The piece was originally commissioned to celebrate the centenary of Jules Verne's death and was first performed in May 2005, in Nantes. The French street theatre company was founded by Jean-Luc Courcoult in 1979 and has performed shows in Europe, Korea, China, Vietnam, Chile and Africa. In the last 12 years they have specialized in making shows using gigantic puppets: Le Géant tombé du ciel, Le géant tombé du ciel: dernier voyage, Retour d'Afrique and Les Chasseurs de girafes. 'The Sultan's Elephant' is the fifth in this series and its London performance was the first time a 'giant' show was staged in a capital city.

4. Clapp, S. (2006), *The Observer*, 14 May.

5. Mantzius, K. (1937), *A History of Theatrical Arts*, New York: Peter Smith.

6. Religious plays were outlawed by Queen Elizabeth and the Council of Trent, 1545–1563.

7. London International Festival of Theatre (LIFT), presenting a one day event called '*How Many Elephants Does It Take?*', explored how the cultural sector and city infrastructures can work creatively together to change the way we experience the city. The proceedings are summarized in a report by Richard Ings,' Conversations with an Elephant.' See: http://www.liftfest.org.uk/festivalsandevents/conversations_about_an_elephant/Conversations_about_an_Elephant.pdf, p. 11.

8. Extracts from an interview with Jean Luc Courcoult by Jean-Christophe Planche http://thesultanselephant.com/assets/downloads/pdf/Interview.pdf

9. Corcadorca was founded in 1991 and has established itself as one of Ireland's leading independent theatre companies. As the company evolved, it established an artistic policy with two main strands: the nurturing of new artists and the production of site-specific work in culturally significant areas of the city. See Corcadorca's website for their performance archive – www.corcordorca.com

10. Ings, Richard, 'Conversations with an Elephant', http://www.liftfest.org.uk/festivalsandevents/conversations_about_an_elephant/Conversations_about_an_Elephant.pdf, p. 5.

11. In the chapter *Dead End Street* from his book *Warped Space*, Anthony Vidler examines Walter Benjamin's idea about why cities are not seen, he writes: 'We seldom look at our surroundings. Streets and buildings, even those considered major monuments, are in everyday life little more than backgrounds for introverted thought, passages through which our bodies pass "on the way to work". In this sense cities are "invisible" to us, felt rather than seen, moved through rather than visually taken in.'

12. Hillman, J. (2005), *Uniform Edition of the writing of James Hillman, Vol. 2: City and Soul,* Leaver, R. (ed.), Putnam Connecticut: Spring Publications.
13. Angharad Wynne-Jones, Director of London International Festival of Theatre, talking at the event 'How many elephants does it take?' Richard Ings, report, 'Conversations with an Elephant', see: http://www.liftfest.org.uk/festivalsandevents/conversations_about_an_elephant/Conversations_about_an_Elephant.pdf, p. 2.
14. de Marinis, M.,Dwyer, P. (1987), 'Dramaturgy of the Spectator', *The Drama Review: TDR,* Vol. 31, No. 2. Summer, pp. 100–14.
15. Wilkie, F. (2002), 'Mapping the Terrain: a Survey of Site-Specific Performance in Britain,' *New Theatre Quarterly,* Volume 18, Issue 02, p. 154.
16. Richard Serra, letter to Donald Thalacker, 1 January 1985, published in Weyergraf-Serra, Clara, Buskirk, Martha (eds.)(1991), *The Destruction of Tilted Arc: Documents,* Cambridge: MIT Press, p. 38.
17. Wilkie, F. (2002), 'Mapping the Terrain: a Survey of Site-Specific Performance in Britain', *New Theatre Quarterly,* Volume 18, Issue 02, p. 154. The phrases replacing 'site-specific' in these situations tend to be either a more detailed description of that company's particular approach – other terms are 'context-sensitive', 'environmental art', 'outdoor performance', 'interactive', 'landscape theatre', 'installation', 'season-specific', 'public', 'promenade', 'contextually reactive', 'street theatre', 'place-orientated work', 'square peg in a square hole', 'one-off specially commissioned performance', 'made specially for...'.
18. Kwon, M., (2004), *One Place after Another: Site-Specific Art and Locational Identity,* MIT Press.
19. de Marinis, M., Dwyer, P. (1987), 'Dramaturgy of the Spectator', *The Drama Review: TDR,* Vol. 31, No. 2. Summer, p. 108.
20. Fricker, K. (2005), *The Guardian,* Theatre Review, Saturday June 18.
21. Ibid.

PART FOUR: THE SITE OF SPECTATING

13

DWELLINGS IN IMAGE-SPACES

Maiju Loukola

The chapter focuses on the processual, spatio-temporal character and conceptualizing of digital image, as well as on the phenomenological body of digital image-space in the light of reading the philosophy of Maurice Merleau-Ponty. Global tele-presence has become the real-time environment of our lived everyday practices, as we find ourselves surrounded by the lightness and accessibility of mobile travelling and communication. How we find ourselves as 'submerged in the world', as it is phrased by Merleau-Ponty, and how we place ourselves in the era of the placeless and the timeless, has a profound impact on how we outline our being. Thus, certain potentialities of sensing the digital image can be contemplated from a particular spatio-temporal body-perspective.

Each act of performance is spatial, temporal, multi-sensory, and connected with its environment. As a meta-stable organ, theatre signifies something happening in a shared place at a shared time, in the 'here and now' of all of its participatory aspects. Theatre constantly renegotiates and re-frames both its spatial and temporal boundaries, to which the essence of all live art reverts. In both visual and performative arts, the reality of the work of art is often seen as equal to, as well as being shared with, the reality of its spectator. In the context of performative arts we are more and more often talking about active audience participation, and of the notion of the work of art and/or an act of art presuming the viewer's phenomenological body – the participant's active bodily presence – through which the piece is actualized and through which it is in its be-coming revealed. Along this process, the act of art is thus made perceivable through the bodily presence of the participating subject. What may the notion of an event as shared, aesthetic, bodily experience bring forward in the means of perception?

In this chapter, I am striving to outline some of the potential modes of perceiving digital image-space, keeping the notion of body as the primary condition of perception as the starting point.

As a ground for reflection in contemplating the theme, I am emphasizing Maurice Merleau-Ponty's notion of 'theory of the body as already a theory of perception'.[1] In Merleau-Ponty's thinking the 'body stands as the existential unity of an open set of equivalences in relation to possible action'.[2] The interpretation and comprehension of digital image as a spatio-temporal entity is based on a phenomenological 'attitude' – the notion of the world colliding with us.

No landscape in itself is unclear

According to Merleau-Ponty our existence in the world is primarily and unconditionally spatial; we exist in relation to space, in the world that surrounds us, in dreams and in our sense perception. From this point of view, 'there are as many spaces as there are separate spatially lived experiences'.[3] Merleau-Ponty points out the weight of learned things affecting our consciousness in perceiving the world. He borrows a concept used by psychologists, 'the experience error', claiming that what we have adopted by learning certain qualities of certain things themselves we take as being in our consciousness of those things; 'We make perception out of things perceived'.[4] An example of an unclear landscape draws out the difference between 'achieving primary consciousness' and 'perceiving the perceived': 'There are many unclear sights, as for a landscape on a misty day, but then we always say that no real landscape is in itself unclear.'[5] It is emphasized that we are caught by the learned expectations, 'caught up by the world',[6] which tends to prevent us succeeding in extricating ourselves from the binding of knowledge in order to achieve primary consciousness of the world – the kind that is direct, and not consciousness 'of' world but rather intentional and thus 'towards' world.

Body perceptions

The phenomenological attitude of Merleau-Ponty strives, as pointed out earlier, towards approaching the origins of the body. Phenomenological body signifies our own, singular body; it is the 'lived', subjective body. By simplification, the lived body is contrary to the 'objective body' as object of observation.[7] Merleau-Ponty's body-unity aims not simply towards brushing away the dichotomy between body/mind – division, but proposes a third unity that would overstep the situation of simply choosing between the physical and the mental, and by this, end up in placing these two attributes in rank order. Therefore, it attempts to overcome the simple division of sense and sensibility by aiming at intensions more complex, namely: for the 'unity of the body as an existential unity'.[8] A.D. Smith claims that in comparison to Edmund Husserl's earlier, to a certain degree equivalent phenomenological ideas, one of the most relevant improvements in Merleau-Ponty's thinking is this very notion of the existential body as a 'third unity'. This notion, he argues, reaches farther than the sole unification of empiricism and intellectualism. The third unity constituted by unifying the physical body and the mental perception, as subject and predicate, exquisitely leads to Merleau-Ponty's central notion; 'the body perceives'.[9]

The notion of multi-sensory perception invites us to reflect on other disciplines concerning sense perception, for instance, neuroscience and synaesthesia. This is a neurologically-based phenomenon in which stimulation of one sensory or cognitive pathway leads to involuntary, automatic experiences in a second sensory or cognitive pathway.[10] The concept of synaesthesia has been influencing the tradition of art since the late nineteenth and early twentieth century. In the late nineteenth century, Vassily Kandinsky created a series of 'synaesthetic paintings' by which he attempted to evoke sound through colour. A contemporary of his, Richard Wagner, introduced the concept of *Gesamtkunstwerk*, 'the total artwork', which was aiming at the synthesis of all the poetic, visual, musical and dramatic arts.

Spaces in places

In terms of perception and reception, how do we see the dwelling in an image-space of a performative event? What kind of bodily consciousness may be located through encountering digital image-spaces in a physical space of a performance or an installation, as immaterial spaces keep appearing through flows of images, as cinematic continuances and layers of image-spaces? As for theatre, it may be defined as a physical location that serves as a location, a dwelling, for any live performance activity in it. Theatre as site thus hosts in itself potential sites for an infinite number of other sites in it. As a location for all potential locations, it resembles those decorative wooden Russian dolls: a doll inside another, and another, and another...

Analyzing the qualities of image-space as an experience through contemplating the spatial qualities, and the orientation of different types of performative spaces offers angles for equivalencies; for example, media researcher Margaret Morse's classic media theory article 'The Body, the Image and the Space-in-Between' still challenges us to evaluate the matter of corporeality and the 'kinaesthetic insight' in contemporary performance practices. Morse pointed out in her early 1990s writing that a vocabulary for learning at the level of the body ego and its orientation in space was missing. The vocabulary was used in the context of video installation art and its poetics, yet it is eminently relevant in the context of contemporary practices of theatre. According to Morse, the most crucial element of an installation is 'the space-in-between', which is in her words 'the actual construction of a passage for bodies or figures in space and time'.[11] Morse emphasizes the role of the presence of the spectator's body, or rather of a 'visitor', as she likes to phrase it, in order to stress the different qualities between installation and (theatrical) performance. It is arguable, though, whether such absolute juxtaposition of emphasizing the division of stage versus auditorium, performances versus everything else, and between types of performances, is needed when regarding today's interdisciplinary practices in performative events. The spatial orientations in different art disciplines have drawn closer to each other by the interdisciplinary approach throughout the cultural practices in the arts and sciences. The significance of an art event more and more frequently thrives on the encountering of the work and the participating visitor.

Immersions

New media, multi-media environments, interactive and immersive installations quite explicitly carry on the continuation of the ongoing, ubiquitous and evolutionary chain of the being-in-the-world project. Taking a look back, we may locate the origin of the viewer-participant discussion to the days of early modernism. The roots of the debate could be placed to times as far back as those of the earliest cave paintings. From there on, we have had in our hands the idea of submerging into images and the theme of immersion. Oliver Grau draws on the beginning of the history of immersion with certain references to the sixteenth century, when the mother of all panorama cylinder simulations, 'Sacri Monti' (Holy Mountain) – the inside of which was fully covered with holy images from the Bible – was constructed in Northern Italy.[12]

More recent examples of physical immersive image-space cylinders are the panorama cylinder multi-media works by Australian media artist Jeffrey Shaw. His works, such as *Place: A User's Manual*, 1995 and *Place: Ruhr*, 2000 – may be seen in the light of carrying the heritage of 'Sacri Monti'. The first one mentioned here, *Place: A User's Manual*, is a 360° cylinder panorama installation combined with a video interface. It is controlled by a joystick, which facilitates navigation of the images as in a typical table computer setting. Viewers/visitors occupy an elevated platform, rotating in the centre, and by means of the joystick manipulate the underwater camera assembled, in order to move about by zooming in and out among the eleven virtual photographic cylinders that re-duplicate, within the illusory space of the image, the cylindrical space, which is contained within the panorama setting.[13]

Image as process

Media researcher Mark B.N. Hansen writes on new media theory following, for example, Henri Bergson's arguments on the foundations of image technology. According to Bergson, affection and memory render perception impure, and we thus select only those particular images precisely relevant to our singular form of embodiment. From there on Hansen defines the digital image as a process rather than as a surface appearance, aiming at going beyond what the eye meets, beyond the visual, and thus places the body in a privileged standing point. It is argued here that digital image presumes the user's bodily presence, through which it penetrates, 'happens', and actualizes as an image. Following the notion of digital image-space as filtered through our bodies to our embodied mind, any singular image is never experienced twice in the same way, but inevitably as another and altered experience.

Lev Manovich comments that the image of new media is no longer something a subject simply looks at, comparing it with memories of represented reality to judge its reality effect. Thus, it can no longer be understood nor theorized merely as a frame, window, reflection/mirror or as early photographs, taken as fixed evidence of reality.[14] Hansen again emphasizes that a more profound look at the digitized image is needed in order to look at the matter of correlation between the user's body and the image; the image of the digital age has itself become a process and as such, it is inevitably bound up with the activity of the body.

In the context of writing on Jeffrey Shaw's works, many of which 'include' multiple sets of various interfaces and therefore possibilities for viewer-user's routes through the work by means of the bodily activities and information process, Hansen constitutes a theoretical constellation in which the concept of body-brain is central:

> ...the body stands over against a virtualized image-space, and thereby acquires a (more) fundamental role as the source of the actualization of images. If the corporeal and intellectual processing it performs still functions to 'give body' to the image, it does

not do so by lending its physical, extended volume as a three-dimensional screen for the image, but rather by creating an image-event out of its own embodied processing of information...the body or the body-brain – rather than existing as a screen or filter (Bergson) within the space of the image – is invested with the task of generating the image through its internal processing of carefully configured information.[15]

The notion of filtering the information received through one's body-filter to create images rather than simply receiving particular images as pre-existing technical packages may be seen as an updating of Bergson's arguments on the digital age. Hansen calls this particular framing function of the body the 'digital image'.[16] He also argues that the embodied status of the frame corresponds directly to the digital revolution, as a digitized image is not a fixed representation of reality, but is defined by its full flexibility and accessibility. It is not just the interactivity of new media that turns viewers into users – the image itself has become the body's process of perceiving it.

How do we define our participatory roles, and the nature of our presence in this play of sensing with not merely eyes, ears and touch but with our whole body as the receptive filter organ? Are we confronting acts of art, performative events, in the means of being present as 'viewer', 'visitor-participator' or 'user' – or a crucible mix of all of these? In which ways do the fundamental conditions of perception diverge and alter, depending on the quality, genre and location of the performative event in question?

As stated earlier, Hansen emphasises the bodily and spatio-temporal aspect of the digital image. The 'body as image filter' as suggested by Bergson or the 'body as digital image-space' strengthens the term 'user' mode as a descriptor for the means of perception. This kind of conclusion may be seen, to my mind, as quite relevant in the means of defining the 'role' of a spectator/visitor/participator. Keeping in mind Merleau-Ponty's notions, though, it seems that we are lacking much by the means of the notion of lived body as a centre of all in-determination, as an 'intentional unity of existence'.[17] Merleau-Ponty: 'The "lived-through" which Bergson sets over against the "thought-about" is for him an experience, an immediate "datum".'[18] Furthermore, Merleau-Ponty claims that 'space, motion and time cannot be elucidated by discovering merely the "inner" layer of experience',[19] but, leaning forward to Immanuel Kant, it must come out of the synthesis of the external and internal. Merleau-Ponty criticizes so called traditional philosophy and psychology for considering 'only the perception of space', whereas he points out his emphasis on 'our body and our perception to always summon us to take as the centre of the world that environment with which they present us'.[20]

Placeless, timeless dance

How should we approach the subject of bodily perception in regarding tele-presence or VR (virtual reality) projects? Media artist Simon Penny has linked in several of his works the concepts of tele-presence and immersion. He made a point of blasting Cartesian dualism in his work from the mid 1990s. The Cartesian mind versus body division has been a notion thoroughly rooted in western philosophy all the way up to the last decades, but has been 'in denial' for a good number of years now – particularly among visual and performance arts since the 1960s. Penny claimed, on striking against the notion of disembodiment through technology and announced in the 1990s, 'we exist within and through our bodies and we should use new technologies to make technology a celebration of our bodies'.[21] Penny carried out a tele-presence project called 'Traces: Wireless full body tracking in the CAVE' – as if celebrating his previous declaration in co-operation with Andre Bernhardt. 'Traces' was first introduced at 'Ars Electronica' in 1999. In this project, several CAVEs (Cave Automatic Virtual Environment) were networked in separate locations, geographically distant from each other, to create one single electronic image-space. Visitors entered the 'Traces'-CAVE, a rectangular room in which they were confronted with a digital image of their own body. As the visitors moved, so did their digital counterparts in the other 'Traces' locations. No navigation interfaces were used. The body movements of the visitors were the interfaces; as the users/visitors entered the CAVE space they interacted with traces of light, and the bodies of the visitors were sculpted by the traces of light. Simultaneously in the other 'Traces' locations, the visitors entering their rectangular rooms noticed that they were not in the 'Traces' image-space alone but they had come to join and to dance with their virtual, telematic partners. The piece referenced the military use of surveillance technology but turned this technology around – given that the bodies the visitors surveyed were their own.[22]

Imagine walking into a rectangular room to discover a digital reflection of yourself as you move through the room. A reflection composed of small cubic bits that reconstruct themselves in real time to reflect your every movement within the room. What would be your first reaction? Perhaps, to dance with your projected virtual self just to test whether or not it's really you being monitored and reconstructed in real time. As the digital reflection remains consistent you become captivated with your own movements. Now imagine taking this interaction a step further. Rather than simply you and your digital reflection dancing about the room, imagine three such rooms in three distant locations networked to one another, so that you find yourself interacting with the real time digital projections of other distant users. [23]

Intentional user

The modes of perception and the role of spectator in performative events seem to be dependent on whether the presence is that of a 'viewer'. Therefore, resembling the traditional stage-audience arrangement of a proscenium theatre with the 'stage' and the 'auditorium' physically separated. A 'visitor' (following Margaret Morse's definition), is provided with the ability to move freely 'as active bodies' in the space,[24] or a 'user' where the image-space experience is controlled by the user's body or another interface of some kind, with the spatial orientation being mapped/guided or free.

As a 'user' the participator would most likely be regarded as the interface herself – the interface being her own body. In a 'Bergsonian' sense the participator's bodily activity – as correlation between the user's body as a filter – might be considered relevant and possible in all of the three cases; in addition, in the situation when the spatial orientation most resembles traditional stage/auditorium arrangements.

Being in an image-space, in the case of 'visitor' and 'user' perception, does not necessarily presume any technical device, nor does it presume any particular arrangements in the organization of the physical space, either. In all of these cases, the perception may be conceived, as described earlier; the body filters all images in relation to the individual experience. The body-filter keeps processing, regardless of whether you sit tight in the chair through the performance or move about actively around the space. As formulated before, the notion of body-subject as the filtering organ is as follows: 'The image no longer can be restricted to the level of merely a surface appearance, but must be extended to encompass the entire process by which information is made perceivable through embodied experience.'[25]

The experience of a tele-presence installation such as 'Traces' may be seen as a transient flux of variations of audience participation; 'positions' and 'roles' of a visitor and of a user. The body serves as the interface or as a device in the information-formulation process and also through the accessibility of moving freely in the space.

Thinking about the different positions of how we are situated in a space of a performative event, Merleau-Ponty's 'unity of the body as an existential unity' calls for clarification. In Merleau-Ponty's philosophy of perception 'being-in-world', existence is defined in terms of 'motility' which, again refers to 'motor intentions' or 'motor intentionality'.[26] By these terms, it is emphasized that moving actively 'towards something' – instead of staying still – means that the spatial position of the perceptive body is active and unstable – it has a direction; it is intentional.[27]

Where is place

The verb 'perform' essentially signifies representation of something, as a mirror reflection of the world. Walter Benjamin makes a comparison between theatre and film in his essay 'The Work of Art in the Age of Technical Reproduction'. He draws an implicit comparison between the two: 'Any thorough study proves that there is indeed no greater contrast than that of stage play to a work of art that is completely subject to or, like film, founded in mechanical reproduction'.[28] Benjamin claims that the fateful hour for the traditional work of art was the invention of photography. Benjamin's criticism is sometimes interpreted lightly; as an opposition for anything technical, whereas, on the contrary, his notion of the 'decay of aura' is not supposed to be taken as longing for nostalgia.[29]

> In Benjamin's thinking the notion of human experience and the conditions of perception are quite central and the concept of medium is most relevant in his theoretical survey. By the phrase 'loss of aura' Benjamin refers to the 're-arrangement of space and time' and to the historical changes, which have altered the fundamental nature of e.g. the meaning of 'place'.[30]

Paul Virilio's literal brush paints before us an image of cybernetic mankind, whose real-time tele-presence is an allegory for the experience of placeless place, the timeless time and out-of-gravity experience familiar to an astronaut.[31] Global 'tele-presenciation' and VR are part of our everyday real-time experience, where we may experience closer connection with someone oceans away, than we do with the next-door neighbour. As cultural lived practices, the lightness and accessibility of mobile travelling has a profound effect on how we outline our existence and on how we place ourselves in the world.

In the be-coming

In focusing on experience, it is notable that persistent questioning, evaluating and re-framing of concepts such as 'presence' and 'reality' is substantially presumed. The interpretations keep escaping fixed definitions and stay unstable, for it must be emphasized, too, that it is much to do with individuation; of some-thing being in its be-coming-one, and thus in all of its potentialities of be-coming-one, indivisible yet never accomplished.

Phenomenological 'attitude' focuses on matters in their be-coming, striving to make way for the matters to appear from and in their own essence; in their being. The challenge for phenomenology is in its contemplating on 'reality'; not in the sense of reality versus illusion, nor in terms of what the reality is – but rather as 'how' reality is. Nietzsche writes on the primary conditions of tragic art, pointing out the perpetual, un-resolvable tension between impartial, chaotic fluidity ('embodied' by the 'Dionysian') and the individuated subjectivity ('embodied' by the 'Apollonian') that lies between these two opposing aspects of nature. In *The Birth of Tragedy*, Nietzsche emphasizes that it is this fundamental dichotomy that fosters the conditions necessary for creation of art. Hence, the primary conditions of (tragic) art are to be found in its be-coming and in its individuation, which are sketched in Nietzsche's words as follows:

> Both very different drives go hand in hand, for the most part in open conflict with each other and simultaneously provoking each other all the time to new and more powerful offspring, in order to perpetuate for themselves the contest of opposites which the common word 'Art' only seems to bridge, until they finally, through a marvellous metaphysical act, seem to pair up with each other and, as this pair, produce Attic tragedy, just as much a Dionysian as an Apollonian work of art.[32]

Though these opposite 'artistic forming powers' (*Künstlerische Mächte*) for Nietzsche are forces that occur 'in and by nature', they presume an 'artist to work on them', to put them in operation in order to strive for higher intensions.[33] When the formulation process becomes carried out by the human figure, the artist, the outcome on one side shines in 'Apollonian' image-form, and on the other, appears in 'Dionysian', non-imaginal form.

John Sallis argues that as the 'imaginality' of an image has been freed from its objectivity, it thus should no longer be conceived through its object-character. It should no longer be ruled by the logic of the Cartesian eye. An image should, rather, be conceived through the way it is, in its 'mode of being'. Thus, it is approached rather through the idea of an 'image in its actualization than as a representational object.[34] The phenomenological approach is quite relevant, as 'the image is letting the showing as imaging come to pass from the (very existence of the image) – objects themselves.'[35] When we are confronted by images, we are not confronted by an already existing original. Instead, what is ahead of us is a be-coming present of the original. The image conceived as a process is nothing solid by its nature, but rather intentional, unstable, active and potential – as any process is. In the context of phenomenological contemplation of image, the matter of dwelling in digital image-space approaches the idea of actualization and be-coming of the 'imaginal experience'. This might be called 'the be-coming' of a sensuous process.

Notes

1. Merleau-Ponty, M. (2002), *Phenomenology of Perception*, New York, NY: Routledge Classics, pp. 235–9, (Original (1945), *Phénomènologie de la perception*, (trans.) Routledge & Kegan, Paul, 1st English edition published in 1962).

2. Smith, A.D. (2007), 'The Flesh of Perception. Merleau-Ponty and Husserl' in Baldwin, T., (ed.), *Reading Merleau-Ponty. On Phenomenology of Perception*, London: Routledge, p. 16.

3. Merleau-Ponty, M., *Phenomenology of Perception*, p.340.

4. Ibid., p.5.

5. Ibid., p.7.

6. Ibid., p.5.

7. For Merleau-Ponty, and also for Edmund Husserl the 'lived body' (*Leib*) is essential for perception of the world and for being-in-the-world as he writes that the body is 'necessary in all perception'. In German language the 'objective body' is called *Körper*. In Finnish language the difference of 'lived body' and 'object-body' the distinction is also drawn out by separate words; '*keho*' standing for the lived, singular, sensing body and '*ruumis*' for object-body, corpse, or body in the meaning of a dead person.

8. Smith, A.D. (2007), 'The Flesh of Perception. Merleau-Ponty and Husserl', in Baldwin, T., (ed.), *Reading Merleau-Ponty. On Phenomenology of Perception*, pp. 16–17.

9. Ibid., p. 2.

10. Cytowic, R. (1998), *The Man who Tasted Shapes*, New York, NY: The MIT Press, pp. 73–80.

11. Morse, M. (1992), 'Video Installation Art: the Body, the Image, and the Space-in-Between', in Hall, D., Fifer, S.J., (eds.), *Illuminating Video: An Essential Guide to Video Art*, London: Aperture, pp. 153–62.

12. Grau, O. (2002), *Virtual Art. From Illusion to Immersion*, Cambridge, Mass: The MIT Press, pp. 41–6.

13. Hansen, M.B.N. (2006), *New Philosophy for New Media*, 2nd edition, Cambridge, Mass: The MIT Press, pp. 44–5.

14. Manovich, L. (2001), *The Language of New Media*, Cambridge, Mass: The MIT Press, p. 183.

15. ibid., pp. 60–1.

16. Hansen, M.B.N. (2006), *New Philosophy for New Media*, 2nd edition, Cambridge, Mass: The MIT Press, pp. 10–70.

17. Merleau-Ponty speaks of the unity of the body as an 'existential unity'. In terms of existence, he defines the body by it's 'tasks' and its 'projects'. The unity of a body thus, in his thinking, is element in relation to potential action. Furthermore, spatiality of the body is not to be approached in terms of a 'location', but in terms of a *situation* – again something active and unstable. A.D.Smith points out that existence, or being-in-world in Merleau-Ponty's philosophy of perception is to be conceived in terms of 'motility': 'not just as an active moment, but action on or *towards* objects'. Smith, (2007), pp. 16–17.

18. Merleau-Ponty, M., *Phenomenology of Perception*, pp. 321–2.
19. ibid., p. 322.
20. ibid., p. 333.
21. Zuniga, R.M. (2000), 'Penny's Robotic Madness', *The Spleen,* 13, also http://www.ambriente.com/ writing/simon.html
22. Grau, O. (2002), *Virtual Art. From Illusion to Immersion*, pp. 276–8.
23. Zuniga, R.M. (2000), 'Penny's Robotic Madness', *The Spleen,* 13, also http://www.ambriente.com/ writing/simon.html
24. Morse, M. (1992), 'Video Installation Art: the Body, the Image, and the Space-in-Between', in Hall, D., Fifer, S.J., (eds.), *Illuminating Video: An Essential Guide to Video Art*, London: Aperture.
25. Hansen, M.B.N. (2006), *New Philosophy for New Media*, p. 10.
26. Smith, A.D. (2007), 'The Flesh of Perception. Merleau-Ponty and Husserl' in Baldwin, T., (ed.), *Reading Merleau-Ponty. On Phenomenology of Perception*, p. 17.
27. ibid., pp. 13–18.
28. Benjamin, W. (1992), *Illuminations*, 2nd edition, London: Fontana Press, p. 223. (Original: *Gesammelte Schriften*, 1955, (ed.) by Arendt, Hannah , English trans. Zohn, H.)
29. Benjamin, W. (1969), *Illuminations*, 1st edition, New York: Schocken Verlag, pp. 104–5.
30. Elo, M., (2007) 'Image Captured – the Exile and Asylum of the Actor', a lecture in the Academy of Fine Art/ Doctoral seminar, 2 February 2007. (Translated from Finnish by writer).
31. Virilio, P. (1998), *La vitesse de libération*, Paris: Galilee, pp. 136–40.
32. Nietzsche, F. (1993), *The Birth of Tragedy*, London: Penguin Books, pp. 32–3. (Original: *Die Gebut der Tragödie*, 1871, English translated, Johnston, Ian C.)
33. Luoto, M. (2004), 'The Beauty of an Image. Of Apollonian Appearing', *Tiede & Edistys,* 2, pp. 112–23. Translated from Finnish by writer.
34. Sallis, J. (1995), *Phenomenology and the end of metaphysics*, Bloomington: Indiana University Press, pp. 70–1.
35. ibid., p. 75.

14

EMBODIMENT, AMBULATION AND DURATION

Craig G. Staff

Within the context of post-war avant-garde artistic practice, minimalism attempted to formulate a conception of the artwork that was given through an embodied viewer. Specifically, the experiential basis of the minimalist artwork entailed a kinaesthetic exchange that unfolded within a set of spatio-temporal coordinates that were necessarily 'real' or actual as opposed to being fictive or illusionistic. On one level, the separate epistemological reception of the artwork became engendered because of minimalism's desire to differentiate itself from the condition of the artwork as constituted by late or so-called 'high' modernist criticism. To this end, the claim that the object, in the instant of viewing became hypostatized appeared no longer tenable. Specifically, by attempting to counter the dominant experiential model, a model that was synectic, disembodied and atemporal, and moreover had first been ratified within the context of quattrocentro painting, minimalism sought to recast the categorical boundaries that separated the viewer from the viewed. The corollary of this strategy meant that the act of viewing, now conceived as ambulatory and episodic, could potentially coalesce into a more dynamic 'event.' By seeking to address the implications held for the 'viewer' by minimalism, the aim of this chapter is to consider one antecedental model that pertains to the new modes of spectating.

> 'Poems are just like pictures: with some, the nearer you go, the better you like them; with others, you must stand back.'[1]

Of the eight installations that have been commissioned so far for the Turbine Hall, Tate Modern's cavernous gallery space, certainly the most physically engaging, if not wholly exhilarating has been Carsten Höller's *Test Site*, 2006. Positioned at different levels of the hall were five steel slides, spiralling down to the ground and appearing out of the hall's architecture somewhat like a series of futuristic, mechanical tendrils. According to Jessica Morgan, the curator of *Test Site*, Höller's installation is symptomatic of a:

> recent history of art concerned with staging the everyday...incorporating willing participants into the arena of the work...Here, the physical object of art has on occasion been completely eliminated, and the institutional or public space turned into a changeable and constantly performed or staged field in which the audience is central as player or performer.[2]

One's first impression of this spectacle was that the ephemeral, seemingly thrill-seeking demands it placed upon the viewer appeared to bracket out the conditions of possibility for any sustained critique or meditation into the place of art and its ascribed role. However, by the very fact that it did transform the vast, echoic space of the Turbine Hall into a 'performed stage or field' meant that *Test Site* nevertheless aligned itself with, albeit in a somewhat eccentric fashion, a set of debates which today centre upon affectivity within the visual arts. Primarily, if the work, as the title would appear to imply, was some form of speculative enquiry, then what was being 'tested,' on one level, was the extent to which an artwork could become fore-grounded by a relationship with the spectator that was dynamic, participatory and markedly democratic. The corollary of which, as one watched an endless succession of willing participants cascade down the steel helixes, was the dissolution of the categorical boundaries that separated the viewer from the viewed. Working with these two basic admissions, the aim of this chapter is to attempt to locate and to a certain extent unpick the prehistory of what is now a prevalent strategy within the repertoire of the contemporary artist. For example, 'Commonwealth', a group exhibition that was held at Tate Modern in 2003 and which included a piece by Carsten Höller, which was inherently 'interactive' in scope. As well as including a semi-operational billiard table and a room where people could sit and read facsimiles of political and philosophical texts, viewers could also inhabit Höller's *Frisbee House*, a tent-like structure containing 30 frisbees that could be thrown either at other viewers or through holes that had been cut into the fabric.[3] This will entail a consideration of the proclivity for minimalism, as one salient form of late modernist practice, to entail a dramaturgy of the viewer that was dynamic, equivocal and episodic. As such, the theoretical positioning of the object entailed and was partly given through the mobilization of an embodied viewer. Within a broader sense, the over-arching intention is directed towards the means by which we might begin to map out a prehistory of the thematics that today pertain to so-called 'spectatorship mediums'.

The equivocal object

From its historical inception, the minimalist object was a repudiation of a certain intellectual and aesthetic dogma that the criticism of Clement Greenberg was considered broadly representative of. Indeed, the differentiation of minimalism from previous critical models of avant-garde artistic practice, on one level, took the form of an attempted withdrawal from the dictates of the canonical western pictorial tradition. Such an attitude is evident in the transcript of an interview between Donald Judd and Frank Stella and Bruce Glaser. Originally broadcast as 'New Nihilism or New Art?' on WBAI-FM, New York in February of 1964, the discussion was subsequently edited by Lucy Lippard and published in 'Art News' in September 1966. Within the first part of the interview, Glaser is keen to establish a set of historical precedents for the work of Frank Stella, whose paintings had developed from the sombre, black-stripe series begun during the latter half of 1958 towards a body of work that encompassed differing configurations of colour, pattern and line. Indeed the first section of the interview in its entirety entails an attempt, on the part of all three speakers to negotiate a credible position for the various three-dimensional forms that were now being produced and that purportedly were 'minimalist' in scope and intent. For his part Judd, keen to repudiate any claim of continuity between previous models of non-representational, geometric art and the 'new' art that was being produced, attempts to position his own work in diametrical opposition to both the visual and philosophical tradition of Europe. Upon being asked by Glaser why he chose to avoid compositional effects, Judd claimed that there was a tendency 'to carry with them all the structures, values, feelings of the whole European tradition. It suits me fine if they are all down the drain.'[4] Moreover, because the qualities of European art were 'linked up with a philosophy – rationalism, rationalistic philosophy',[5] Judd attempted to bracket out the conditions of possibility for his own work to be read on these terms by claiming that the parts that went to make up his own sculptures were necessarily unrelated. Therefore, as Glaser observed, they were based upon 'an abdication of logical thinking.'[6] Compounded as it was by the object's 'brute physical presence,'[7] the corollary of this abdication resulted in a wholly separate set of demands being placed upon the agency of the viewer. The production of an ostensibly new category of object proffered the viewer with what one observer called an 'embarrassing freedom,'[8] the incidence of critics framing their discussion through a basic admission of perturbation is notably high, with feelings of uneasiness, unhappiness and even, in one case, a feeling of bewilderment being openly expressed.[9] This problem which one might assume stems from the ostensible equivocality the object was understood as having, is evident if one considers the artist's intentions themselves. In 'Notes on Sculpture 2', originally published in October 1966, Robert Morris included a statement by another minimalist, Tony Smith, which entailed the artist's intention to produce a work that neither loomed over the observer nor, equally, was capable of being loomed over. Of course, this physical positioning of the work in relation to the viewer is also a theoretical positioning, and one whose apparent indeterminacy resists straightforward assimilation into the realm of 'meaning.'[10] Anyway, such a set of responses are telling. Collectively, one would misconstrue such remarks if one was to take them simply as anecdotal evidence of a general feeling of antipathy directed towards a range of objects that the critic was unaccustomed to. Rather, the observations I think are indicative of a more fundamental sense of uncertainty, which directly stemmed from minimalism's fundamental problematization of the received protocols of viewing.

Although such protocols first became figured within the interpretive framework of quattrocentro painting, a framework wherein art was conceived, perhaps for the first time, as a theoretical form of practice as much as a social or liturgical form, to a certain extent these protocols continued to underwrite the formalist account of high modernism. It was exactly viewing conditions necessitated by late modernist abstraction that the contingent, speculative object of minimalism attempted to dismantle, and, potentially, re-imagine.

The inception of corporeal space

Within the context of the quattrocentro, and partly as a result of the increasing prevalence of humanist doctrines, the formation of subjectivity inscribed the 'body' as the primary epistemological locus. As Ian Harvie has noted, the body became 'both the key instrument and the prime specimen of a new, practically oriented, curiosity. The body divided outside from inside, so that all investigations of the structure of reality took the body as the point of departure and most significant reference point.'[11] Implicit within the logic of painting at this time had been a specific set of precepts that had been valorized within the highly rationalised conception of pictorial space given through the 'new science' of perspective. According to John White, artificial perspective, as it came to be conceived during the quattrocentro was constituted by four principle characteristics:

> (a) There is no distortion of straight lines. (b) There is no distortion, or foreshortening, of objects or distances parallel to the picture plane, which is therefore given a particular emphasis. (c) Orthogonals converge to a single vanishing point dependent on the fixed position of the observer's eye. (d) The size of objects diminishes in an exact proportion to the distance from the observer, so that all quantities are measurable.[12]

As John Shearman writes: 'the synthesis (of mathematical perspective) occurred...when a shift of priorities produced an urgent need driven by evolving expressive purposes, a new mode of experience, and to that end a newly conceived reality of the spectator.'[13] Shearman's account of the role of the spectator in Renaissance art is taken up, in part, by what he describes as a *transitive* relationship. He writes: '...to say that the spectator on the street finds himself in the position of the other Apostles, or in other words to say that Verrochio's subject is completed only by the presence of a spectator in the narrative, is to realize that the relationship between work of art and spectator is now fully transitive.'[14] Up until this point, according to Norman Bryson, there was:

> no requirement that the text be articulated from the viewpoint of the individual craftsman or be received by an individuated spectator: just the reverse – for the schema to be guaranteed precise recognition, it must keep to its minimal form. The viewing subject is addressed liturgically, as a member of the faith, and communally, as a generated presence.[15]

As a rational means by which pictorial or fictive space could be organized, the corollary of perspective was that the viewer herself would be rendered complicit within the perspectival schema as it became mapped out. As Victor Burgin explains: 'Perspective provided, quite literally, the "common ground" on which the identification of architectural space and corporeal space could "take place". In the Renaissance, the inaugural act in constructing this parity was to lay out the horizontal plane that united the illusory space of the image with the real space of the viewer.'[16] More specifically, as Norman Bryson notes:

> In its production of the centric ray between viewpoint and vanishing point, the Albertian regime assumes the viewer not simply as an ambient witness...but as a physical presence;

and in this sense the vanishing point is the anchor of a system which *incarnates* the viewer, renders him tangible and corporeal, a measurable, and above all a visible object in a world of absolute visibility.[17]

Reading the generation of a viewer upon these terms, both Burgin's and Bryson's claims are further qualified by the *braccio*. What marked this standardized unit of measurement that determined a painting's 'true' proportions was its correlation with the human body. Alberti observes that: 'three braccia is just about the average height of a man's body.'[18] However, the efficacy of what was now, ostensibly, a regimented experience of the work of art through one-point mathematical perspective was dependent upon the viewer assuming a specific station point in relation to the picture plane. Adhering to the protocol of this visual system, and having assumed the painting's station point, the percipient was now in the position to receive the entirety of its effects instantaneously or *un' occhiata*.[19] Of course, the delimitation of the percipient or viewer through a prescribed station point was never entirely watertight. Indeed, that painting, from its historical inception as a theoretical object was conditioned by indeterminacy and can be attributed, at least in part, to what Erwin Panofsky identified as perspectival distance. To this end, the laws of perspective brought into focus the question of the specificity of the viewer's station point and, furthermore, whether the experience of the work of art by the viewer should primarily be conceived, in the first instance, according to actual or fictive space. According to Erwin Panofsky: 'It had to be asked (and indeed it was asked) whether the perspectival configuration of a painting was to be oriented toward the factual standpoint of the beholder...or whether conversely the beholder ought ideally to adapt himself to the perspectival configuration of the painting.' The corollary that inevitably follows from this observation, as Panofsky adds, was 'how close or how far the perpendicular distance ought to be measured.'[20]

This infra-logic, which constituted the reception of painting, continued into the sixteenth century. Leonardo for his part wrote that: 'Painting presents its essence to you, through the visual power and the means by which the *imprensiva* receives natural objects, in an instant [un' subito]...'[21] Leonardo's writings in relation to identifying a role for the viewer are interesting because in terms of ascertaining the correct perpendicular distance, his suggestions range from a distance of anything between ten to twenty times the size of the greatest object represented.[22] Additionally, he challenges the efficacy of the stationary viewpoint. Firstly, in his estimation, 'a picture will look correct from a number of positions if its perspective construction has been carried out using a viewing distance at least three times the size of the object.'[23] Secondly, Leonardo's recent invention of curvilinear perspective 'would allow the picture to be viewed from any position. This curvilinear perspective projects a spherical intersection of the visual cone on the surface of the picture, and since all the points of the intersection are at the same distance from the eye the viewer is free to move in front of the painting.'[24] Whether Leonardo's general level of indeterminacy more widely denotes the artist's inability to be unequivocal or whether it can be read as denoting the possibilities for a degree of contingency is difficult to conclusively say. Frangenberg observes that his 'approach to the optical tradition...changed over time and he seems never to have worked out a unified theory of the relationship between the process of vision and the construction of artificial perspective in paintings.'[25]

Even at the beginning of the seventeenth century, considerations of how the act of vision became inscribed within the theoretical correlates of one-point mathematical perspective are discussed in terms of immediacy. Guidobaldo de Monte, in his exposition *Perspectivae libri sex* echoes the critical set of precedents that had emerged with the publication of *De Pictura* by conflating the viewer's comportment with the 'laying bare' (*appraehendere possit*) of the image within an instant. According to de Monte, for this to occur three things must necessarily be taken into consideration: 'namely position, then distance and finally the possible angle of view: so that the object as a whole can become visible to the eye; so that the eye can take in the object at a single glance.'[26] It is important to add to these observations by noting that between the publication of *De Pictura* and *Perspectivae libri sex*, a diametrical conception of time within Renaissance painting became posited. In 1567 Pietro Cataneo, in his own treatise on the operation of the perspectival laws, clearly identifies the process of viewing a painting as a series of successive and episodic stages: 'Note that in whatever thing one looks at one cannot see all its parts at a glance but one judges with the eye one part at a time...'[27] As Frangenberg notes, the Islamic scholar Alhazen had originally introduced this durational conception of vision: 'And some particular visual intentions from which the forms of visual things are composed appear at first glance onto the thing seen: and some do not appear except after scrutiny and considerable consideration.'[28]

From presentness to presence

Whilst the organization of late modernist painting, with its wholesale rejection of verisimilitude clearly was not organized around such a set of visual predicates, implicit within the logic of this model of painting remained the assumption that painting could be 'received' by the viewer all at once, or instantaneously.[29] More specifically, as Rosalind Krauss has noted, the singularity of the object, an account of the object, whose operation was synectic, was keyed into and given through the primacy of vision:

> If the Renaissance had diagrammed the punctuality of [a] viewing point, it was modernism that insisted on it, underscored it, made the issue of the indivisible instant of seeing serve as a fundamental principle in the doctrine of aesthetic truth. Modernism was to absolutize this 'now' to insist that painting exist within the indivisible present of the extremist possible perceptual intensity...[30]

That the experiential basis of late modernist art had become underscored by a specific temporality is evident in 'Art and Objecthood', Michael Fried's riposte to and attack on the presence of 'theatre', which, in turn, he claimed worked to legitimise 'literal art', a pejorative term Fried coined in 1967 for minimalism:

> It is as though one's experience of modernist painting *has* no duration – not because one *in fact* experiences a picture by Noland or Olitski...in no time at all, but because *at every moment the work itself is wholly manifest.* [...] It is this continuous and entire presentness, amounting, as it were, to the perpetual creation of itself, that one experiences as a kind of *instantaneousness*...[31]

Indeed, this conception of painting, and specifically the viewing conditions engendered by reading painting on these terms, were reiterated by the philosopher Stanley Cavell four years later. Although Cavell appears willing to concede that the viewer could be involved in an exchange that was broadly reciprocal, painting remains delimited by a temporality that is theoretically consonant with that of Fried's:

> There may be any number of ways of acknowledging the condition of painting as total thereness...For example, a painting may acknowledge its frontedness, or its finitude, or its specific thereness – that is, its presentness; and your accepting it will accordingly mean acknowledging your frontedness, or directionality, or verticality towards its world, or any world – or your presentness, in its aspect of absolute hereness and nowness.[32]

However, whilst Fried, and to a certain extent Cavell attempted to frame painting, and specifically the appropriate mode of painting's address through a dialectic of presentness, it was the idea of presence, which on one level was more readily bound up with a phenomenological mode of address, which minimalism gravitated towards as a means of legitimizing the objects they produced.[33] Contained within the dialectic of presence were the conditions of possibility for both a different conception of the object to be engendered and, as a corollary, a radically different set of viewing conditions.

This is evidenced in 'Allusion and Illusion in Donald Judd', an article Rosalind Krauss wrote for *Artforum* in 1966.[34] Describing a long wall-hung piece by Donald Judd made of brushed aluminium and punctuated by a series of irregular shorter bars, Krauss attempts to track the operation of the work by assuming a series of contrasting viewpoints in relation to it. After reading the work from being directly in front of it, she notes that the tendency to perceive the main bar as a support for the 'voluptuous' lower bars is in fact disingenuous. For an oblique reading of the work denies this possibility by making apparent the fact that the aluminium bars are in fact hollow and it is the actual shorter bars which are, in fact, directly attached to the wall.[35] As a means of attempting to account for this reversal of the work's form, and because it further confounds the viewer's intention to perceive it within a set of unequivocal terms due to the unequal intervals which separate the smaller violet bars, Krauss draws upon the terms of perception as they were set out by Maurice Merleau-Ponty. The actual length of the piece requires that it be seen in 'perspective', but also partly because when this is attempted it does not readily adhere to the rationalisation of optical space as it was given within the quattrocentro. The sculpture can be seen and sensed, and here she quotes from Merleau-Ponty, 'only in terms of its present coming into being as an object given in the imperious unity, the presence, the insurpassable plenitude which is for us the definition of the real.'[36] Moreover, and again drawing upon Merleau-Ponty's phenomenological enquiry into vision, she notes that perception 'does not give me truths like geometry, but presences' and as such the 'lived perspective' of which Merleau-Ponty speaks is very different from the rational perspective of geometrical laws.[37]

The coalescent 'event'

During the same year within which Krauss wrote 'Allusion and Illusion', the artist Robert Morris had begun his own enquiry into the contingent object minimalism had proffered. Firstly, in 'Notes on Sculpture 1', originally published in *Artforum* in February 1966, Morris tackles the issue of divisibility, anticipating Fried's own remarks in relation to the object being considered within a singular set of terms:

> ...art objects have clearly divisible parts that set up...relationships. Such a condition suggests the alternative question: could a work exist that has only one property? Obviously not, since nothing exists that has only one property. A single, pure sensation cannot be transmissable precisely because one perceives simultaneously more than one property as parts in any given situation.[38]

In 'Notes on Sculpture: Part II', written eight months later, Morris develops his initial claims by attempting to consider the ontology of the artwork in relation to its epistemology. Firstly, he posits the idea that the object, and here we can assume he is speaking of the minimalist object, whilst still rendering the viewer complicit, does so on a very different set of terms than those attributable to the logic of one-point mathematical perspective. Such complicity now becomes figured through the fact that she/he is palpably more aware of their own situatedness, their own *presence*, in relation to the object: 'The object is but one of the terms in the newer aesthetic. It is in some way more reflexive because one's awareness of oneself existing in the same space as the work is stronger than in previous work...'[39] Heavily bound up with the idea that the experiential basis of the object was necessarily reflexive, is the related notion that the 'space' within which the object is both located and viewed is mutable. Therefore, creating the conditions of possibility for an unregimented experience of the artwork that encompasses multiple viewpoints: 'One is more aware than before that he himself is establishing relationships as he apprehends the object from various positions and under varying conditions of light and spatial context.'[40] It is worth noting that in the same year that Morris was attempting to formulate the experiential basis of minimalism through an interpretive framework that was fore-grounded by multiple viewpoints, parallax and ambulatory space, the psychologist James J. Gibson had begun to formulate a set of mutually inclusive ideas within the framework of visual perception:

> the identity of a thing, its constancy, can emerge in perception only when it is observed under changing circumstances in various aspects. The static form of a thing, its image or picture, is not at all what is permanent about it. A form frozen in time is ambiguous information and is not a typical stimulus for our receptive surfaces. Only when the perspectives flow can one notice the distinctive features of the solid object.[41]

Some of the best of the new work, being more open and neutral in terms of surface incident, is more sensitive to the varying contexts of space and light in which it exists. Even its most patently unalterable property – shape – does not remain constant. For it is the viewer who changes the shape constantly by his change in position relative to the work.[42]

Specifically though, what this analogous model of spectatorship affirms is the fact that the experiential basis of the minimalist artwork entailed a dynamic, and to this end kinaesthetic exchange that unfolded within a set of spatio-temporal coordinates that were necessarily 'real' or actual as opposed to being fictive or illusionistic. To this end, the claim that the object, in the instant of viewing became hypostatized appeared no longer tenable. By bracketing out the experiential model as set out by both Clement Greenberg and Michael Fried, a model that was synectic, disembodied and atemporal, minimalism conceived the terms upon which the viewer and the viewed were conceived as mutually inclusive. The corollary of which meant that the act of viewing, now conceived as embodied, ambulatory and episodic, could potentially coalesce into a more dynamic 'event'. In an article published after these debates had become all but played out, Morris claims that the concerns of such work, namely the coexistence between the 'space' of the work and the 'space' of the viewer, the multiple, parallactic viewpoints and the specific conception of time such work necessitated, were also ideas one finds in the Baroque.[43] A point of fascination, albeit a paradoxical one then was the fact that although Baroque art and minimalism would initially appear to offer two wholly separate conceptions of 'art,' upon closer inspection both movements appear to be premised upon an equivalent modality of address and a consonant dramaturgy of the viewer.

Coda

By way of a coda to what has been discussed, it would appear appropriate to briefly consider a piece Olafur Eliasson made in 2001. Conceived for the windows of MoMA's Garden Hall in New York, Seeing yourself sensing consisted of 50 sheets of striped transparent and mirrored glass which extended over the first and second floors of the museum. As you moved in front of it, the experiential basis of the piece became fore-grounded by a certain switching between two separate modes of spectating, if not realities. On the one hand, by looking immediately through the transparent vertical slats, one became inscribed within the work as a perceiving subject, capable of looking out onto the world and finding oneself somehow situated within it. On the other hand, if one looked at one's reflection within the mirrored slats, this phenomenological purview became short-circuited, and one became cast as a mere reflection or apparition, objectified and caught in the petrified instant of the image of one's gaze. Indeed, as one attempted to situate oneself within a visual field that switched between two seemingly mutually exclusive realms, such an encounter appeared to directly echo Morris's own claim that our 'encounter with objects in space forces us to reflect on our selves, which can never become "other", which can never become objects for our external examination. In the domain of real space the subject-object dilemma can never be resolved.'[44]

Whilst certainly, this piece can be seen, on one level, as a continuation of a certain line of enquiry that had first been mobilized by minimalism, its efficacy, and its relevance to the discussion generally, is the fact that it places under question, in both a succinct and highly subtle way, minimalism's originating claim; that the phenomenological body could still be conceived as the primary locus by which the exterior world might be palpably felt. Certainly, as Rosalind Krauss observes, 'this corporeal condition...which was still directed at a body-in-general within a rather generalized sense of space-at-large – that condition became ever more particularized in work that...followed in the '70s and '80s.'[45]

Although, antithetically to minimalism, obdurate matter has now been entirely absented, (and by doing so, lays itself open to accusations that it veers dangerously close to merely re-staging a dialectic minimalism sought to critique, if not entirely repudiate, namely that of opticality), *Seeing yourself sensing* still seems entirely in accordance with the new type of art Morgan has identified. A category of art that mobilizes the viewer within its arena as a willing participant and one wherein the physical object has entirely been eradicated. However, it should be noted that the mobilization of the viewer for Eliasson is never automatically a given; rather, the relationship which becomes inscribed between the viewer and that which is viewed, is in harmony with the terms that were first described by Morgan. Therefore, it must necessarily entail a reflexive form of consciousness that is capable of making the viewer aware of her own situatedness and cultural conditioning. As a means of attempting to articulate the mechanics of this process, the artist describes a viewing situation analogous with that of cinema:

> At certain times you can sit in a cinema and become so engaged with the film that you kind of feel the level of representation, but then the next moment you flip back out. And I think the ability to go in and out of the work – showing the machinery – is important today. My work is very much about positioning the subject.[46]

To this end what *Seeing yourself sensing* as a theoretical object, renders visible is the actual cultural, social and phenomenological apparatus of the performed field within which the act of viewing, and by extension the viewer, becomes inextricably inscribed within.

Notes

1. Sisson, C. H. (1975), *The Poetic Art A Translation of Horace's Ars Poetica*, Cheshire: Carcanet Press, p. 34.
2. Morgan, J. (2006), *Carsten Höller: Test Site,* The Unilever Series, London: Tate Publishing, p. 13.
3. See Morgan, J. (ed.) (2003), *Commonwealth*, London: Tate Publications.
4. Battcock, G. (ed.) (1995), *Minimal Art A Critical Anthology*, USA: University of California Press, p. 150.
5. ibid., p.151.
6. ibid.
7. Krauss, R. (1966), 'Allusion and Illusion in Donald Judd,' *Artforum*, 4, No.9, p. 24.
8. Battcock, G. (ed.) (1995), *Minimal Art A Critical Anthology*, USA: University of California Press, p. 203.
9. Bryson, N. (1983), *Vision and Painting: The Logic of the Gaze*, London: Macmillan, p. 96. For example, see Wagstaff Jr, S. J. (1964), 'Paintings to Think About', *ARTnews*, January, reproduced in Meyer, J., (ed.) (2002), *Minimalism*, London: Phaidon, p.203 and Rose, B., 'ABC Art', in Battcock, G., p. 281.
10. Morris, R. (1992), 'Notes on Sculpture 2', in Harrison, C., Wood, P., (eds.), *Art in Theory 1900–1990*, Oxford: Blackwell, p. 816.

11. Harvie, I. (1997), 'Me and My Shadow: On the Accumulation of Body-Images in Western Society. Part One: The Image and the Image of the Body in Pre-Modern Society, *Body and Society* 3, p. 25.

12. White, J. (1967), *Birth and Rebirth of Pictorial Space*, London: Faber, pp. 123–4.

13. Shearman, J. (1992), *Only Connect...Art and the Spectator in the Italian Renaissance*, Princeton: Princeton University Press, p. 62.

14. Shearman, J. (1992), p. 33.

15. Bryson, N. (1983), *Vision and Painting: The Logic of the Gaze*, London: Macmillan, p. 96.

16. Burgin, V. (1996), *In/Different Spaces: Place and Memory in Visual Culture*, Berkeley, London: University of California Press, p. 142.

17. Bryson, N. (1983), *Vision and Painting: The Logic of the Gaze,* p. 106.

18. Alberti, L. B. (1972), *On Painting and Sculpture*, Grayson, Cecil (ed.) (trans.), London: Phaidon, p. 5.

19. ibid., p. 49.

20. Panofsky, E. (1991), *Perspective as Symbolic Form*, Wood, C.S. (trans.), New York: Zone Books, p. 68.

21. da Vinci, Leonardo (1270) *Codex Urbinas Latinus* , quoted in Andrews (1995), p. 62.

22. da Vinci, Leonardo, *The Literary Works of Leonardo da Vinci*, Richter, J. P. (ed.) (1939), London: Oxford University Press, no. 543 MS A. 406, no. 544 MS A 41a, no. 544 MS A 416.

23. Frangenberg, T. (1986), 'The Image and the Moving Eye: Jean Pélerin (Viator) to Guidobaldo Del Monte,' *Journal of the Warburg and Courthauld Institutes*, p. 167.

24. ibid.

25. ibid., p. 167.

26. De Monte, Guidobaldo, *Perspectivae libri sex*, n. 46, quoted in Frangenberg, p. 165.

27. Cataneo, Pietro (1567), *L'archirttura*, Venice, 179, quoted in Frangenberg, p. 151.

28. Frangenberg, p. 152.

29. In fact, as early as 1945 Clement Greenberg attempted to frame the viewing conditions of the work of art through such a temporality. See 'On Looking at Pictures: Review of Painting and painters: How to Look at a Picture: From Giotto to Chagall by Lionel Venturi' quoted in *The Collected Essays and Criticism*, O' Brian, J. (ed.) (1993), vol. 2, *Arrogant Purpose, 1945–9*, Chicago: The University of Chicago Press, pp. 34–5.

30. Krauss, R. (1993), *The Optical Unconscious*, Cambridge, Mass: MIT Press, pp. 213–214. For example of its prevalence within the discourses of modernism generally, see Mangold, R. (2000), *Flat Art*, quoted in Meyer, J., *Minimalism*, London: Phaidon, pp. 230–1. See also Rose, B. (1971), 'Quality in Lewis', *Artforum* 10, October, pp. 62–3.

31. Fried, M., 'Art and Objecthood', reprinted in *Art in Theory 1900–1990*, p. 832.

32. Cavell, S. (1971), *The World Viewed: Reflections on the Ontology of Film*, New York: Viking Press, p. 110.

33. By making this broad assertion one immediately invokes the figure of Maurice Merleau-Ponty and his writings that attempted to formulate an account of experience that was phenomenological in scope and intent. As Foster et al. note, since his 'phenomenology places the subject's body – its bilateral symmetry, its vertical axis, its having a front and a back, the latter invisible to the subject him – or herself – at the center of the subject's intention towards meaning – those artistic projects

dependent upon bodily vectors for their aesthetic experience are particularly open to phenomenological analysis.' Foster, et al. (2004), *Art Since 1900: Modernism, Antimodernism, Postmodernism*, London: Thames and Hudson, p. 495.

34. Krauss, R. (1966), 'Allusion and Illusion in Donald Judd,' *Artforum*, 4, No.9, May, pp. 24–6.

35. ibid., p. 25.

36. ibid. The text from which the quotation of Merleau-Ponty's is taken from is 'Cézanne's Doubt', reproduced in *Sense and NonSense*, which was first published in its translated version in 1964.

37. ibid.

38. 'Notes on Sculpture: Part 1', reproduced in Morris, Robert (1995), *Continuous Project Altered Daily: The Writings of Robert Morris*, Cambridge, Mass: MIT Press, p. 6.

39. ibid., p. 15

40. ibid.

41. Gibson, J. (1966), 'The Problem of Temporal Order in Stimulation and Perception', *Journal of Psychology*, No.62, p. 148.

42. ibid., p. 16. In fact, as Nick Kaye has noted, by attaching mirrored surfaces on to the unitary, serial structures that he had produced during the first half of the 1960s, Morris, 'radically extended his address to the viewer's encounter with the inter-related spaces in which the work is defined.' Kaye, N. (2000), *Site-specific art Performance, Place and Documentation*, London, New York: Routledge, p. 26.

43. Morris, R., 'The Present tense of Space,' in *Continuous Project Altered Daily*, p. 199. For example, Leo Steinberg, writing about *The Crucifixion of St Peter* and *The Conversion of St Paul*, two canvases that hang in the Cerasi Chapel in Rome, attempts to posit the idea that a process of ambulation is a necessary factor by which the viewer experiences these paintings: 'These are paintings, in fact, which no longer conceive of the beholder as a fixed witness...what they presuppose is a being in motion who is never perfectly placed.' Leo Steinberg, Leo (1959), 'Observations in the Cerasi Chapel', *Art Bulletin*, 49, p. 187. In addition, the two paintings by Caravaggio 'are so conceived as to assume movement in the spectator; and they are composed as to promote in him a sense of potential intrusion among its elements.' ibid., p. 187.

44. *Continuous Project Altered Daily*, p. 165.

45. Foster, H., (ed.) (1987), *Discussions in Contemporary Culture*, Seattle: Bay Press, pp. 63–4.

46. Olafur Eliasson in conversation with Daniel Burnbaum in *Pressplay: Contemporary Artists in Conversation*, London, Phaidon, 2005, p. 179.

15

ODD ANONYMIZED NEEDS: PUNCHDRUNK'S MASKED SPECTATOR

Gareth White

What is the role of the spectator in interactive performance? What is spectatorship in a one-to-one encounter, in the dark, with a performer? What does it mean to be a masked spectator? Punchdrunk takes a peculiar approach to the problem of audience participation, and offers their audiences strange encounters with their work. Spectators are separated and isolated, then released into vast, dark environments; and it is they, not the performers, who are masked. This chapter examines how this intervention into the practice of spectatorship facilitates interaction, and how the mask enables spectators to become performers in ways that might surprise them. It compares this strategy to other contemporary ways of dealing with the failure of theatre to provide an exchange between performer and audience.

Punchdrunk have been producing immersive site-sympathetic theatre since 1999, most often in the form of interpretations of canonical texts in very large environments built within empty buildings. Their work is predicated on the agency of the spectator, and there are a number of strategies they employ to engineer this agency that are interesting from the point of view of spectatorship. For example, they separate spectators from each other, they disorientate audiences using darkness and noise, they dissolve narratives so that audiences need to seek out the performance, and conversely they provide opportunities to enjoy the environment for its own sake. However, I will consider, in detail, only one of their audience strategies, which I think is the most decisive and radical: the masking of the spectator. I want to consider how their use of masks facilitates active participation, and how it influences the spectator's reception of the performance and of the experience as a whole. These events, and this particular strategy, suggest much about the practice of theatre-going, and of being a spectator, and how people are responding to theatre and theatre-going, early in the twenty-first century. My discussion is based upon my own experience as an audience-participant in several different events, and interviews with the directors, Felix Barrett and Maxine Doyle, and four of the performers, Hector Harkness, Katy Balfour, Rob McNeill and Kath Duggan. My own experiences seem to be typical, and I will draw on them in my analysis, but they are far from exhaustive: each participant takes a very different journey through these events, so I also draw on examples of representative or remarkable moments given by the company.

Punchdrunk's immersive environmental theatre

Since 2001, I have attended Punchdrunk productions in two disused industrial buildings, an empty school, a theatre's attic and a field. All but one of these was inspired by a canonical theatre text (*The Tempest*, *Macbeth*, Goethe's *Faust* and Büchner's *Woyzeck*) and the other by a folk tale.[1] In each, I was introduced to an environment and invited to explore it, freely. In three of them, I was given a mask to wear, while the performers wore none, and it is these performances of the audience in masks, that I am most interested in, as they represent the core of Punchdrunk's work, and their most successful innovation. *Woyzeck* was the exception, the audience was not masked, and as exceptions are wont to do, it will benefit this analysis.

In the programme to *Faust*, Punchdrunk describe the work thus:

> The audience is invited to rediscover the childlike excitement and anticipation of exploring the unknown, to experience a natural sense of adventure. You are free to roam the production in your own time, follow any theme, storyline or performer you wish, or simply to soak up the atmosphere of magical, fleeting worlds.[2]

In these 'magical fleeting worlds' I have discovered cornfields and forests, libraries, workshops, bars, and bedrooms. I have witnessed plots and murders, love affairs and betrayals, scenes of domesticity and formal dance, ensemble performances and isolated, intimate moments. As the programme note says, 'the spectator is given freedom to roam', and really is left alone, unguarded and unwatched, and is likely to spend much of these performances away from any performers, exploring, and examining the environment and its contents. We have space and time to explore, unguided. One of the most pleasing things that the company achieve is to avoid the feeling of molly-coddling that emerges in some environmental, promenade or site-specific performance. Nothing is cordoned off, little is out of bounds, the stewards, when you can identify them (they are also masked) are satisfyingly obtuse and unobstructive. It is easy to settle into a space and make it your own, and it is very possible to interfere with the *mise-en-scene*, or to help yourself to souvenirs. Although the work's interactivity reflects the zeitgeist, it seems to lack the heavy hands of health-and-safety and customer service.

Another freedom offered to the spectator is to choose their encounters with the events of the performance. Action happens simultaneously throughout the spaces of the environment, to audiences of one or many, or perhaps no audience at all. The spectator has to choose tactics for discovering the performance – following characters as they make their journeys, attempting to follow the action of the play, if it is familiar, or staying in one spot to see what will develop there. The rhythms of the activity of the audience can become fascinating in themselves, as we gather into mobs, surge in pursuit of a character, jostle for position, and dissipate, sometimes in frustration. The performers work on a 'loop' of action which is repeated a number of times in a performance, and which reflects a character's journey through the text; their journeys take them through the environment and into scenes with other performers, and into encounters with audience members. The work on the text is rigorous and serious, but few spectators will see anything resembling a 'whole' performance, even from a single performer/character. A performance of the text can only be assembled from fragments.

The other choices that arise come in response to the direct invitations of performers, who have many games to play with individuals and groups of spectators – they might grab hands and run through corridors, initiate dances, separate people from the crowd and take them into a secluded space for a private encounter. After the show, as a participant, you hear tales of things you have missed, of others' special moments. The performers, too, tell stories about the responses to their carefully constructed, but always unpredictable 'one-on-ones'.

The mask is crucial to the effect of the show, to the way the audience are able to view the action and the environment, and to the interactions that occur between audience and performers and between individual spectators. In *Faust*, the masks were conspicuously long-beaked carnival masks, and it can be said that they carry a carnivalesque significance. Masking in carnival is supposed to stimulate licentiousness, both because of the learnt associations of holiday time and because of the practical benefits of anonymity, but there is more to it than this. The mask is not just about being anonymous, and therefore free from censure – we are not anonymous, in any case, as we can always be identified by our clothing, and we aren't going to get away with anything. Neither is it entirely about the resurrected folk memory of carnival practice. It is about the inhibition of various kinds of interactions between spectators, which, paradoxically, facilitates interactions of other sorts.

Agency in interactive performance

The activity – the agency – of the participant in this event takes forms that are found in all performances: the power to interpret, to take viewpoints, to shape our own experience, to follow invitations to active participation, and to initiate participation. The powers to interpret, to take viewpoints and to shape experience are significant and interesting aspects of any audience experience, and are present in all performance experiences, whether there is scope for significant invitations to active participation or self-initiated participation or not. But in this case the agency to choose how and whether to participate has a fundamental effect on these more conventional elements of agency, and so I shall explore them first. As Jan Murray puts it in her discussion of narrative practices in computerized entertainments: 'agency is the satisfying power to take meaningful action and see the results of our decisions and choices.'[3] In Punchdrunk's work, we have many opportunities for action; how satisfying and meaningful they become is open to question, though the popularity of their work suggests it satisfies many, and I will show how it is meaningful, at least in relation to other audience-practices in contemporary performance.

When theorizing audience participation, I take a lead from Anthony Jackson,[4] who uses *Goffman's Frame Analysis* to show a way to map the moves from one mode of interaction – the attentiveness, applause, and perhaps laughter of what he calls the 'outer theatrical frame' – to a variety of 'inner frames' in which the participations of Theatre in Education can be differentiated. But we need to go further, with Goffman and beyond him, in order to make sense of a wider variety of audience interactions. Goffman's idea is that we manage perception and social interaction through 'organisational premises'[5] that make the situation real to us as well as manageable: we have ways of understanding what kind of activity is going on and what kind of activity we should use that is appropriate and beneficial to us. When Goffman uses frame to describe our functional understanding of interactions in everyday life, he indicates a network of shared assumptions about what an interaction means for its participants, and what is appropriate behaviour at these interactions. A key phrase for Goffman is the 'definition of the situation'[6] the agreement between the people involved in an interaction about what it is they are engaged in, and what can or should happen.

Two terms Goffman uses to understand the 'anchoring' of frames in the activity that surrounds them are the 'episoding conventions' and 'resource continuity'. The episoding conventions[7] of a frame are the signals through which an activity is 'marked off' from other activities, from the 'ongoing flow of surrounding events'.[8] This might be the opening of a curtain in a theatre or merely the opening remarks of a conversation. These conversations help us to learn from others what kind of activity is going on, and to signal what role we are going to take in an activity and when we are doing so. They also allow us to move – not always seamlessly, but fluently – from one mode of behaviour to another, assuming that the conventions used have made it clear and acceptable to all that a change in frame has happened. Having accepted a change of frame, it is 'resource continuity',[9] that allows us to bring aspects of ourselves to different frames and maintain a connection across various activities. Our meaning-providing attributes are the resources that can continue from one frame to another, so that we do not have to re-stage every interaction from scratch. Among other things this might constitute what we could call an individual's style, but it is also the recourse within the framed activity to the cultural and personal skills they possess. Episoding conventions and resource continuity are helpful to an understanding of audience participation, as they account for the signalling of a transition from one theatrical frame to another, and also for the resources that a participant has to deploy within the frame of participation; and they allow us to describe the characteristics of different interactive frames without resorting to a simple taxonomy of interactive strategies.

In Punchdrunk's work, the framing begins in the marketing and promotion, continues in the welcome to the building and in the way the spectators are separated from each other before being introduced to the performance environment, and further in the characteristics of the environment itself – its lack of seating or stage, its darkness and size. There are re-framings within this, however, as performances shift in and out of overt interactivity, and in these we see different episoding conventions at work, as performers verbally and non-verbally address spectators and invite them to join the action. Though fictional place and time are represented, as in a conventional stage set, the frame implies an invitation to inhabit these environments in a different way, and it does this through a lack of overt instruction more than through articulation of the company's aims as in the programme note above, or any performative suggestions by the company. Initially introduced to the environment alone, without a performance to attend to, we have to make our own entertainment. It is soon clear that if there is a chair, there is no reason not to sit on it, and if there is a library, we can pick up the books and read them. Until we encounter a performer, and some action to follow, these are the resources we have from which to assemble an understanding of the event. If we have prior knowledge of the text we have another important resource to draw on: the scene becomes Dr Faust's library, and we can look for evidence of his magical researches. This resource becomes more important when encounters with performers begin, and isolated incidents can be identified as part of a known narrative, and choices about who to follow can be made on this basis.

This difference in resources available to participants suggests that the matter needs to be developed to take greater account of difference. Though the idea of a 'definition of a situation' hints at a power struggle for this definition – whoever defines the situation defines what goes on – Goffman's frame analysis tends towards the a-political, and does little to recognize differences in power or differences between the capabilities of those who operate under the regimes of his various metaphors for social life. Augmenting Goffman with a key concept from Bourdieu goes some way to putting this right. Bourdieu takes account of differences in capability by insisting that social, symbolic and cultural capital (the consonances with Goffman's 'resources' are obvious) cannot be used without recourse to the 'structuring mechanism' which indicates what its value is, and how it is to be deployed, in an appropriate field; this mechanism is the habitus:

> [...] the strategy generating principle enabling agents to cope with unforeseen and ever-changing situations [...] a system of lasting and transposable dispositions which, integrating past experiences, functions at every moment as a matrix of perceptions, appreciation and actions and makes possible the achievement of infinitely diversified tasks.[10]

Bourdieu's habitus can suggest the way that the capital of social skills can be made liquid when the subject is presented with unexpected social situations, such as interactive theatre events. It also indicates how difficult it can be to transpose dispositions and assemble appropriate perceptions and actions, when past experience does not provide useful reference points. In Bourdieu's metaphor, social life is not a work of art in which we paint ourselves according to the appropriate convention, but a marketplace where we hope to get the most for our capital, but need to have learnt its value before we can do so with skill.

The metaphor can be productively stretched a little further, however, with a return to Goffman, who writes of 'gambling' public esteem in an essay called 'Where the Action Is'.[11] Theatre events are rarefied social marketplaces, where we may hope that the fictional nature of the action can protect our investments, and save us from the losses of esteem that come with embarrassing performances. But we are often very careful to protect ourselves by refusing participation when it is offered; the gamble seems too great, and the odds in favour of losing social capital too steep. If we view performance as the defining trope of late-capitalist culture, as Jon McKenzie[12] says we should, then the demands to produce effective performance, and to do so in circumstances that we can control, seems more pressing.

The masked spectator

The mask is part of the episoding convention of the overall framing of the event, but it is also a resource, that has continuity across the different interactive frames, and has different functions within them. Wearing identical masks, it is easy for spectators to ignore the crowds of people gathering around a scene, or alternatively to stand and watch a scene alone. Barrett says that the initial impulse to mask the audience was to 'enable them to explore, and to do what they wanted without the distraction of other people';[13] when masked each spectator becomes part of the scenery. An audience is prevented from doing what they might in another promenade performance: looking at each others' faces for reaction to the play, and laughing together with nervousness when approached by performers. The result is that a crowd does not form to the same degree, instead a string of – literally – faceless strangers mill around, each having very individual experiences. It is possible, wearing these masks, to identify people by their clothing, and it is of course possible to take off the mask (most don't) but communication is inhibited by the lack of visible facial expression and the muffling of the voice.

Entering the event alone also frames the work as a solitary experience, and makes it more difficult to begin to interact – it is necessary first to find someone in the maze-like environment. When characters address spectators – for example when Mephistopheles seductively takes someone by the hand and pours them a shot of vodka – people do seem to respond less self-consciously, hidden behind the mask, than they might if openly visible to an audience. The actor may have to do an even greater share of the work than in other actor/audience interactions, as the actor is restricted by the mask in using facial expression, and also to a degree their voice, but the spectators are consistently more willing to become part of the performance. This is the second major consequence of the mask, according to Barrett, an unintended but very welcome one. It was not until it became clear that the audience were empowered to behave in very different ways while they were masked, to become participants in the action as well as part of the scenery of the show, that he realized how significant a discovery this was; one that has become the hallmark of Punchdrunk's work.

The participants are hidden from view and become parts of the performance, but with their identities hidden far more deliberately than is usually the case through the framing devices of a participatory procedure. The process of putting participants on display is interrupted, so that a participatory performance can take place with a much more exclusive emphasis on the experiential. This strategy hides the public persona rather than putting it on display, so that the individual is placed in the performance, and yet remains absent from it to those watching. At times this becomes an experience of pure gaze, like the spectator of conventional theatre but with more voyeuristic privileges. The small eyeholes of the mask exaggerate the directness and the disembodied feel of the gaze.

The performance I attended of *Woyzeck* at 'The Big Chill', (a music festival) serves as a useful comparison. It had a noticeably different atmosphere and different kinds of interaction to the other performances I have seen, which all took place in London. This may be partly because it was presented in a situation where more participants were likely to have less knowledge of the play or its plot, while *The Tempest* and *Sleep No More*, and to a degree *Faust*, were attended by a theatre-going audience who may have selected the play from among many available in London on a particular evening; it is also because on this occasion the audience were not masked. There was far more interaction of certain kinds, for example, in questions addressed to the characters: people were to be heard asking the reasons for Woyzeck's diet of peas, or speculating aloud about Marie's relationship with the Drum Major. Masked audiences are much more reticent, less inclined to interact unless invited and are more inclined to follow the characters from a distance, watching scenes unfold. The unmasked audience spent more time speaking to each other, with far more self-conscious laughter; they were more present to each other, there to exchange glances, to confirm reactions to the performance, and to conform to them. When direct interaction was invited from this unmasked audience, there were more refusals, accompanied by embarrassed clinging to fellow spectators, or displays of reluctant or ironic detachment. The experience seems to have been less immersive, and more self-conscious, confirming for me that for most participants, under these conditions, the habitus asserts normative behaviours that do not allow for immersion in the experience, and asserts the protective self-presentations of scepticism and resistance.

So there are contradictory licences and inhibitions that come with this mask. It seems to inhibit interaction amongst spectators, and some kinds of interaction between spectators and performers, while it facilitates more experimental interaction between these two positions. The mask affects how participants attend to each other or do not, and how they bring their colleagues into their frame of perception. It is the attention of the participant to others in the audience that generates the embarrassment and sense of risk that makes participation so difficult for us. By removing our co-spectators from our vision, Punchdrunk disrupt our identification with the crowd, and facilitate a more immersive and less performative experience. Re-framing the theatrical contract through the physical environment and through the activity of performers can achieve a lot in stimulating interaction and active spectatorship, but it will always come up against the learnt habits – and the habitus – of theatre culture. Theatres are places where we put ourselves on show, as well as watching other people's shows, but within the parameters of everyday frames of behaviour. This is why so many people dread audience participation: it calls upon them to take part in extra-everyday performance, for which they fear they do not have the resources.

The blank masks used by Punchdrunk, when seen on figures moving with us in the dark, and surrounding the action, are not legible as other audience members, and if we don't identify with them in a crowd-like way, we may identify with them enough to come to believe in our own blankness, and a kind of invisibility. It is telling that when Punchdrunk have experimented with other kinds of mask, for example, a kind of melancholic Greek chorus mask, for a combined version of *Oedipus* and *Antigone*, it has not had the same success in stimulating interaction. This mask, which is so legible, makes the masked figure part of the action whether they are active or not, and creates impressions in the viewer which feedback again to the wearer. The feedback from a characterful mask creates an obligation to produce a performance, in a process, which is famously productive in masked performance, but in this context, on the evidence of Punchdrunk's experimentation, produces the opposite effect on audience-participants. In this situation the obligation to produce a performance to fit the mask inhibits such a performance more than it facilitates one, as audience members anticipate failure and embarrassment.

Resisting intimacy

In the essay from which I have borrowed my title – Herbert Blau's 'Odd Anonymous Needs' of 1986, which became the opening chapter of 1990's *The Audience*,[14] there is an impression of a disturbingly unknowable audience, as the diffuse and unreliable remnant of a theatrical constituency. While Blau portrays the performance maker's horror of the absence of an audience, he is deeply suspicious of any practice, which makes claims for community of communion: he prefers that which, 'foregoes the blessed moment of intimacy in favour of the rigorous moment of perception'.[15] He both scorns and misses a coherent public, and he is embarrassed by attempts to create intimacy.

Punchdrunk's audience strategies don't offer a solution to Blau's dilemma: they provide more treats than shocks, whereas he is looking for the sublime confrontation with solitude that is the gift of post-modernity. However, they do swim in the same water. Their anonymized spectator, protected into participation and seduced into a kind of intimacy, and then often placed in compromising situations, speaks of the necessity of peculiar and paradoxical interventions in audience practice in contemporary theatre. Punchdrunk render their audience incoherent, anonymous, and exaggeratedly absent. They hint at subversive desires in the experience of being masked for a long time, in the dark, in the presence of provocations to voyeurism. There is an idealism in the promises to give freedom to move, to roam, and to soak up, an idealism that has echoes of Boal's 'spect-actor', but there is an implicit scepticism in the masking of the participant. It acknowledges the desire for anonymity, for protection from the social risk that comes with re-staging precious and much performed social selves in the treacherous landscape of theatrical performance.

Nicholas Ridout, in *Stage Fright, Animals and Other Theatrical Problems*,[16] does offer a solution, or at least he charts the way some seminal performance companies have made a feature of difficulties of this sort. He considers his own embarrassment when he catches the eye of a performer directly addressing him, an unease caused by his inability to place himself, either as a fellow performer with a duty to maintain the fictional narrative, or as a spectator who has become invisible to the circuit of reception that usually operates in the theatre. The intimacy of direct address which many actors and many spectators find stimulating for its apparent honesty about their mutual presence in the place (if not the specific space) of performance, for Ridout reveals the awkward dishonesty of playing the game of theatrical belief:

> Someone is making claims on me and it's not entirely clear who. On the one hand, I feel obliged as a responsible and professional theatre-goer to comply with the contract

I am being offered. Look for look is the deal. To turn my eyes away from his would be rude, and what's more, a betrayal of my own principles (those Brechtian principles of my youth). [...] But who exactly is it making this claim on me? Is it Samuel West or is it Richard II? When the ethical claim of the face-to-face encounter is deployed in this way, I feel I am entitled to know. And I am embarrassed because the utter foolishness of the theatrical contract I have been going on with overwhelms me.[17]

This, once again, is part of a set of imbalances in power that I have already outlined. If Ridout, a theatre maker and critic with a hoard of cultural capital to draw on, finds it hard to produce the appropriate performance, what hope for spectators with lesser resources? The imbalance in power cuts across the actor/audience divide, as well as across the audience itself. Sam West, in Ridout's example, has the power to act, and the licence to perform with conviction, drawing on a professional's skill and the resources of rehearsal, while Ridout, when the light falls on him, finds only his own uneasy experience of other similar occasions. It is an imbalance that he casts in economic terms, avoiding Bourdieusian metaphor and referring directly to the conditions of production of performance: '[...] in the theatre of capitalism, the reverse gaze must always acknowledge, however tacitly, an intimate economic relation: I paid to have this man look at me, and he is paid to look. Our intimacy is always already alienated. It is a difficult intimacy.'[18]

Ridout sustains this analysis by considering the controversy over the exploitation of animals and children in the theatre: controversies, which rarely arise when adult human beings are concerned, unless there is an element of sexual exploitation.

This, then, has relevance in two ways: the difficulty of participating in interactions in theatre can be traced to the roots of the contract between spectators and performers and the enjoyment of theatrical interaction is an exploitation of alienated labour. Ridout completes his thesis by showing that it is through the repeated theatrical revelations of this kind that the masters of performative failure – Societas Raffaelo Sanzio and Forced Entertainment for example – expose us to keener understandings of what theatre, and our intensely performative social lives, consist of. What remains to be discussed is how Punchdrunk, who are self-confessedly escapist, tell us anything about these matters.

Conclusion

This peculiar ontology of theatre, that it is a 'machine which sets out to undo itself',[19] appears initially to be at odds with ideologies of presence in performance. In fact, this is a notion that recognizes that a meaningful co-presence between performer and audience cannot happen through the architecture of mimesis, where one either pretends that the other is absent, or recognizes the other while in such a situation of imbalance that embarrassment is the only response. The familiar response to this failure in the theatre has been to become un-theatrical through, for example, disposing of mimesis in making 'non-matrixed' performance, as in much of performance art, or disposing of distance, as in Grotowski's 'para-theatre', where all those in attendance participate in a 'real' event. What Ridout notes is a return to the theatrical, but in order to witness its collapse.

This is not Punchdrunk's strategy, and not their aim: they claim to be in the business of escapism. Nevertheless, what they do is another return to theatrical intimacy which does not seek communion, but which plays a different game with the theatrical contract and the distance between the spectator and the performer. The mask maintains distance, while allowing proximity of a controlled kind. Performer and spectator-participant can occupy the same physical and fictive space, without the latter having to reveal themselves, without them having to be present as a recognizable social subject. Ridout might still find this embarrassing, but the success of the company shows that many others do not. Again, it is telling that when performers try to take off the participants' masks, as they often do in the isolated, one-on-one interactions, they produce the strongest reactions. They report that they are often resisted, and when they do succeed in removing it they might be met with tears, confessions, and sometimes anger.[20] In these moments they have achieved an intimacy, which is sometimes disturbing, to both parties, and which brings into question that this work is as purely escapist as they believe it is. The company have learnt to handle these encounters with care, and to provide a staged exit from the event, with spaces that allow participants to be part-in and part-out of the environment and to cool off before leaving the building.

Daphna Ben Chaim has shown how important the manipulation of aesthetic distance was to the formal experiments of twentieth century theatre. That large audiences appreciate further experiments of this kind, and can treat them largely as escapist entertainment, testifies to how these challenges have been absorbed into a mainstream conception of what theatre can be, and a broadened set of audience practices. Punchdrunk's approach to distance is peculiar, however, as they bring the audience very close to the aesthetic objects of the theatre – performers' bodies, action, set and setting – while allowing them to maintain a feeling of distance. It is only when the mask is taken off that proximity makes its full impact, and the shock to the system – the habitus that tells us so persuasively to stay off stage when we are at the theatre – can produce such powerful effects. Returning to Blau, as he acknowledges the importance of aesthetic distance to theatrical form, we see how sharply he perceives what can be at stake when audiences are brought into participatory encounters:

There have in the course of modernism been all kinds of experiments in the theatre to activate the spectator, achieve intimacy, or collapse distance; yet whenever the spectator is restored to the environs of the stage, what opens is another disjuncture, between that narcissistic figure and the audience in a collective sense. It makes us aware of the incremental and sometimes radical differences between such notions as community, public, audience and spectator, all of which alter as the eye alters, thus – as Blake perceived – altering all.[21]

Punchdrunk produce disjuncture between the individual spectator and the crowd-like audience, and do so quite deliberately. One can often leave their productions asking questions about community, public, audience and spectator, but the work itself does not foreground these things. They produce experiences in which we appear to forget ourselves as social subjects, but what they do not have, so far, is a programme to draw attention to this remarkable achievement.

Notes

1. At the time of writing they are about to open *The Masque of the Red Death*, for once inside a theatre building (Battersea Arts Centre), but after a radical transformation in which cellars, kitchens, corridors and workshops have become performance spaces.
2. Punchdrunk, *Faust*, (Programme), 2007.
3. Murray, J. (1999), *Hamlet on the Holodeck – The Future of Narrative in Cyberspace*, Cambridge, Mass: The MIT Press, p. 152.
4. Jackson, A. (1997), 'Positioning the Audience: Inter-Active Strategies and the Aesthetic in Educational Theatre', *Theatre Research International*, Vol. 22, No. 1., pp. 48–60.
5. Goffman, A. (1986), *Frame Analysis*, Harmondsworth: Penguin, p. 247.
6. ibid., p. 1.
7. ibid., pp. 251–69.
8. ibid., p. 251.
9. ibid., pp. 287–92.
10. Bourdieu, P., Wacquant, L. (1992), *An Invitation to Reflexive Sociology*, Chicago: University of Chicago Press, p. 18.
11. Goffman, E. (1972), *Interaction Ritual*, Harmondsworth: Allen Lane.
12. McKenzie, J. (2001), *Perform or Else – from Discipline to Performance*, London: Routledge.
13. Personal Interview, Felix Barrett, Interviewed 22 August 2007, (transcript with author).
14. Blau, H. (1990), *The Audience*, Baltimore: John Hopkins University Press.
15. ibid., p. 6.
16. Ridout, N. (2006), *Stage Fright, Animals and Other Theatrical Problems*, London: Cambridge University Press.
17. ibid., p. 87.
18. ibid., p. 80.
19. ibid., p. 168.
20. Personal Interviews, Hector Harkness, Katy Balfour and Rob McNeill, Interviewed 5 September 2007, (transcript with author).
21. Blau, H (1990), p. 18.

16

SITES OF PERFORMANCE:
THE WOLLSTONECRAFT LIVE EXPERIENCE!

Anna Birch

Fragments & Monuments has a unique scenography and dramaturgy that has emerged through the aim of the company to produce a form of site-specific theatre to re-activate the stories of women's achievement, linking performers, site and audience to make compelling experiences. The first word goes to one of our valued audience members recorded at *The Wollstonecraft Live Experience!* 2007:

> The outdoor experience gives a historical resonance where you see a history in the modern day and we can look back on it. It's really neat how you look at the screen and it cuts away to the road and you cut away and look at the road and a bus is going around the green in the same place! I think it's fantastic! Events like this give a personality to the locality. Civil society started by people meeting in public places and it's very important to re-kindle this if we have any chance of surviving.[1]

The choice of site, or where a performance is located, can be motivated by the desire to create a space where the production of readings and meanings are different to those produced in the conventional building-based theatre. In western theatre, plays have been produced behind a proscenium arch to an audience seated facing the stage. In site-specific theatre practices, performances are located outside the theatre building in places which can include public parks, disused warehouses or car parks. This re-contextualization from the theatre building to outside the theatre building has the effect of exteriorizing the conventional theatrical codes produced and maintained by building-based theatre practices. The context of the theatre building includes the history of theatre and plays, the people who have run and continue to run the theatre, those who have performed, designed/directed for the theatre, plus countless others. By moving outside the theatre building, the relationship that the performed or recorded material and the personnel have to the means of production is disturbed in a way that helps the messages produced be less taken for granted and more fluid between audience, site and performer. The blurred boundaries created by this approach can create a space where groups, who have been excluded from the theatre historically, can negotiate a new position in a different context.

The history and context of the female theatre director in the building-based theatre environment has been well recorded and the number remains low even in 2008.[2] Fragments & Monuments was set up in 1998 to produce site-specific theatre and by engaging a predominantly female artistic and production team the company began to work outside the theatre. Working outside the theatre building has enabled Fragments & Monuments to commission new work that is site-specific and accessible to non-theatre going audiences. As Artistic Director for the company, I have observed how the shift from working inside the theatre building to outside has shaped our work and the way that it is looked at by our audiences.

Fragments & Monuments present their work in a variety of different formats. These multi-modal presentations in themselves encourage the audience as spectators to look in a number of different ways. Since 1998, the Fragments & Monuments audience has looked at our work from a variety of points of view including rail and bus passengers, hotel and millennium party guests, film extras and as people having a picnic. The audience has been choreographed to travel around our performances and this entails physical movement, which in itself creates the possibility of an embodied experience, for example as a film extra or party guest. The sequence of movements performed by our audience produces a strand of the scenographic and dramaturgical score contributing to the overall concept. The company mission statement explains that by linking performers, site and audience Fragments & Monuments make compelling experiences. Our focus on the experiential aspect of our work is linked to developing the dynamic between the audience and the performance through different levels of participation. It is through this embodied relationship to the site and performers that a space can be created where the audience can start to spectate differently.

The focus for this chapter is *The Wollstonecraft Live Experience!*, a presentation of the artefacts generated in the site-specific, live and recorded production *Wollstonecraft Live!*,[3] a multimedia history of Mary Wollstonecraft (1759–1797). By analyzing the processes entailed in the construction and production of this large-scale and international on-going multimedia project, I investigate how 'modes of spectating' can be challenged through the event itself. By blurring the boundaries between spectator, performer and the site the possibility for a different way of looking can be produced. Fragments & Monuments conjures up the life and times of Mary Wollstonecraft, a spectacular woman of achievement, to bring the past into the present through text, costume, location and audience participation. During the live and mediated performance, the audience found out how Mary Wollstonecraft articulated the case for women's suffrage in her famous treatise called *A Vindication of the Rights of Woman*, and went on to marry philosopher William Godwin and gave birth to Mary Shelley the author.

In 2005, Fragments & Monuments commissioned Kaethe Fine, a playwright with film experience, to write a hybrid multimedia script based on the life of Mary Wollstonecraft, which included a script for *VINDICATION*, a moment of fiction when Wollstonecraft meets William Godwin, her future husband to be, on Newington Green.[4] Tina Lonergan[5] was engaged as the production designer and designed three white 'box' dresses for dressing the three performers who were playing Mary Wollstonecraft. The show was presented twice a night over four nights and filmed by a team of professional camera-operators.

Fragments & Monuments had arranged access to two sites: the Unitarian Chapel where the performance started (and Mary Wollstonecraft had prayed in pew nineteen during the eighteenth century) and a walk outside to Newington Green, a regenerated 'Greenspace',[6] where Wollstonecraft had run a school for girls. Fine set up a tracking-shot in her script where William Godwin proposes marriage to Mary Wollstonecraft with the audience playing 'film extras.' The audience expect to see themselves on film, but instead a 360 degree shot of Newington Green was projected onto the screen. This dramaturgical choice opened up the possibility that multiple versions of history are possible and cast the audience in the role of the history-makers.

The documentary of *Wollstonecraft Live!*, which was filmed at the 2005 performance, was projected onto Newington Green in 2007. The storyboard for the film was constructed to give the site, audience and performers equal weighting. The plot was not the driving force in this instance – we were using film to investigate Newington Green, Mary Wollstonecraft, local audiences and history. Fragments & Monuments invited the audience back to see themselves enjoying the Newington Green site and with a new audience in 2007 and re- launched the project as *The Wollstonecraft Live Experience!*

Mary Wollstonecraft has played a major role in the lives of women across the western world. She was the first British feminist, human rights activist. She lived and worked on Newington Green, just around the corner from where I live in Stoke Newington, North East London. Newington Green has a history of political dissent, which is 300 years old. The rights of all human beings were fought for as a matter of principle and for the assorted historical figures including Daniel Defoe, Anne Lettitia Barabauld, Joseph Johnson and Tom Paine the discourse for the fight revolved around anti-monarchist ideology. When I discovered that Mary Wollstonecraft was a neighbour of mine from the eighteenth century I became fascinated with the contribution her life had made on so many levels and what that contribution could continue to offer. This neighbourhood history became more available through the ritual of performance and returning with my production company Fragments & Monuments to the site of Newington Green repeatedly, as if to conjure up the ghosts of the past.

As a visiting director for the MA in Scenography under Pamela Howard at Central Saint Martin's College of Art and Design I met and collaborated with a Dutch scenographer on the course. We set up Fragments & Monuments in the late 1990s and the company now has a reputation for working outside the theatre building and developing new performance languages to investigate hidden histories through technology and location.

In a collection of post-feminist discourses,[7] I have written of the semiotic shift of meanings achieved through the re-contextualization of theatre from new writing based in the theatre building to site-specific performance. From the 1980s to the mid-1990s, I developed scripts and produced plays written by women writers.[8]

Key to the development of a theoretical base for my practice are the plays of Caryl Churchill, in particular *Top Girls*,[9] which gave a new perspective on travelling through time and space, and *Ironmistress* by April de Angelis, where I discovered how setting the interior/domestic space in the exterior/public space presented a potent scenographic shift from the conventional to a progressive topography. Marina Warner's seminal book *Monuments and Maidens: the Allegory of the Female Form*, 1985, inspired me to 're-view' the representation of women and femininity in civic monuments, for example Britannia and Liberty. Fragments & Monuments continue to draw on the work of Churchill, de Angelis and Warner to re-activate lost histories of women of achievement and to bring women together across history.

The work on historicization by Elin Diamond in *Unmaking Mimesis* has contributed to my current practice as a theatre director now choosing to site my projects outside the theatre building. Her argument that the ideological construction of gendered meanings can be dismantled through theatre in a strategy to challenge the role of mimesis in consolidating and perpetuating the status quo, points towards a new role for the spectator:

> With Brechtian hindsight we know that realism, more than any other form of theatre representation, mystifies the process of theatrical signification. Because it naturalises the relation between character and actor, setting and world, realism operates in concert with ideology and because it depends on, insists on stability of reference, an objective world as the source and guarantor of knowledge, realism surreptitiously reinforces (even if it argues with) the arrangements of that world.[10]

The changed 'arrangement' of the spectator to site-specific performance and the re-contextualization[11] is offered as a strategy to breathe new life into gendered readings, in both live and mediated performances. In this context, the topography includes the relationship of the audience to the site, to the performers and the history of the site. In this way race, gender, sexuality, age and disability are brought into the re-presentational frame by the audience themselves and the constructions of ideology and power are put centre stage.

A focal point for feminist performance critics and theorists is the historical fact that young men performed femininity on the western stage primarily in the period leading up to the 1660s. During the 1980s and 1990s a new aesthetic of feminist performance based on lesbian desire was developed by feminist theorists. [12] Lizbeth Goodman has argued this case since the mid 1990s and Leslie Hill and Helen Paris[13] have built a body of work using live and mediated strategies to explore agency and identity. Since femininity is a performative state, endorsed in part by the history of young men playing women on stage, then feminist art practices are interested in discovering new spaces through live and mediated performance, and site-specific performance, where the discovery of what femininity might be, can continue.

New spaces for performance offered by the opportunity of the developments in digital technologies for live and mediated performance are being utilized by companies such as Station House Opera, for example in *Views from Paradise*, where a single performance was re-enacted in three separate sites and projected between the sites.[14] In *Performance and Place*, Julian Maynard-Smith discusses some impressions of Station House Opera performance spaces:

> The company has primarily always been architectural, trying to sequence space into narrative, space which obviously contains objects – inevitably mundane/everyday/ 'found' objects in order to foreground their use, their position in space, their physical presence rather than their design or style – which is then used as the performance world. At times, instead of a physical object or material, a means of presenting space is used – light or video in one of its forms.[15]

These liminal spaces created by digital technologies can offer new sites for the spectator to produce meanings by developing a relationship with the site, text, performers and technology. In this way, the decoding process can be encouraged and made explicit. In his article 'Encoding, Decoding', Stuart Hall argued that there can be no meaning without consumption; in other words, that the process of encoding cultural artefacts is as important as the process of decoding in performance and performance making.[16]

The Wollstonecraft Live Experience!

In 2007 Fragments & Monuments were invited to display the objects and materials assembled from the live and mediated performance *Wollstonecraft Live!* enabling the company to move into the gallery space and start looking at our work from a fine art as well as a performance perspective. The relationship of the audience/spectator to our work could now be investigated through a new lens:[17] 'Mother of feminism reborn in triplicate. Wollstonecraft makes for a great multimedia heroine. Long may she live!'[18]

In the site-specific performance *Wollstonecraft Live!*, 2005, reviewed above, the artefacts and remnants included the three dresses and three tool belts worn by the three performers each playing Mary Wollstonecraft; a script re-drafted and re-written to show the stages that the script development process covered; fragments of Mary Wollstonecraft's writing from her published books and letters, a visitor's book and candles.

In February 2007, Fragments & Monuments were invited by artist, Daria Dorush[19] to present the *Wollstonecraft Live!* artefacts and to talk about the work of Fragments & Monuments in New York at the A.I.R. Gallery. This re-presentation of *Wollstonecraft Live!* became *The Wollstonecraft Live Experience!* and the objects from the show were hung in the gallery and the dresses worn in a performance installation spin-off. A transatlantic connection was made between Newington Green, London the home of Mary Wollstonecraft and Tom Paine (1737–1809), her friend and colleague, who made a major contribution to the development of the American Constitution. Harvard University, was originally founded by Charles Morton, who led a dissenter's academy on Newington Green in the eighteenth century.

Subsequently, the objects and materials were installed at the Ruskin Gallery, Cambridge as part of the 'Modes of Spectating' conference.[20] The remnants from the 2005 production were re-visited again this time to include traces of our New York trip in the form of air tickets and 100ml vials of liquid from the flight. These artefacts included A1 posters of the writings of Mary Wollstonecraft in the style of Barbara Kruger.[21] The typographic style of Kruger was selected to bring the writings of Mary Wollstonecraft into the twenty-first century making a trans-historical link across two important periods of feminist thought and practice. Recently produced films and costumes from the live show were also included in the exhibition. The films were looped to emphasize the repetition and re-play dimension of the exhibition. The three box dresses and tool belts were suspended and turned slowly with the wind current of people walking in the gallery. Conference delegates were invited to view the labelled artefacts and discuss themes from a worksheet prepared for the workshop. In this way, delegates were explicitly positioned as engaged spectators and their response to the exhibition was recorded. The scenographic choices made in hanging the exhibition, invited the audience to initiate a relationship to *The Wollstonecraft Live Experience!* including the Newington Green site, the Unitarian Church and Mary Wollstonecraft herself.

In September 2007, Fragments & Monuments returned to the site at Newington Green and produced *The Wollstonecraft Live Experience!* on the original site of *Wollstonecraft Live! 2005.*

Fig. 39: The set up for the picnic with mats spread across Newington Green printed with fragments of Wollstonecraft's writing.

This was a picnic event with an outdoor film screening and broadband Internet connection broadcast across the world-wide-web. A safe and lit space was provided for our audience and in particular women who may not have felt safe to be out at night. The Deidre Cartwright Trio, (international women jazz musicians based in Stoke Newington, London) performed their own compositions and modern jazz under-scoring the live video mix projected by Fragments & Monuments onto Newington Green. The picnic mats were designed and made by Tina Lonergan incorporating fragments of Wollstonecraft's writing and extending the idea of handkerchiefs reminiscent of Wollstonecraft's father, who was a handkerchief weaver in Spitalfields, East London. By sitting on the picnic mat on Newington Green the possibility of an embodied relationship between the audience and the legacy of Mary Wollstonecraft's work was offered. Resources about her work and life, for example films, time-lines and historical documentation for the audience to view and reflect on later, were displayed.

Fragments & Monuments constructed the possibility for the audience to visit the event bringing a picnic and sitting on Newington Green side by side with other people with picnics. The picnic mats supplied by Fragments & Monuments created a context by quoting the writing of Mary Wollstonecraft in fragments and single words.

The announcements over the public address system gave the history of Fragments & Monuments' interventions on Newington Green and planned future events to which the audience were invited.

Fragments & Monuments' events commemorated the achievements of women world-wide. The use of ghosts is a popular theatrical device, for example, in *Hamlet* by William Shakespeare, we see the ghost of Hamlet's dead father at the beginning of the play. In *The Haunted Stage*,[22] Carlson argues that the need to renegotiate our memories and pasts is best done in the theatre. In this way, we create a trans-historical link shared by the community. The excavation and commemoration of hidden achievements and everyday lives are layered and the materials recycled, repeated and multiplied. This layering and recycling creates a space where an opportunity for participation between audience, performer and site is invited. The aesthetic outcomes we develop in this way drive the company onto the next stage – over-laying and re-visiting our digital archives is a part of this.[23]

Monuments

Even when the narrative does not itself explicitly support a rethinking of landscape, the counter-monumental potential of theatre can create a significant effect in the cultural landscape. That effect may disrupt traditional representations of space or it may generate a specifically oppositional representational space that can intervene in the production of social space.[24]

Fragments & Monuments seek to generate on-going monuments through the different incarnations of the *Wollstonecraft* project as a whole. The aim is to create a community around a particular aspect of political dissent driven by Mary Wollstonecraft through her writing by encouraging the participation of the audience in our events. In 2005 the audience played the role of extras in the film-making of a biopic about the life of Mary Wollstonecraft, and in 2007 the audience were invited to bring their own picnics to Newington Green and to take part in an event, which included seeing themselves projected on the Green attending the show in 2005. In this way, the bodies of our audience are mixed with the bodies of performers, pedestrians and drivers passing-by Newington Green and the ghosted bodies of Wollstonecraft and her eighteenth century contemporaries, to develop the language of monument making for both our local and global spectators.

Wollstonecraft Live! 2005, the live and mediated performance was repeated each night, and as the first show finished the second show began. This schedule created a new space for audiences to interact and queue up to witness one show begin as the other finished. This repetition mirrors the repetition of 'takes' on a film set and the technical re-plays of sound and picture in editing processes. The sculptural[25] potential of including the audience in our scenographic concept demonstrates the commitment to challenge the conventional audience/performer relationship found in the building-based theatre.

The separation between the audience and the performed action is consciously erased by *Fragments & Monuments*, again in *Di's Midsummer Night Party*, 2000,[26] Diana, Princess of Wales was represented in multiples by a mask and the chorus of Dianas moved together as one body. This parodic gesture reminds us of the multiple images circulating of Diana as the most photographed woman in the world. In *Wollstonecraft Live!* three Mary Wollstonecraft's were cast: Ros Phillips played Mary Wollstonecraft in the biopic *VINDICATION* and was the focus-puller on the film set, Katherine Vernez played the film director and Saddiqa Akhtar played Mary Wollstonecraft in the tracking scene where she agrees to marry William Godwin in the performance on the Green. As the film crew, the three Mary Wollstonecraft's worked closely adjusting the track ready for the shot to take place. Their bodies, dressed in the box dresses, continually re-formed in sculptural patterns of threes, twos and a single Mary all contributing to the construction of a live and fragmented monument to Mary Wollstonecraft herself. In South Africa 2007, Fragments & Monuments' drive to re-discover monuments and make open monuments in which people could feel ownership and belonging[27] in order to encourage reparation was received with enthusiasm by artists and academics.[28] In the outdoor screening of the film the three Mary Wollstonecrafts, back projected onto a twelve by twelve foot screen, became mapped and embedded onto Newington

Fig. 40: Three Mary Wollstonecrafts in the Unitarian Chapel dressed in eighteenth century costume and projected onto the 'green' in 2007.

Green in the photographs and video footage of the event, producing a view of viewing and re-viewing history.

Repeat, repeat

The concept of 'repetition' is a key feature of performance, for example in rehearsals for actors repeating lines from the script as a part of the process of constructing a role. An example is where, William Godwin is seen rehearsing his lines from the script and Katherine Vernez is seen as Mary rehearsing her lines back-stage before the audience/extras arrive at Newington Green. The repetitions enacted by Fragments & Monuments include returning to the site of the first performances of *Wollstonecraft Live!* with a documentary film of the show and re-visiting the fragments and artefacts in different spaces and for new audiences. These re-visits and repetitions create an ongoing ritual to conjure up the memory of Mary Wollstonecraft and her legacy.

I would like to draw together some of the findings from our most recent work, discussing the impact of this working method on modes of spectating. The physicality of Fragments & Monuments' performers has increased and the amount of dialogue has decreased in our development of a performative event. The work is increasingly driven by visual imperatives and although the seeds for the progressive exteriorization of Fragments & Monuments work were sewn from play scripts developed, directed and produced professionally, the move outside the theatre offers an opportunity to record work as an integral part of the production. Here the performance site doubles as a film location with a camera crew integrated into the dramaturgical and scenographic vocabulary.

Di's Midsummer Night Party, 2000, was filmed by camera operators in the role of the paparazzi. In 2005, a film crew roved around the live and mediated site-specific performance mirroring the film crew (three Mary Wollstonecrafts) inside the show. In 2007, camera operators filmed and broadcast the picnic event live over the Internet, which included placards with messages to our audience beyond Newington Green who had logged on, to document the picnic, outdoor screening and live band and to talk to the audience as they enjoyed their evening picnic on Newington Green live. The screen and the camera are now found in the space that was once reserved for live performance. As Judith Butler argues, the construction of identity occurs in and through interaction in the social space. The opportunity to perform roles over the Internet emphasizes the multiple meanings available once identity is released from its closed circuit and the widening nature of social space.

Digital artist Jana Riedel, who has worked with us for seven years, selected Isadora[29] software to mix the digital assets that Fragments & Monuments had collected during their travels since 2000. Mary Wollstonecraft was said to be the first woman travel writer[30] and now Fragments & Monuments travel around the globe in person and remotely in her name.[31]

The progressive exteriorization achieved by working outside the theatre, at the site of performance and by harnessing new technologies creates a space where gender coding can be tested. The excessive visibility that disempowers women can be challenged through this trans-historical approach and working outside the theatre points towards transcending the conventional topography of the domestic and public use of space. Mary Wollstonecraft met and spoke to her audience in *Di's Midsummer Night Party*. In 2000, she inquired about the history of photography, in 2005 she filmed the audience in their role as extras in her biopic and in 2007 she projected herself onto Newington Green, juxtaposed against an audience who had met her at a previous live performance alongside a new audience.

Our audience is now both local and global. On the website www.wollstonecraftlive.com members can write to the 'dear mary' blog about human rights issues and campaigns that effect women across the world. Fragments & Monuments has analysed the live and digital scenography created for these events in the open access website *The Performance Kit*.[32] On the website members contribute their own work and a space is created to develop and analyze site-specific, multimedia performances and to investigate what the nature of spectating might be in the various site-specific multimedia represented.

Fragments & Monuments' plans for the future are indicative of the modes of spectating that the company have developed. This emerging multi-modal scenography includes an invitation from The Hackney Museum, London, to develop a special exhibition on Mary Wollstonecraft. Artefacts arising from our five-year project will be curated alongside more conventional historical materials held by the museum about Mary Wollstonecraft.

In the summer of 2008 Fragments & Monuments travel to Seoul, Korea to the International Federation of Theatre Research Conference (IFTR/FIRT) where the Asian strand of the project is launched. This will include the development of the 'dear mary' blog where 'mary' answers questions and letters from interested members of the developing Fragments & Monuments community.

Notes

1. Richard Reiser, Director of Disability Equality in Education, UK.
2. For an up to date survey of the position of women in the arts see Costa, M. (2008), 'Thinking outside the box' *The Guardian* 9th June.
3. The multi-modal arenas where the work has been shown are Newington Green, London UK 21–24 September 2005; 'Spit-Lit Festival', East London; 'SPICE Festival', Hackney, London; A.I.R. Gallery, New York; Ruskin Gallery, Cambridge; Outdoor screening with live music Newington Green, London, UK, Saturday 15 September 2007.
4. *Wollstonecraft Live!* and *VINDICATION* written by Kaethe Fine. Produced and Directed by Anna Birch are available from www.wollstonecraftlive.com and www.youtube.com
5. Tina Lonergan Production Designer for *Wollstonecraft Live!* and *The Wollstonecraft Live Experience!* based in Hamburg, Germany. Central Saint Martins, University of the Arts London alumni – www.buehnenbraut.com
6. Islington Greenspace is run by Islington Council with regeneration funds.

7. Birch, A. (2006), 'Staging and Citing Gendered Meanings: A practice-based study of representational strategies in live and mediated performance', in Haas, Birgit (Hg.): *Der Postfeministische Diskurs*, Würzburg: Königshausen & Neumann, pp. 79–100.

8. De Angelis, April (1999), *Ironmistress, Hush, Playhouse Creature*, London: Faber; and Trainor, K., *Bad Girls*, Old Red Lion, Islington, (1991).

9. *Top Girls*, (1982), The Royal Court Theatre, London. Directed by Max Stafford-Clark, designed by Peter Hartwell; *Cloud Nine*, (1979), Joint Stock Theatre Group, The Royal Court Theatre, London. Directed by Max Stafford-Clark and designed by Peter Hartwell.

10. Diamond, E. (1997), *Unmaking Mimesis*, 1997, p. 4.

11. DV8's *Enter Achilles* (World Première, 7 June 1995, Vienna Festwochen, Vienna, Austria. UK Première 15 September 1995 Newcastle Playhouse, Newcastle), is a great example of re-contextualization. This film of a dance piece set in an East End London pub brings dance outside the dance space into a male-coded space (the public house) and films the piece from the inside and outside of the window of the pub itself to show the interior, exterior and public and private spatial relationships.

12. Dolan, J., (ed.) (1988), *Performing Feminisms: Feminist critical theory and theatre*, Baltimore: John Hopkins University Press; Feminism and Theatre, Macmillan, 1988; Dolan, J. (1993), *Presence and Desire: Essays on gender, sexuality, performance*, University of Michigan Press; Dolan, J. (1991), *The Feminist critic as Spectator*, Michigan Press; Goodman, L., de Gay, J., (eds.) (1998), *The Routledge Reader in Gender and Performance*, London, New York: Routledge. www.smartlab.uk.com

13. www.placelessness.com

14. Station House Opera: Views from Paradise at www.stationhouseopera.com

15. Hill, L., Paris, H. (2006), *Performance and Place*, Palgrave, p. 233.

16. Hall, S. (1993), 'Encoding and Decoding in Television Discourse', in *The Cultural Studies Reader*, (ed.), During, S.

17. Artangel, *Battle of Orgreave* at Tate Modern, in 'The World as a Stage' exhibition October 2007 where the artefacts and research were assembled and reviewed in a new art gallery context. Also Mark Wallinger, *State Britain* at Tate Britain, 15 January-27 August 2007.

18. Eyre, H. (2005), 'Talk of the Town', *Independent on Sunday*, 25 September.

19. Daria Dorush's 'The Changing Room'.

20. Different Directions Symposia – 'Modes of Spectating', Cambridge School of Art, March 2007.

21. www.barbarakruger.com

22. Carlson, M. (2001), *The Haunted Stage*, The University of Michigan Press, p167. 'The simultaneous attraction to and fear of the dead, the need continually to rehearse and renegotiate the relationship with memory and the past, is nowhere more specifically expressed in human culture than in theatrical performance.'

23. It is interesting to note Carlson, when he describes the Wooster Group aesthetic as follows: 'Using "what you have in the closet" has become an important part of the Wooster Group aesthetic, which consciously and regularly practices every sort of recycling so far discussed: the theatre itself, its stage, its texts, the bodies of the actors, their costumes and properties, as well as the modern technological recycling offered by film, sound tape, and most important, video.' (2001), p. 172.

24. Tompkins, J. (2006), *Unsettling Space*, Palgrave, p. 49.

25. www.ecole-jacqueslecoq.com learning about the Le Coq method of performance with Pascal le Coq inspired the design development of the 'box' dresses and now helps in understanding how the audience embody the Newington Green site – how the bodies of the audience can be read sculpturally in both live and mediated contexts.

26. *Di's Midsummer Night Party*, is a live, site-based, devised show using non-traditional theatrical resources. Birch, A. (2004), *Staging and Citing gendered Meanings: A practice-based study of representational strategies in live and mediated performance*, Produced by Fragments & Monuments for Stoke Newington Festival, London, UK.

27. A living monument to Ken Saro-Wiwa toured the UK from 2006 using a bus. Nigerian born sculptor Sokari Douglas-Camp's mobile memorial takes the form of a giant bus made out of steel and loaded with oil drums – the idea of a travelling memorial was conceived as an antidote to the colonial notion of the fixed, figurative monuments. The memorial is large enough to serve as a miniature venue for film screenings and exhibitions. www.remembersarowiwa.com and 'in heritage' 2006, produced by Myer Taub is involved in projects such as 'in heritage' around the University of Cape Town and 'Injunction,' around Cape Town, South Africa.

28. 'International Federation for Theatre Research', conference Stellenbosch, South Africa 2007.

29. Isadora is a proprietary graphic programming environment for Mac OS X and Microsoft Windows, with emphasis on real-time manipulation of digital video. It has support for OpenSound Control. Isadora was designed by Mark Coniglio.

30. Cashden, L. (1995), *Dear Mary; A Journey through Sweden & Norway in the footsteps of Mary Wollstonecraft*, Sheffield: Sterndale Press. Dr. Cashden retraces Wollstonecraft's footsteps and writes letters to her as she travels.

31. Films produced and directed by Fragments & Monuments can be seen at www.theperformancekit.com and www.youtube.

32. Designed and curated by Anna Birch in collaboration with 'I-Dat' Plymouth University, funded by Manchester Metropolitan University.

Selected Bibliography

d'Ardenne, P., and Mahtani, A. (1989) *Transcultural Counselling in Action,* London: Sage.

Achterberg, J. (1985) *Imagery in Healing*, Boston: Shambala.

Achterberg, J., Dossey, B., and Kolkmeier, L. (1994) *Rituals of Healing*, New York: Bantam.

Alberti, L. B. (1972) *On Painting and Sculpture*, edited and translated by Cecil Grayson, London: Phaidon.

Andrews, L. (1995) *Story and Space in Renaissance Art: The Rebirth of Continuous Narrative*, Cambridge: Cambridge University Press.

Anzieu, D. (1989) *The Skin Ego: A Psychoanalytical Approach to Self*, translated by C., Turner, New Haven & London: Yale University Press.

Aronson, E. (1995) *The Social Animal*, New York: W.H. Freeman and Co., 7th Edition.

Audi, R. (1998) *Epistemology: A Contemporary Introduction to the Theory of Knowledge,* London: Routledge.

Bakhtin, M. (1993) *Rabelais and His World*, translated by Helene Isowolsky, Indiana University Press.

Bal, M. (1996) *Double Exposures: The Subject of Cultural Analysis*, New York & London: Routledge.

Baldwin, T., (ed.) (2007) *Reading Merleau-Ponty. On Phenomenology of Perception*, London: Routledge.

Bandura, A. (1973) *Aggression: A social learning analysis*, Englewood Cliffs, NJ: Prentice-Hall.

Balsamo, A. (1997) *Technologies of the Gendered Body*, Durham & London: Duke University Press.

Baron-Cohen, S., and Harrison, J.E. (1997) *Synaesthesia: classic and contemporary readings*, Blackwell London.

Battcock, G., (ed.) (1995) *Minimal Art A Critical Anthology*, USA: University of California Press.

Baudrillard, J. (1996) *Simulcra and Simulation*, translated by Glaser, S., University of Michigan Press.

Baugh, C. (2005) *Theatre, Performance and Technology: The Development of Scenography in the Twentieth Century*, London: Palgrave Macmillan.

Benjamin, W. (1992) *Illuminations*, London: Fontana Press.

Bennett, S. (1997) *Theatre Audiences: a Theory of Production and Reception*, London: Routledge.

Berkowitz, L. (1962) *Aggression: a social psychological analysis*, New York: McGraw-Hill.

Bhaba, H.K. (1994) *The Location of Culture*, Routledge.

Blau, H. (1990) *The Audience*, Baltimore, John Hopkins University Press.

Blesser, B., and Salter, L-R, (2007) *Spaces Speak, Are You Listening? Experiencing Aural Architecture*, Cambridge, Massachusetts and London, England: The MIT Press.

Boal, A. (1985) *Theatre of the Oppressed*, New York, Theater Communications Group.

Botler, D., and Grusin, R. (1999) *Remediation: Understanding New Media*. London: The MIT Press.

Bourdieu, P., and Wacquant, L. (1992) *An Invitation to Reflexive Sociology*, Chicago: University of Chicago Press.

Braddon, R. (1965) *Roy Thomson of Fleet Street – and How He Got There*, London: Collins.

Brigham, D.D. (1994) *Imagery for Getting Well: Clinical Applications for Behavioural Medicine*, New York: Norton.

Bryson, N. (1983) *Vision and Painting: The Logic of the Gaze*, London: Macmillan.

Bull, M., and Back, L., (eds.) (2003) *The Auditory Culture Reader*, Oxford: Berg.

Burgin, V. (1996) *In/Different Spaces: Place and Memory in Visual Culture*, Berkeley; London: University of California Press.

Carr, C., (ed.) (1983) *On Edge: Performance at the End of the Twentieth Century*, Middletown: Wesleyan University Press.

Cassell, J., and Jenkins, H. (1998) *From Barbie to Mortal Kombat Gender and Computer Games*, London: The MIT Press.

Cavell, S. (1971) *The World Viewed: Reflections on the Ontology of Film*, New York: Viking Press.

Corbin, A. (1998) *Village Bells: Sound and Meaning in the Nineteenth-Century French Countryside*, translated by Thom, M., New York: Columbia University Press.

Cytowic, R. (1998) *The Man who Tasted Shapes*, NY: The MIT Press.

de Certeau, M. (1984) *The Practice of Everyday Life*, Berkeley & London: University of California Press.

Deleuze, G., and Guattari, F. (1987) *A Thousand Plateaus*, Minneapolis: University of Minnesota Press.

Dixon, S. (2007) *Digital Performance*, London; Cambridge, Mas.: The MIT Press.

Eliade, M (1989) *Shamanism: Archaic Techniques of Ecstasy*, New York: Pantheon Bollingen Foundation.

Elkins, J. (1999) *Pictures of the Body: Pain and Metamorphosis*, Stanford: Stanford University Press.

Ermann, D.E., and Shauf, M.S. (2003) *Computers Ethics and Society*, 3rd edition, Oxford University Press.

Erlmann, V., (ed.) (2004) *Hearing Cultures Essays on Sound, Listening and Modernity*, Berg: Oxford, New York.

Fava, A. (2007) *The Comic Mask in the Commedia dell'Arte*, Evanston: Northwestern University Press.

Foster, H. et al (2004) *Art Since 1900 Modernism Antimodernism Postmodernism*, London: Thames and Hudson.

Foster, H., (ed.) (1987) *Discussions in Contemporary Culture*, Seattle: Bay Press.

Freud S. (1990) *The Interpretation of Dreams*, Standard Edition 5, London: Hogarth Press.

Giannachi, G. (2004) *Virtual Theatres: An Introduction*. London: Routledge.

Gere, C. (2002) *Digital Culture*, London: Reaktion Books.

Goffman, A. (1986) *Frame Analysis*, Harmondsworth: Penguin.

Goffman, E. (1972) *Interaction Ritual*, Harmondsworth: Allen Lane.

Grau, O. (2003) *Virtual Art. From Illusion to Immersion*, Cambridge, Mass.: The MIT Press.

Grau, O. (2007) *Media Art Histories*, London; Cambridge, Mass.: The MIT Press.

Gray, A. (1984) *An Introduction to the Therapeutic Frame*, London: Routledge.

Grayling, A,C. (2006) *Descartes: the life and times of a genius*, 1st edition, New York: Walker Company.

Greenfield, S. (2000) *The Private Life of the Brain*, London: Penguin.

Hall, D. & Fifer, S., (eds.) (1992) *Illuminating Video: An Essential Guide to Video Art*, London: Aperture.

Hall, E. et al. (2007) *Guided Imagery*, London: Sage.

Hansen, M.B.N. (2006) *New Philosophy for New Media*, Cambridge, Mass.: The MIT Press.

Harrison, C. and Wood, P., (eds.) (1992) *Art in Theory 1900–1990*, Oxford: Blackwell.

Hill, L., and Paris, H., (eds.) (2006) *Performance and Place*, Palgrave Macmillan.

Howes, D., (ed.) (2005) *Empire of the Senses The Sensual Culture Reader*, Oxford: Berg.

Huizinga, J. (1938) *Homo Ludens: a study of play-element in culture*, Beacon Press.

Iverson, M (1993) *Alois Riegl: Art History and Theory*, Massachusetts: The MIT Press.

Jackins, H. et al. (1999) *The Human Male: A Men's Liberation Draft Policy*, 1st edition, Seattle: Rational Island Publishers.

Jones, C., (ed.) (2006) *Sensorium embodied experience, technology and contemporary art*, The MIT Press.

Jones, P. (2007) *Drama as Therapy*, 2nd Edition, London: Sage.

Jung, C.G. (1954) *The Archetypes and The Collective Unconscious, The Collected Works of C.G. Jung, Vol. 9.*, New Jersey: Princeton University Press.

Kaye, N. (2000) *Site-specific art Performance, Place and Documentation*, London; New York: Routledge.

Kershaw, B. (1999) *The Radical in Performance: Between Brecht and Baudrillard*, Routledge: New edition.

King, L., (ed.) (2002) *Game On*, London: Laurence King Publishers.

Krauss, R. (1993) *The Optical Unconscious*, Cambridge, Mass.: The MIT Press.

Kristeva, J. (1982) *Powers of Horror: An Essay on Abjection*, translated by Roudiez, L.S., New York: Columbia University Press.

Kuhn, T. S. (1962) *The Structure of Scientific Revolutions*, Chicago: University of Chicago Press.

Kuniavsky, M. (2003) *Observing the User Experience: a Practitioner's Guide to User Research*, San Francisco: Morgan Kaufmann.

Kwon, M. (2004) *One Place After Another: Site-specific Art and Locational Identity*, The MIT Press.

Lacan, J., Millar, J-A, and Sheridan, A. (2004) *The Four Fundamental Concepts of Psycho-analysis*, London: Karnac Books.

Lago, C., and Smith, B., (eds.) (2003) *Anti-Discriminatory Counselling Practice*, London: Sage.

Leadbetter, C. (1999) *Living on Thin Air: the new economy*, London: Penguin.

Lewis, M. (2002) *The Future Just Happened*, Hodder & Stoughton.

Lloyd, M. (2005) *Beyond Identity Politics: Feminism, Power and Politics*, 1stedition, London: Sage.

Lodge, D. and Wood, N., (eds.) (2000) *Modern Criticism and Theory: A Reader*, UK and New York: Longman.

Long, R. (2002) *Walking the Line*, Thames & Hudson: London.

Lucretius, (1951) *On the Nature of the Universe*, translated by Latham, R., Harmondsworth, Penguin Books.

McKenzie, J. (2001) *Perform or Else – from Discipline to Performance*, London: Routledge.

Manovich, L. (2001) *The Language of New Media*, Cambridge, Mass.: The MIT Press.

Mantzius, K. (1937) *A History of Theatrical Arts*, New York: Peter Smith.

Marks, L. U. (2000) *The Skin of the Film: Intercultural Cinema, Embodiment and the Senses*, Durham: Duke University Press.

Mason, B. (1992) *Street Theatre and Other Outdoor Performance*, Routledge.

McLeod J. (1994) *Doing Counselling Research,* London: Sage.

McLeod J. (1997) *Narrative and Psychotherapy*. London: Sage.

McLuhan, M., and Fiore, Q. (1967) *The Medium is the Message: An inventory of Effects*, New York, Bantam Books.

Merleau-Ponty, M. (2003) *Phenomenology of Perception*, NY: Routledge.

Meyer, J. P., (ed.) (2002) *Minimalism,* London: Phaidon.

Morgan, J., (ed.) (2003) *Commonwealth*, London: Tate Publications.

Morgan, J. (2006) *Carsten Höller: Test Site, The Unilever Series*, London: Tate Publishing.

Morris, R. (1995) *Continuous Project Altered Daily: The Writings of Robert Morris*, Cambridge, Mass: The MIT Press.

Mulvey, J.F. and Joiner B.S.(1996) *Men and Masculinities*, London: University of Westminster.

Mulvey J.F., and Joiner B.S. (1999) *Machos y munecas: images of masculinity*, London: University of Westminster.

Murray, J. (1999) *Hamlet on the Holodeck – The Future of Narrative in Cyberspace*, Cambridge, Mass.: The MIT Press.

Naughton, J. (1999) *A Brief History of the Future*, Weidenfeld & Nicolson, Limited, London.

Nietzsche, F. (1993) *Birth of Tragedy*, London: Penguin Books.

Oddey, A. (2007) *Re-Framing the Theatrical, Interdisciplinary Landscapes for Performance*, Hampshire & New York: Palgrave Macmillan.

Oddey, A. and White, C., (eds.) (2006) *The Potentials of Spaces*, Bristol: Intellect.

Packer, R., and Jordan, K. (2001) *Multimedia: From Wagner to Virtual Reality*, New York: W.W.Norton & Co. Inc.

Panofsky, E. (1991) *Perspective as Symbolic Form*, translated by Wood, C., New York: Zone Books.

Perchuck, A. and Posner, H. (1995) *The Masculine Masquerade*, Cambridge, Mass.: The MIT Press.

Perls, F.S. (1969) *Gestalt Therapy Verbatim*, New York: Bantam.

Poole, S. (2000) *Trigger Happy: Video Games and the Entertainment Revolution*.

Porter, R., (ed.) (1997) *Rewriting the Self: Histories from the Renaissance to the Present*, London & New York: Routledge.

Postlewait, T., and McConachie, B., (eds.) (1989) *Interpreting the Theatrical Past: Essays in the Historiography of Performance*, Iowa City: University of Iowa Press.

Reiser, M., and Zapp, A., (eds.) (2002) *New Screen Media:Cinema/Art/Narrative*, London, British Film Institute.

Richter, J.P., (ed.) (1939) *The Literary Works of Leonardo da Vinci*, translated by Bell, R. C., London; New York; Toronto: Oxford University Press.

Ridout, N. (2006) *Stage Fright, Animals and Other Theatrical Problems*, London: Cambridge University Press.

Rowan, J. (1990) *Subpersonalities: The People Inside us*, London: Routledge.

Rush, M. (1999) *New Media in Late 20th Century Art*, London: Thames & Hudson.

Rutherford, J., and Chapman, R., (eds.) (1988) *Male Order: Unwrapping Masculinity*, 1st edition, London: Lawrence and Wishart.

Rymaszewski, M. (2007) *Second Life: The Official Guide*, Hoboken: J. Wiley.

Sallis, J. (1995) *Phenomenology and the end of metaphysics*, Bloomington: Indiana University Press.

Sarris, A. (1968) *The American Cinema: Directors and Directions, 1929–1968*, New York: E.P. Duttton.

Sartre, J-P. (1963) *St Genet: Actor and Martyr*, translated by Frechtman, B., New York: George Braziller.

Schneider, R. (1997) *The Explicit Body in Performance*, London & New York: Routledge.

Schafer, M.(1997) *The Tuning of the World*, Random House.

Shearman, J. (1992) *Only Connect...Art and the Spectator in the Italian Renaissance*, Princeton: Princeton University Press.

Schechner, R. (1973) *Environmental Theater*, New York: Hawthorn Books.

Shneiderman, B. (1998) *Designing the User Interface: Strategies for Effective Human-Computer Interaction*, 3rd Edition, Reading, Mass: Addison-Wesley.

Sisson, C. H. (1975) *The Poetic Art A Translation of Horace's Ars Poetica*, Cheshire: Carcanet Press.

Spinelli, E. (1989) *The Interpreted World: An Introduction to Phenomenonological Psychology*, London: Sage.

Spolin, V. (1999) *Improvisation for the Theatre*, 3rd edition, Evanston: Northwestern University Press.

Toffler, A. (1970) *Future Shock*, New York: Random House Publishing.

Toffler, A. (1980) *The Third Wave*, New York: Bantam Books.

Toop, D. (2000) *Sonic Boom: The Art of Sound*, London: Hayward Gallery Publishing.

Virilio, P. (1998) *La vitesse de libération*, Paris: Galilee.

Weeks, J. (1991) *Against Nature: Essay on History, Sexuality and Identity*, 1st edition, London: Rivers Oram Press.

Weiss, G. and Haber, H., (eds.) (1999) *Perspectives on Embodiment*, London: Routledge.

White, J., (1987) *Birth and Rebirth of Pictorial Space*, London: Faber.

Wilber, K. (2003) *Integral Psychology*, Boston and London: Shambala.

Willett, J., (ed.) (1957) *Brecht on Theatre: the Development of an Aesthetic*, New York: Hill and Wang.

Wilson, E. and Goldfarb, A. (2003) *Living Theatre: A History*, 4th edition, McGraw-Hill Higher Education.

Winnicott, D. W. (2005) *Playing and Reality*, London: Routledge.

Wisnowsky, R. (2005) *Avicenna's metaphysics in context*, London: Duckworth and Co.

Youngblood, G. (1970) *Expanded Cinema*. New York: E. P. Dutton.

Authors Biographies

Dr Anna Birch is Research Fellow in Theatre and Drama at Manchester Metropolitan University, and Artistic Director for the site based, multimedia performance company Fragments & Monuments. She has recently published the chapter, 'Staging and Citing Gendered Meanings: A practice-based study of representational strategies in live and mediated performance' in Birgit Haas (Hg.): *Der postfeministische Diskurs*, Würzburg: Königshausen & Neumann, 2006. She has directed many premieres of new plays by women writers, including April de Angelis and Marina Carr. She was an assistant director to Max Stafford-Clark at the Royal Court, winning the first Gerald Chapman Award. Her current research focuses on contemporary performance, directing, curating, gender and feminist art practices and models of Practice as Research. She is an honorary research fellow for SMARTlab, University of East London and visiting artist to the University of the Arts London. www.wollstonecraftlive.com, www.fragments.

Dr Gianna Bouchard is Principal Lecturer in Drama at Anglia Ruskin University, Cambridge. Her work has been published in *Performance Research*, for which she is currently Reviews Editor. She has also just contributed to an edited collection: *The Anatomical Theatre Revisited* (Amsterdam University Press & Chicago University Press), forthcoming in 2008.

Professor Lizbeth Goodman directs studies for a group of professional new media artists and technology developers from industry. She is the author and editor of some thirteen books including a range of titles on women and theatre, the arts, representation and creativity. Lizbeth has also written and produced a wide range of multimedia programmes ranging from educational CDROMs and video/media packs to more experimental online performance events. She is known as a professional performer and presenter, with many years of experience in live and telematic writing, improvisation, performance and direction. She is Director of SMARTlab at University of East London.

Dr Chris Hales is a specialist in exploring the interactive moving image, as practitioner, educator and researcher. His CDROMs have been selected at numerous film/multimedia festivals and his touch-screen installation (showing a dozen or more of his interactive films) has been presented in Seoul, Helsinki, Warsaw, Nagoya, San Francisco and Sydney. His work was included in the landmark 2003 'Future Cinema' exhibition curated by the ZKM. He writes frequently about the interactive moving image, has taught 90 short workshop courses on this subject in numerous institutions in Europe, and is a regular speaker at international events. Recent projects include 'Cause and Effect', an experimental interactive cinema performance which has been staged with Finnish colleagues in more than thirty international venues, and a research project in Prague to rediscover the *Kinoautomat* from 1967 – the world's first interactive movie.

Dr Iryna Kuksa researches the dialogue between design, education and new media technologies. She explores the role of multimedia within the field of theatre studies and cultural heritage research, investigating how novel methodologies, including 3D reconstruction of historical artefacts, can be applied to pedagogical practices. Her creative practice includes the development of the 'Set-SPECTRUM' project, which aims to strengthen the established approach to research and teaching, and also, to transform the passive consumers of yet another digital product into active participants. She is a member of IFTR's 'Digital Technologies, Visualisation and New Media in Performance'. She has taught on the MA International Design and Communication Management at the Centre for Cultural Policy Studies at Warwick and she is currently Research Fellow for Narrative and Interactive Arts at Nottingham Trent University.

Maiju Loukola is a scenographer, research scholar and lecturer living and working in Helsinki, Finland. Maiju is a post-graduate researcher and assistant in the Department of Film, TV and Scenography/School of Scenography in the University of Art & Design, Helsinki, working with theatre, performance and installations. She is a member of the International Federation for Theatre Research's 'Digital Technologies, Visualisation and New Media in Performance', Finnish Oistat Centre governing board and the History and Theory Commission of Oistat International, Finnish Artist's Association MUUry and Union of Finnish film and video employees/SET. She is currently working on an interdisciplinary research project, teaching and organizing an international conference on scenography education and research.

Dr Esther MacCallum-Stewart is a post-doctorate research fellow at SMARTlab, University of East London. She is currently part of the Microsoft Community Affairs funded project on IT for Development, as sub-editor and research associate for related publications in this domain. Her work beyond this project investigates digital narratives, in particular the relationship between role-playing, history and popular cultural representations through games, online resources and interactive media.

Jeremy Mulvey is an artist who specializes in painting and drawing. His exhibition 'Heures et Malheurs de Heures du Bureau' (Office Hours: routine and rapture) at the World Trade Organisation in Geneva, in November 2005 took a wry look at the patterns of office life for men and women. He exhibits regularly with the New English Art Club at the Mall Galleries. His work can also be seen on his own website, www.jeremymulvey.co.uk He is Research Convenor at Cambridge School of Art, Anglia Ruskin University, where he is collaborating on a project with artists and curators that looks at issue-based painting about identity, gender and masculinity. Mulvey is currently working on an exhibition about men and war.

Vicki Munsell is a leading expert in technology tool development and training for youth at risk. She is the original creator of the 'YouthNet' Programme for Microsoft/BGCA, and is now an MS-funded PhD candidate studying the potential for 'YouthNet' for Europe and then for roll out to the Middle East and Africa regions.

Professor Alison Oddey is Visiting Professor of Contemporary Performance and Visual Culture at The University of Northampton. Previously, she was Head of the Drama Department in the School of Drama, Film and Visual Arts at the University of Kent and Professor of Theatre and Contemporary Performance at Loughborough University. She is a writer, broadcaster and academic, and has chaired 'Platform Events' at the Royal National Theatre. Her most recent book publication, *Re-Framing the Theatrical*, (Palgrave Macmillan), takes the reader on a spectator's journey engaging with art forms that cross boundaries of categorization. She makes some radical claims about performance, discussing spirituality and how the work becomes meditative, whilst considering the relationship of silence in performance and how the spectator emerges into the performer-protagonist within secular and non-secular sacred spaces. Other book publications include two editions of *Performing Women* (Palgrave), *Devising Theatre* (Taylor and Francis) and *The Potentials of Spaces* (Intellect), co-authored with Dr Christine White. She is currently completing her first novel.

Roma Patel is Senior Lecturer in Digital Creativity and the Research Co-ordinator for Narrative and Interactive Arts at Nottingham Trent University. She has presented papers on interactivity and theatre in Britain and Germany. She is mostly involved in the designing of sets and projection for theatre and collaborative digital art installations. She is a committee member of the Society of Theatre Designers and her work has been exhibited internationally at the 'Prague Quadrennial, International Exhibition of Scenography and Theatre Architecture' in 2007 and at a national exhibition for Theatre Design, 'Collaborators', V&A, 2008. She is currently one of a team of London International Theatre Festival International Associates, who are central to the development of 'The Lift', a mobile venue and meeting place, contributing to its design, protocols and programme for the 'Lift Festival', 2008. Her most recent design include sets for *Romeo in the City* (2007) for The Theatre Centre, site-specific production of *The Tempest* (2006) and *The Merchant of Venice* (2005) for Corcadorca Theatre Company, Cork and *A Hip Hopstory* for Kompany Malakhi, Bristol (2006).

Dr Gregory Sporton had a career in dance performance before becoming Head of Research and Graduate Studies at Laban. He is currently Director of the Visualisation Research Unit at Birmingham City University, where his research team work on the application of new technologies to the performing and visual Arts. He has been a prominent contributor to the e-Science in the Arts and Humanities programme run by AHESSC and is currently developing movement-based sound generators with Jonathan Green from MediaInterakt.

Dr Craig G. Staff is an artist and writer based in Northamptonshire. His research is geared towards rendering explicable the ontological basis of non-representational painting. His current research encompasses the production of both visual and text based outcomes. He has exhibited in a number of galleries, including the Pumphouse Gallery in London, the Angel Row Gallery in Nottingham and the Cheltenham Art Gallery and Museum. He is currently Course Leader for the History of Art and Design degree at The University of Northampton.

Valerie Thomas spent over a decade developing the use of therapeutic imagery in the treatment of substance misuse. She currently lectures in counselling at Anglia Ruskin University, Cambridge and is undertaking doctoral research into the use of imagery in counselling training.

Saint John Walker is Lecturer in Digital Animation and Visual Effects at Anglia Ruskin University, and a Co-ordinator for FDMX (The Film and Digital Media Exchange), where he co-organized 'Megapixel: the impact of HD technologies on the screen arts and education' conference in 2007, (with Dr Chris White) and 'The NEXT next-gen', a competition to envisage future games. In 2007, Saint was nominated for the Times Higher Awards for his FDMX work in widening participation. Previously, Saint ran the first Visual Effects training centre in the UK for the National Film and Television School, and was a lead animator on BBC TV's cult comedy *Look Around You*.

Dr Christine White is Head of Narrative and Interactive Arts at Nottingham Trent University. She has lectured in lighting, sound, multimedia, drama and performance design for film, television and theatre. Her book *Technical Theatre* (Arnold Press) documents productions from the 1990s, which have shaped her professional career, and she has worked for a variety of UK companies and events in the arts. Her book with co-author Gavin Carver, *Computer Visualisations: 3D Modelling for Theatre Designers*, (Focal Press), is a key text for theatre designers. She is editor of *Scenography International*, www.scenography-international.com. She has been the convenor for the International Federation for Theatre Research for the 'Scenography Working Group' and more recently the 'Digital Technologies, Visualisation and New Media in Performance Group'. She has organized a number of international conferences and symposia including the 'Transliteracy' conference at the Prague Quadrennial, 2007. She is a member of the AHRC Peer Review College for Scenography and Performance. Her last book, co-authored with Professor Alison Oddey, *The Potentials of Spaces*, 2006 is a key text for the study of performance and scenography both in the UK and North America. She has developed MA study opportunities in interactive arts, film, TV event and production design, interactivity and technology.

Dr Gareth White is an actor, director and facilitator, who teaches at Central School of Speech and Drama, Goldsmiths College and Wimbledon College of Art. He has researched agency and control in audience participation, in a range of settings from Theatre in Education to live art, and his current research and practice pursues the problems of active audiences and interactive performers.

Dan Zellner has worked with theatre, multimedia, and the Internet for over 15 years. His focus is the combination and study of improvisation and digital multimedia. He serves as a multimedia services specialist at Northwestern University and is the Artistic Director of Studio Z, a Chicago based multimedia improvisation production company. He has taught classes in multimedia theatre and authoring both at Studio Z and at Northwestern University. His plays have been presented both nationally and internationally at venues that include the American Conservatory Theatre (San Francisco) and the South Australian Writers Workshop. He was the Interactive Writer for 'Virtual Vaudeville': a project funded in part by the National Science Foundation and headquartered at the University of Georgia. He produced the Commedia dell'Arte Master Antonio Fava's first Chicago visit and the premiere of his play *Pulcinella's War* and continues his improv and directing work in Second Life. He is a member of IFTR's 'Digital Technologies, Visualisation and New Media in Performance'.

INDEX